Kashmir

A Tale of Shame

Kashmir

A Tale of Shame

Hari Jaisingh

 **UBSPD**

UBS Publishers' Distributors Ltd.
New Delhi • Bombay • Bangalore • Madras
Calcutta • Patna • Kanpur • London

UBS Publishers' Distributors Ltd.
5 Ansari Road, New Delhi-110 002
Bombay Bangalore Madras Calcutta
Patna Kanpur London

First Published **1996**

Cover Design : Ilaksha/UBS Art Studio

Designed & Typeset at UBSPD in 10.5 pt Souvenir
Printed at Rajkamal Electric Press, Delhi

To
The people of
J&K

Acknowledgements

I am deeply indebted to Mr. H.K. Dua, who actually prompted me to write this book. He told me during his days as editor of *The Hindustan Times* that Kashmir would continue to be in focus for years to come and, therefore, any reasonably good work on Kashmir would always generate interest.

It is also my pleasure to acknowledge the great help I have received from the comments, criticisms and suggestions of some of my close friends and well-wishers, especially Mr. M.S.N. Menon. I should like to mention the name of Dr. Y.P. Chathley for providing many useful suggestions.

The availability of computer hardware at CRRID (Centre for Research in Rural and Industrial Development), Chandigarh, helped me a lot in preparing the manuscript. I am grateful to the staff of CRRID Computer Centre.

My wife, Neena, smilingly provided a helping hand in compiling research notes whenever I sought her assistance before I joined *The Tribune* at Chandigarh. My young children, Rahul and Bhavna, understood and appreciated my efforts and left me free to do my job.

My book is dedicated to the people of J&K who never say die, whatever be the range and dimensions of the turbulence and the turmoil.

Hari Jaisingh

Contents

Introduction

Crises have become endemic to Kashmir. Violence has begotten violence, and, in the end, paralysed virtually everything. Amidst the on-going tragedy, the voice of sanity in the Valley is hardly audible.

Some people in the Valley, no doubt, feel alienated. On this issue, we have no authentic details. But, such alienation is something that they themselves chose under foreign inspiration. They look upon India with hatred. Not that the Indian nation deserves this. It has always done what it has thought to be good for the people of the Valley. This approach, however, has not won their love and affection. Willingly or unwillingly, the people blame New Delhi for the misdeeds of their leaders.

Should we ask: do here live a people steeped in ignorance and prone to wiles and temptation? They do need an enlightened leadership. Instead, most of their leaders are among the most opportunistic. Perhaps the history of Kashmir and its circumstances have made them so. Such leaders have played a dangerous game with their own people and with the Central Government basically to stay in power and to enrich themselves. Today, they are on the defensive and find themselves virtually irrelevant, if not already relegated to the refuse dump of history. Men with guns have taken over the centrestage, and are enacting a macabre drama.

One can never be sure who really represents the people. The Central leaders, as usual, love to put the "Humpty Dumpties" back on the wall. This will not work for the simple reason that these men have no credibility. There is need to identify new leaders. This process may take time. But there is no other alternative. Why should the Centre put some of these discredited men on the seats of power again when, while in power, they did nothing to improve their standing with the people? In the meantime, the militants continue to rule over the minds of many through fear or through acquiescence. Which of the two factors has been decisive is difficult to say.

The Central leaders give the impression that they know the answers best. Alas, they know so little. Neither the Congress leaders nor the Opposition leaders have so far shown that they know how to deal with the situation. They have only been groping in the dark since 1947. Merely changing governors or power brokers does not constitute a policy or strategy. We did not have a policy in 1947. We do not have one today. In its absence, we look towards the political poltroons, strutting about in the streets of Srinagar, to bail us out of the impasse we have landed ourselves in. As for those who are entrusted with Kashmir affairs at the Centre, their thoughts are concentrated on their rating with their seniors in New Delhi, and not on what is good for the country or the people. Such exercises can only be futile.

The state of Jammu and Kashmir is rather unique. It contains three distinct ethnic groups. Why was the state not trifurcated during the reorganisation of states on the basis of language? Perhaps this was yet another concession to Sheikh Abdullah by Jawaharlal Nehru? Can't we take courage and follow the example we have set in the north-east? This three-legged race will do no good to anyone.

And what of the northern territories which were of vital importance to India from the strategic point of view? There are a million and a half Shias in the Gilgit area, living in almost primitive conditions. The Pakistan forces not only occupied the "Azad Kashmir" areas, but also the icy and rocky northern territories. Out of the total area of the present-day Jammu & Kashmir (2.22 lakh sq. km), about 35 per cent (78,000 sq. km) is under illegal occupation of Pakistan, about 2 per cent (5000 sq. km) has been handed over by it to China, which is already in illegal occupation of an additional area of about 17 per cent (35,000 sq. km). This means that the area under the effective control of the state is only about 46 per cent (1.01 lakh sq. km). Out of this area, about 26 per cent forms part of the Jammu division, 16 per cent the Kashmir division and the remaining 58 per cent the Ladakh division. But the proportional distribution of population in these divisions is about 45 per cent, 53 per cent and 2 per cent, respectively (Y.P. Chathley, *Education, Population and Development: A Regional Perspective of Northwest India, 1995*).

The Pakistan strategists, as is evident, had far more foresight than their Indian counterparts. To the north-east of this region lies the Chinese border; further north is Kazakhastan and to the north-west is Afghanistan. The Karakorum highway runs through this region and the Siachin glacier commands a strategic position. How come India did not press its claim over this area? This uncertainty needs to be resolved. One should also investigate why this matter remained suppressed all these years.

Our politicians have made many mistakes while dealing with Kashmir. One was the delayed decision by Nehru on the question of accession of Kashmir. This delay enabled Pakistan to mount the aggression which subsequently resulted in the Kashmir problem. Nehru was undoubtedly a great man, but like all great men he had his weaknesses. His closeness to the Sheikh created terror in the mind of Maharaja Hari Singh, who did not want to be humiliated by the Sheikh.

At heart, Maharaja Hari Singh was for independence like many others. Another Nepal or Bhutan? Could that have been the best course? The answer to this question depends on one's perspective. In any case, history gave Nehru no choice. As for the leaders of Pakistan, they wanted to acquire the state by hook or by crook. So, Maharaja Hari Singh waited and watched and did nothing till the tribal raiders, unleashed by Pakistan, reached his doorstep.

When the Maharaja asked for Indian military assistance against the raiders, after indicating in a letter that the state would accede to India, Lord Louis Mountbatten and Nehru wanted him to sign the Instrument of Accession as a precondition for help.

There was no need for this precondition. India could have straightaway given assistance to protect the independence of the Maharaja. The question of accession could have been dealt with in a more peaceful atmosphere. Apparently, our constitutional experts failed to give Nehru proper advice.

Even after the Instrument of Accession had been signed Mountbatten wanted the question of accession to be referred to the people. Why this concession in the case of Kashmir? Partition was not based on a referendum. As regards the territory under British rule, the religious complexion of the area was the decisive factor. This factor, however, did not apply to princely states. Many historians have claimed that Mountbatten was pursuing some imperialist objectives. There is a great deal of evidence to support this claim, but, then, we would credit him with less than average intelligence if he thought that in the event of a reference to the people, the will of Sheikh Abdullah, the most popular leader, could have been defeated. The people of the Valley could not have voted either for Pakistan or for independence against his wishes. In any case, in the final analysis, it was Nehru who was responsible for policy, not Mountbatten. The latter was only a constitutional head. Why Nehru offered to ascertain the wishes of the people, when no one was asking for it (Sheikh Abdullah certainly did not ask for it then), has not been convincingly explained by anyone. Nehru must have known then that, in response to the Sheikh's call, the people of the state, including the Valley's Muslims, would have voted overwhelmingly for accession to India. This being so, he should have promptly arranged reference to the people under UN auspices. One wonders why he did not do so? We could have at least legitimised the accession of the area in our possession. In that case, the issue could have been closed once for all. We do not know why Nehru did not choose this option.

The leaders of Pakistan knew that the Maharaja would not join Pakistan. They also knew that Sheikh Abdullah held the same position because of Mohammad Ali Jinnah's antipathy towards him. That is why Pakistan decided to seize Kashmir by force. Anyway, the crucial point is that the Maharaja signed the

Instrument of Accession, and Jammu and Kashmir became a part of India.

However, instead of getting the Valley cleared of the raiders, the Indian leaders decided to halt the advance of the Indian army and preferred to refer the matter to the UN Security Council. This was yet another blunder. This act of Nehru, no doubt under Mountbatten's prompting, brought Kashmir into the vortex of geopolitics. The Anglo-Americans desperately wanted a foothold in Kashmir so as to keep a watch on China and the USSR. This was possible only if the state remained independent or became a part of a smaller state, in this case, Pakistan. In the circumstances, only Sheikh Abdullah could have advanced the idea of Kashmir's independence. It was with this objective that the Anglo-Americans wooed the Sheikh. Only when the Sheikh fell foul of New Delhi, did the Anglo-Americans shift their focus to plebiscite in the hope that the angry followers of the Sheikh would vote for accession to Pakistan.

Historians will one day declare that the masses of both Hindus and Muslims sleepwalked into the partition of India, for they were only vaguely conscious of the real consequences of the two-nation theory. The Congress opposed this theory but yet finally allowed the break-up of the country precisely on the basis of this theory. But everything was done in half-measures. Why didn't the leaders think of the future of the minorities that would be left behind in each dominion? It is clear today that not a thought was given to this matter by Britain or the Congress or Jinnah. Theoretically, India could have accepted the full consequences of the two-nation theory (if not the theory itself) and allowed total transfer of populations. This would not have made India a theocratic state; far from it.

It is no use going into the ifs and buts of history. Partition did take place at a cost no other people on earth have paid before, unless we take into account the price paid by the Russians and the Chinese for the Utopia that they wanted to usher in. Pakistan had driven out most of the Hindus from its territory. On this issue, it was true to its declarations. It wanted a pure Islamic state. The advocates of the two-nation theory lacked the insight of the ultimate reality that they must learn to co-exist with others. If they had had that intelligence, they would have accepted a less-than-ideal solution. We human beings are not perfect so as to create a perfect world. The Pakistanis are no different from the rest of us.

India refused to become a theocratic state because that would have done grave injury to the genius of our people and their civilisation. But the leaders should have realised (and should continue to realise) the clear implications of such a stand. We must allow our quest for truth to continue, preserve the right to differ, and remain secular, multiethnic and multireligious. But we should be bold enough to state the precise obligations that we, as a society and as individuals, must assume to carry forward such a civilisation. If we fail to do this, we will invite new perils. Our civilisation is imbued with the spirit of enquiry and it cannot close its quest. The day Hindus close their minds and become less tolerant, their civilisation will perish. Nor can they accept the mortuary existence of repetitive thoughts. It is tolerance that creates diversity. We will not allow fear of diversity to snuff out our tolerance and create an intolerant society.

If Kashmir has become a problem, it is because we chose to live in a make-believe world. We made a mess of accession. We allowed personal factors to determine national issues. We did not know how to deal with a Muslim-majority state. We thought that we had to purchase the loyalty of the Kashmiri Muslims by giving them concessions. Even after the two-nation theory had brought about partition, we accepted the "separateness" of Jammu and Kashmir by instituting Article 370. This was a grave error. We went too far. We have made concessions to Goa, Nagaland, Mizoram and some other states too, but only the Kashmir Valley has remained insatiable. Its plea for autonomy has turned into a demand for separation.

But membership of a union of states is not like membership of a society. Once you become a member of a federation of states, you cannot withdraw from it except under extreme circumstances. We have seen its consequences in America in the latter half of the nineteenth century. The Americans fought a bloody civil war to prevent secession. And look at the mind-boggling events in former Yugoslavia! This is because in matters of such crucial importance, we cannot allow passions and prejudices of the times to overwhelm us. Whether the militants are mercenaries of Pakistan's intelligence agency or "soldiers of Islam" financed by fundamentalist forces, they cannot be allowed to dictate solutions to basic issues by force. For, we know by now that there are no easy solutions to most of the basic problems, whether political or economic. We have seen what such attempts to create Utopias have resulted in. That is why in Kashmir the Kalashnikov cult cannot be allowed to win. That will be a precedent too costly for us. Like in Punjab, we must bring the militants to their knees through the process of attrition, however slow its progress. The militants must know that they are living in an era in which few have faith in "new saviours" – religious, political, economic or social. Their cause carries no conviction. We are seeing what damage fanatics can do; a poignant example is Afghanistan!

We have already paid a heavy price for appeasement. Ours is not an activist civilisation, crusading for causes. In Kashmir, it was undue dependence on the Sheikh which brought us to the present pass. And how many of us really know the history of Kashmir? How many members of the council of ministers of the Central Government are knowledgeable about the Kashmir problem? Our problems started with appeasing Sheikh Abdullah and his family. We did not search for alternatives. But did not all political parties (except the Jana Sangh) and the media join hands to raise this man – Sheikh Abdullah – to the status of a superhero? He was called the "lion of Kashmir!" If he was tall among his people, that was no reason to make him a hero in India. He refused to be called an Indian. And where is that superhero today? Protected in his mausoleum by an Indian regiment !

Sheikh Abdullah was a fanatic at heart – perhaps a "Valley Muslim" – and he remained one till the end. He was not secular in the true sense of the word. He cared little for Jammu and Ladakh or for Hindus and Buddhists. His concern was essentially for the Muslims of the Valley. That was all. He opted for accession to India because he knew that he had no place in Pakistan, having burnt his bridges with Jinnah and other leaders of that country. And he could not have opted for freedom of a landlocked Kashmir. It was only later that he discovered that the Americans were willing to promote Jammu and Kashmir as an independent country.

Today, we argue that if Kashmir decides to join Pakistan, it would cause another holocaust as in 1947. This may be true to some extent, but it speaks volumes about our inability to get across the message that we will not tolerate another division. In the past four decades we – Hindus, Muslims, Sikhs, Christians and others – have failed to arrive at a clear understanding of what is expected of a citizen of this country of immense diversity. If you want to be in America, you have to first of all be an American, then only everything else follows. But here in Bharat, a man is an Indian last of all. And this position has not changed. In fact, we have allowed a situation of perpetual conflict of one kind or another to develop. This is the Dead Sea fruit of our political process. The multiplicity of demands made on our society will not be met by turning the country into a soft state and making its system of governance permissive. On the contrary, a state like India can be governed only with a measure of firmness. But firmness should be based on irrevocable principles. We have, alas, allowed our principles to be eroded for the expediencies of electoral politics. Power has become the objective of most politicians.

Nehru was opposed to Kashmir's independence. But he proceeded to grant the state all the attributes of a sovereign nation – a separate flag and Constitution, a Sadr-i-Riyasat and prime minister. In fact, Article 370 gave Sheikh Abdullah the first exulting feel of independence from New Delhi.

Are our politicians not responsible for much of what is happening in Kashmir today? How is it that only in Kashmir the question of autonomy has become a matter of life and death, whereas in all other states, there is a recognition that autonomy is the product of an evolving Centre-state relationship, of a process of give and take? How is it that we failed to tell the Kashmiris that they already have more autonomy than any other people of India? Instead, we started haggling with their leaders on the "quantum" of autonomy to be given to the Kashmiris!

The Sarkaria Commission report showed how the autonomy question could be solved. But we have hardly given this report any importance.

Kashmir was part of the Indian civilisation from time immemorial. Is *Kashmiriat* not a part of this civilisation? No one is going to extinguish Kashmir's identity, just as nobody is going to wipe out the identity of Kerala. The fear of losing Kashmir's identity is a false alarm and part of the pressure tactics of those who are opposed to India. In any case, how can we take these critics seriously when they have given up their own language, Kashmiri, for Urdu, as the official language? A people who can give up their mother tongue cannot be in love with their motherland. What is worse, they are trying to impose Urdu on others – for example, on Buddhists of Ladakh – who want to preserve and promote their own mother tongue. And let the Pandits of Kashmir know that part of their history, of which they are so proud, is rejected by their Muslim compatriots. The Sheikh had a particular aversion to it.

Sanskritisation of India over the past 1000 years has failed to destroy the unique elements in the cultural life of our states. Then what is it that Article 370 tries to protect? It has certainly failed to promote democracy or self-government, not to speak of a good and efficient administration. In fact, the leaders of Kashmir misused autonomy from New Delhi to run the most obnoxious government in the country. Nothing better could have been expected. The Kashmiri politicians did not suffer from the natural inhibitions common to the rest of the people. They were not restrained by any considerations. This explains the rampant corruption in every walk of life. They could give full vent to their acquisitive instincts. But this is not to say that Article 370 should be abolished. Indeed, we should proceed with the process of integration of Kashmir slowly so that the fears of Kashmiris are assuaged through a gradual process of adjustment. There are several odd elements in the Jammu and Kashmir situation. How is it that the Valley seems to dominate all discussions? How is it that we hear so little of the voice of Jammu and Ladakh? All the six chief ministers (and, earlier, prime ministers) were from the Kashmir division; most of the presidents of political parties were, again, from the Kashmir division; as also 15 out of 20 secretaries/commissioners and 90 per cent employees in the Secretariat (Y.P. Chathley, *op. cit.*). That is so because, here again, the Sheikh had given the Valley a predominant place in the affairs of the state. Through manipulation of the electoral system, the representation of the people in the State Assembly has been distorted. The Valley people are given a permanent majority over the rest of the state (reminds one of the Fiji Constitution which gives permanent majority to the minority aborigines). The amazing thing is that we have allowed this outrage to continue.

Because of the Valley's immense tourist attraction (tourism alone can make the Valley viable), the region has always enjoyed a fairly high per capita income, which it has refused to share with the less fortunate Jammu and Ladakh. The path of sustained progress got interrupted from 1989 onwards with the outbreak of militant violence, inspired by foreign countries. The worst affected sector was tourism. A large proportion of the population in the Valley (about 50,000) depended on tourism for their livelihood, directy or indirectly. The earnings from this sector were about Rs. 5000 million per year. But the disturbed conditions brought tourism in the Valley to almost nil (Y.P. Chathley, *op. cit.*). According to one estimate, the Centre has spent by now about a hundred thousand crores of rupees, including military and security outlays, in the state. This is no small amount. Considering the small population of the state, the people could have built up a prosperous economy, had its politicians been earnest about their job. However, only the rich have become richer.

The Indian media refuses to educate the people about the realities of the situation there. I must admit that no reporter posted in Srinagar can be really fearless, for he or she is likely to be threatened for being candid. This process began years ago. Many journalists have been put to shame and agony. That is why the truth will not be known easily. And, there is a well-established disinformation network in the Valley – an ISI (Inter-Services Intelligence, a Pakistani agency) creation – which regularly feeds both domestic and foreign mediapersons and human rights activists with sensational stories.

Many people believe the present militancy is the result of accumulated grievances against New Delhi. What are these grievances about? Kashmir has enjoyed a large measure of autonomy. In any case, more than in any other state, Kashmiri leaders have been at the helm of affairs. So how can the Centre be blamed for the lapses of their own leaders? The people of Jammu and Ladakh, however, have legitimate economic grievances, but that is not the case with the Valley people, whose per capita income is the highest among the three regions of the state. So this talk of neglect and poverty is a calculated canard. There was no poverty in the Valley. If life is hard today, this is a fate the Valley people themselves have chosen to invite. It is militancy which has destroyed the tourist trade.

In any case, if there are political or economic grievances, these can be redressed. There are many redressal measures available to states. Then, why this armed revolt? Is it that no peaceful way is available to them to get their grievances redressed? Are all ways blocked to them? If, however. they want India to hand over Kashmir to Pakistan, this will never happen. As for the option of independence, we know that Kashmir can never remain independent. Even the fundamentalists are opposed to it. So is Pakistan. So are the people of Pakistan-occupied Kashmir (PoK). The fundamentalists will subvert Kashmir's independence and join forces with Pakistan. India cannot be party to this process.

Many Valley politicians hold the grouse that J & K gets only a low share of 0.03 per cent of the Central investment resources. In fact, J & K is one of the states which fall under the special category for Central economic assistance. The state received Rs. 934 per capita Central assistance as compared to Rs. 100 for the non-special category states in India (1991-92). Even among the special category states, of which there are ten, J & K received more than many others, including Assam and Himachal Pradesh (Y.P. Chathley, *op.cit.*). But how can public and private investment flows reach the state when its leaders have erected a "Berlin Wall"? When nobody from outside the state can acquire property there, how can enterprises be set up?

Enterprises need land, factory sites and workers' colonies. And some of the workers may want to settle down. All these facilities must be provided. There is an effort today to prevent bank money from flowing out of the state. Well, the reverse flow can also be blocked. As far as growing educated unemployment is concerned, this is the direct result of the state's educational policy – free education up to the graduate level and beyond and the reluctance of Kashmiri youth to move out of the state.

It is true that the Valley was not communalised before partition. But after that, both the National Conference and the Congress in their competition for power have contributed to the growth of communalism. Sheikh Abdullah did not hesitate to make communal appeals. But there were not many Hindu-Muslim clashes. With the Dogra army and Dogra police at hand, there was no scope for such clashes. It is the inexorable drive for power which has finally communalised the politics of the state. Indira Gandhi ran a purely communal election campaign in Jammu in 1983. The Jamaat-i-Islami and its hundreds of *madrasas* (Islamic religious schools), supported by the National Conference, poured out a constant stream of fundamentalist propaganda. The Central Government did not take corrective measures. Statements by leading Kashmiri politicians like Saifuddin Soz only added to the confusion. He claimed that the factor most responsible for the alienation of the Kashmiris is the treatment meted out to them by New Delhi. According to Soz, the Kashmiris feel that New Delhi's behaviour has been atrocious in that it has chosen to ignore them completely. These are contradictory statements. On the one hand, he charges that the Centre has interfered in Kashmir affairs and, on the other, says that it has neglected the state.

India fought two wars with Pakistan over Kashmir. Yet, our leaders have failed to resolve this problem. It appears as if they had left it to be solved by time. There were several options before our leaders – military, political, economic and administrative. But they never tried any of these in earnest.

The genesis of the present phase lies in the 1971 war, the surrender of the Pakistan army to the Indian forces and the dismemberment of Pakistan. These were tragic and traumatic events for Pakistan. Men like General Zia-ul-Haq had sworn to take revenge. That is why he sponsored and financed secessionism in India. "Operation Topac" was conceived by General Zia in 1983. Arms started flowing into Punjab soon after and into Kashmir in 1986. Now many other parts of India are facing terrorism. With every passing year, the adventure has become bolder. The Government of India is aware of these facts, but it has failed to evolve a suitable low cost response to a low cost war. Perhaps the Indian leaders were under the delusion that Pakistan had no international support, that the issue would die away, and that the end of the Cold War would witness the dawn of a better era in international relations. These were mere hopes. Most of the Islamic states are inclined to back Pakistan. And now the USA is back to its old game of supporting Pakistan and the secessionists in the Valley. Our analysts, except for a few, have failed to explain the American behaviour. This time India cannot bank upon Moscow's veto in the UN Security Council.

There is a sense of outrage of having been let down by America. This is because the members of the pro-West lobby in India have never really understood the nature of global conflicts and the reasons why the West has remained hostile to India. They thought that the end of the Cold War would bring the "green card" to all of them, and that a new era would dawn in Indo-US relations.

India has a good case for going in for strong measures against Pakistan. But such an approach will solve nothing. The international community will not allow India to enjoy the fruits of a victory in war. In any case, we can never have peace in the subcontinent by resorting to wars. We must find other solutions. We must know that human rights and environmental concerns are as much weapons in the US strategy today as were anti-communism and promotion of democracy during the Cold War years. Some useful suggestions have been put forth for a solution to the Kashmir crisis. They should now be considered in earnest. Of these, the recognition of the present line of actual control as the international border and the permanent division of Kashmir should be given serious thought. These were the objectives that the Shimla Agreement had hoped to achieve. But it did not find favour with Pakistan. India can never permit the Kashmir Valley to go to Pakistan just "because there are three million Muslims there". We have about 120 million Muslims in the rest of India, i.e., more than in Pakistan. If the claim is for territory, then it is a different matter. Pakistan was not a product of territorial division. An attempt has been made here to discuss certain possible solutions, keeping in view lessons from history and fast changing situations. India can offer free access to the Valley to the people of Pak-occupied Kashmir (PoK). Whatever the final solution, the Kashmir Valley and the northern territories should not be used for military purposes either against India or Pakistan. Any agreement between India and Pakistan must protect the long-term interests of both countries. In such an event, Kashmir, Jammu and Ladakh should form separate union territories with a common council.

We have handled other insurgencies – of Nagas, Mizos and Sikhs – and we have won through conciliation and firmness. We must follow the same path. A few thousand terrorists and mercenaries cannot hold the rest of India to ransom. But we must remove the defeatists and saboteurs from positions of power. We must take the "softies" out of the settlement process. Pakistan cannot frighten us by rattling the "nuclear sword". It cannot destroy India without destroying itself. Consequently, we may have to meet the low cost war with a low cost response and a proxy war with a proxy war.

Pakistan's case for Kashmir is based on the two-nation theory. But after the creation of Bangladesh, this theory has lost its validity. The Mohajir movement is yet another example. The Biharis are still languishing in Bangladesh. Religion has been found wanting as a cementing factor. This is no new discovery. Throughout history, Muslim countries have waged bloody wars among themselves. The Caliphate and the Turkish empire broke up because of internecine feuds. India, on the other hand, in spite of its vast diversity, has been able to hold together. In Pakistan, deep fissures still threaten to erupt into ethnic conflicts because of the very nature of its birth. People who refuse to co-exist with others soon find that their own differences prevent them from living together. Pakistan is the only defiant theocracy in the world. This experiment will prove a disaster not before long as did the communist experiment in Russia. As against this, the spirit of the Indian civilisation has given greater assurance of justice and fairplay to all its citizens. The Kashmiris should see the advantage.

To say, as some do, that there is no Kashmir problem is a tragic delusion. There *is* a Kashmir problem, and to solve it, we have to deal with Pakistan. The Shimla Agreement admits the existence of a Kashmir problem. It must be resolved and, that too, urgently because delay will hurt both the countries. But, Pakistan must understand that no government in this country can make any concession as regards territory. Pakistan may not tire itself by this proxy war, but the militants will. Pakistan must understand this reality. As for India, it can wage this war for a very long time. Ultimately, its superiority in men and material will win the day. This is the final truth. The point is: India cannot bend to every political poltroon in the Valley – there are dozens of them – who ostensibly have a shortcut to "Nizam-e-Mustafa". We have already seen the devastating results of such experiments. We have, first of all, the case of Pakistan – a country now ruled by warlords and druglords. Is this the "Nizam-e-Mustafa" that the separatist Muslim leaders of India wanted to create? And the irony of it all is that the very same Muslim leaders (and also their offspring) who migrated from India to Pakistan are now called "traitors" by no less a person than Benazir Bhutto. She calls the Mohajhir Qaumi Movement a party of "traitors"! And that the Mojahirs do not have the same blood as Pakistanis!

All these factors might take time to sink in. In the meantime, we cannot mark time. It is necessary to take steps which are easy and effective. The reckless competition for power has been at the root of most of the troubles. This competition must be stopped. And constitutional devices must be found to give balanced representation to the various regions. Politics based on religion should be banned (or, is this going to remain a pious wish?) and economic interest should come to the fore. A veto should be available to non-Muslims to block controversial legislation that would adversely affect their interests.

If there was no policy on Kashmir, it was because the Kashmiri leaders did not want the Centre to have a policy. For the same reason, the Centre has been afraid to appoint a strong minister for Kashmir affairs for fear of offending the Kashmiri politicians. And yet Kashmir was at the heart of our foreign policy activity right from 1947. The tragedy is that there is no clear way out. We have tied ourselves into a knot. Why? Instead of following a policy which is in the country's interest (in which case, the way will be clear), we were following other policies – first, a policy of appeasing Sheikh Abdullah and later, a self-serving policy in which the two major contenders for power – the Congress and the National Conference – were guided by the interests of their party men. This situation must come to an end.

Take the case of the burning of the Chrar-e-Sharief in May 1995. Nothing new. Earlier, in October-November 1993, there was the Hazratbal episode. And the Punjab cases. Yet no lesson was learnt. The government believed that the militants would not go to the extent of torching the shrine. Yet the foremost objective of the Jamaat in Kashmir is to eliminate the Sufi influence. Without that they can never gain control of the Valley. The Chrar was the foremost symbol of Sufi influence in the Valley. It had to go.

And what was the need for the Indian Government to rush in with the statement that the mausoleum will be rebuilt. Was the Centre directly responsible? Why this panic reaction? This reaction was followed by yet another panic reaction – the promise of "anything short of *azadi* (freedom)". If the Centre was ready to concede so much, we could have avoided a lot of bloodshed. But this was never the policy. Then how did Prime Minister P.V. Narasimha Rao offer "anything short of *azadi*"? Are these not constitutional matters which call for a consensus?

As for election, it is difficult to understand why the specific date has become so important. The constitutional obligation to hold the election – if this is the reason – is the least valid. Yet this is what is being repeated *ad nauseam*. The real ground for holding the election is to counter the defiance of the militants and the belligerency of Pakistan and their determination to deny the Fundamental Right to the rest of the population to have a representative form of government. This is the challenge which calls for an immediate response. A minority cannot be allowed to impose its diktat on the rest of the people through violence. The armed revolt has to be put down and the diktat of the militants frustrated. But, in this case, the election is significant for another reason – that is, to demonstrate that the will of the majority will prevail. But the militants and their political representatives have opposed the election and it seems they can prevent most of the people in the Valley from coming out to vote. Unfortunately, there is no consensus on election among the mainstream political parties. In these circumstances, caution is of utmost importance. There can be no hard-and-fast rule about the exact date of election. We should hold it at a time suitable for us. Meanwhile, we should let political activity continue.

An extraordinary situation calls for an extraordinary response. The coming election shall not be a normal one. The world knows this. Even the relative strength of the political parties of the Valley cannot be ascertained in the coming election. The main objective should be to ensure that the will of the majority in the state prevails. Even if 5 to 10 per cent of the people come out to vote in the Valley and thereby demonstrate that they are ready to pay with their lives for their beliefs, no further evidence is necessary that people are for normalcy. Everything will depend on the mobilisation of security personnel to give protection not only to the voters but also to the candidates.

But election and representative government in themselves solve nothing. What is needed is to turn the attention of the people away from militancy to development. They must be convinced that tomorrow is going to be better.

There are many books on Kashmir, and a certain degree of repetition is unavoidable. I have tried to look at the problem dispassionately. I have only one point of reference: whatever the line I took, it should serve the interests of my country. But not in the spirit: "my country right or wrong".

It is time we acknowledged that the Kashmir problem is, first of all, our own creation. It began in 1947. After the horrendous experience of partition, a direct result of Muslim separatism, we should have grown wiser. But we have only made a series of compromises. Even today, we are groping in the dark without a clear policy. There is a demand now that we should go back to the pre-1953 days. The objective of its advocates is clear. They want to undo everything that has been done to integrate the state with India. This is an effort to widen the chasm between the Centre and the state. The root of Kashmir's alienation, as Hari Om, a specialist on Kashmir, pointed out recently, lies in misrule, bureaucratic bungling and the suppression of the legitimate expression of popular will.

Unfortunately, we did not want to call a spade a spade for fear of offending so many interest groups. We have put up with the unscrupulous politicians of the Valley as well as with the naïve Central leaders, who encouraged Muslim fundamentalism and separatism for fear of losing Muslim votes. Above all, the happenings in Kashmir are a reflection of our failure over the past centuries to evolve a proper policy towards the minorities. This situation has forced our leaders to make a series of compromises in Kashmir, which they would not do elsewhere. More often, we have chosen to be mute on the matter in the hope that time will resolve the problems. Time does not resolve such problems. Only political will can. But we have a very short memory. And those who do not learn from history are condemned to repeat it. That is why we continue to repeat the mistakes in Kashmir. Pakistan wants to wage a jehad in Kashmir. Muslims in India must remember what partition has meant to them. They should be in the forefront of the fight against the separatism of Kashmiri fundamentalists. But they are not.

And why double standards? Take, for example, the confusion in our response to the demand of the Pandits for a separate homeland. The Valley politicians see this as the beginning of the break-up of India. The Central leaders continue to have reservations, whereas it is a very simple issue. Sheikh Abdullah carved out a Muslim-majority area in Ladakh (Kargil) when the Muslims demanded self-rule. It was done without any fuss, without any opposition either from the Centre or from any quarter. Is it not possible to identify an area where there are more Pandits? Let the security of this area be handed over to the Pandits themselves. This could be the nucleus of a self-administered district.

I have tried to be frank and objective in my analysis. I strongly believe in pursuing the truth and being objective in the interest of my country and of humanity at large. To me, my country is all. I am not guided by the partisan, sectarian and communal priorities of past and present generations.

1

From the Vedic Age to 1947

Kashmir. The very name evokes powerful images and emotions and stirs up deep-felt memories of a past when Kashmir was one of the major nurseries of Hindu civilisation.

Kashyapa-pur, Kashir, Kashmir, Kashmira: these are the different names by which Kashmir was known, all meaning "reclaimed from water". Legend has it – *Nilamata Purana* is our authority – that sage Kashyapa (Kashyapas were a tribe inhabiting the Caspian Sea region) reclaimed the Valley by draining out a mountain lake called "Satisar". Hence the region was called Kashyapa-pur.

For millennia a Shaivite centre, the Valley was considered the embodiment of Uma, the wife of Shiva. Also, Srinagar was (and is) situated on the banks of the Vitasta (now renamed Jhelum), mentioned in the Rig Veda.

Unlike other parts of India, Kashmir has an uninterrupted record of history. The earliest part, much of it legendary, has been recorded by the great historian of Kashmir, Kalhana, in his work *Rajatarangini*. Kalhana admits that he had himself consulted about eleven compositions on history. They are no more available. Pandit Jonaraja brought this history up to the fifteenth century A.D., while Srivara and Prajyabhatta took it forward to 1586, when the Valley was annexed by the Mughals. Then, there were the works of Birbal Kacheri, and Diwan Kirpa Ram, one of the governors appointed by Maharaja Ranjit Singh. The Europeans too have contributed to our understanding of the history of Kashmir. Among them, credit must go to Walter R. Lawrence's *The Valley of Kashmir*, which stands out as a monumental work. Unfortunately, not much is known of the history of present-day Jammu and Ladakh regions.

The history of Kashmir can be divided into five periods - Hindu, Muslim, Sikh, Dogra and later. This is the broad classification followed in this book. The new phase begins in 1947.

The Golden Age

The Aryan Hindus gave Kashmir its Golden Age. Kashmir emerged as one of the great seats of Hindu learning, producing a distinct Shaivite philosophy. The Vedic Indians, who settled along the banks of the Indus, were familiar with the Valley, and sang in praise of its rivers in the Rig Veda. There is mention of Kashmir in this Veda. It is said that the Pandavas crossed the Valley during their wanderings while they were in exile. Kashmir was thus associated with the childhood of our race and was one of the earliest homes of the Aryans in India.

The *Nilamata Purana* is a goldmine of information on Kashmir's legends and sacred places. The great historian, Kalhana, also throws much light on the legendary past of Kashmir, on the various races which lived in the Valley and its neighbourhood, on how Kashmir became part of the Ashokan empire, on the founding of Srinagara, the capital, by Ashoka, on the spread of Buddhism by Majjhantika, one of Buddha's disciples, who was especially entrusted with this task by the Master, and, finally, how Ashoka gave away the whole of the Valley to the Buddhist *Sangha* as a gift and built 500 *viharas*. Thus, Kashmir also became a major centre of Buddhism and attracted scholars and students from far and wide.

Not much is known of the history of the early period. After Ashoka's death in 232 B.C., Buddhism suffered a setback. Jaluka, a Shaivite, drove out the foreigners from the Valley, and Damodara, also a Shaivite, who succeeded him, followed a similar policy. However, Buddhism continued to flourish and reached new heights under Kanishka, Hushka and Jushka, the Indo-Scythian kings, who established a vast empire that stretched from Central Asia to the Yamuna and included Kashmir and parts of present-day Chinese territories.

During this period, Buddhist scholars are said to have gone out to Central Asia and China. The most famous among them was Kumarajiva. During the reign of the Indo-Scythian kings, Kashmiri Buddhism reached its pinnacle of glory. It was in one of the great monasteries of the Valley that Kanishka held the Third Buddhist Council, which established the Mahayana school of Buddhism in the North. Cities named Kanishkapur, Hushkapur and Jushkapur show that Kanishka and his successors took keen interest in the life of the Valley.

Kashmir regained its freedom from foreign rule in A.D. 530, but soon came under the supremacy of Ujjain. But with the decline of Ujjain after Vikramaditya, Kashmir was again free. During this period, Shaivite philosophers tried to bring about a fusion of Hindu and Buddhist religions. In any case, Buddhism did break down the caste system in Kashmir. Hinduism re-asserted itself soon after, and during the reign of Abhimanyu I, the Shaivites received considerable patronage from the king. The Gonanda dynasty, which followed, continued to promote Hinduism, and was actively opposed to Buddhism. In A.D. 515, Mihirakula, a Hun, seized power. Although known for his extreme cruelty, he was a patron of Kashmiri Shaivism. One of his successors, Gopaditya, built a temple on the Gopa Hills in Srinagar (now called the Shankaracharya Hill). In A.D. 580, Pravasena II conquered Kashmir and founded the Karkota dynasty. He built the city of Pravarapura at the present site of Srinagar. It was during the reign of Durlabhavardhana (A.D. 625-661) that the famous Chinese pilgrim, Hieun Tsang, visited the Valley. The Chinese scholar found ample evidence of religious tolerance and noted that Buddhism was still flourishing in Kashmir. Durlabhavardhana's son, Pratapaditya, (A.D. 661-711) founded the city of Pratapapura. His third son, Muktapida, later known as Lalitaditya (A.D. 724-761), was one of the greatest rulers of Kashmir. He extended his kingdom from Central India to Central Asia. The historian, Al Biruni, claims that he even won a battle against the Turks. Kalhana records that his victories were celebrated regularly. Lalitaditya has been compared to the great European emperor Charlemagne and also to Harun-al-Rashid.

Lalitaditya extended his patronage to both Hinduism and Buddhism and constructed temples for Shiva and *viharas* for Buddhists. He was a great builder, and has left behind immense monuments like the Sun Temple of Martand, the ruins of which evoke wonder even today. The model of this temple became the pattern for future temples in Kashmir. He also built several structures in his capital, Paraspur. Lalitaditya was a great patron of men of letters. He brought to his court such great Sanskrit scholars as Vakpatiraja, the author of *Gaudavah* and *Bhavabhuti*, the author of the great work, *Malatimadhava*.

Lalitaditya was followed by his grandson, Jayapida, a Sanskrit scholar, who ruled for 31 years and was known for his military prowess too. Among others, he defeated the king of Kannauj.

For half a century after Jayapida, Kashmir saw a succession of weak kings who indulged in court intrigues. In A.D. 855, Avantivarman came to the throne and founded the Utpala dynasty. He was a patron of art and culture. During his reign, Suyya, an engineer in the king's court, built the town Suyyapura (now known as Sopore) on the bank of the Jhelum. Suyya also changed the course of the Jhelum so that it flowed through the Wular Lake and prevented regular flooding of the Valley. He built the city of Avantipura and also a temple which is second only to the Sun Temple of Martand in splendour.

With the death of Avantivarman, Kashmir relapsed into anarchy. His son, Sankaravarman, bankrupted the treasury by his profligacy. He was succeeded by a long line of weak rulers who became victims of the intrigues of their relatives, nobles and soldiers. During the tenth century alone, Kashmir had 18 rulers. Tantrine, a military caste, became king-makers, and the landed aristocracy became a deciding factor in the life of the people.

This period was, however, marked by the rise of Didda, the queen of Kshemagupta (A.D. 950-958). After the death of Kshemagupta, Didda, daughter of Simharaja, chief of Loharas, placed her young son Abhimanyu on the throne and became the regent. She retained power till A.D. 981, when she herself ascended the throne. In all, she ruled Kashmir for about 50 years till A.D. 1003. A woman of remarkable beauty, strength and courage, she was an able administrator and a major influence on the women of Kashmir. Kashmiris are still fond of calling their illustrious mothers and ladies as "Didda".

The Lohara dynasty established by Didda ruled for three centuries, but had little achievement to speak of. Only King Harsha (A.D. 1089-1101) managed to distinguish himself because Kalhana's father served in his court. Uchala, his brother, usurped power and established the second line of the Loharas. He was killed by traitors and was succeeded by his brother Sussala (A.D. 1112-1120). It was during his son Jayasimha's rule (A.D. 1128-1155) that Kalhana wrote the *Rajatarangini*. The successors of Jayasimha turned out to be weak and incompetent and inadvertently prepared the ground for the end of Hindu rule in the Valley. Islam entered during the rule of Sahadeva (A.D. 1301-1320) when many people embraced this religion.

With the entry of Islam, Kashmir lay open to constant threats from Afghanistan and Central Asia. In A.D. 1319, Dulchu, a Tartar of Central Asia, said to be a descendant of Genghis Khan, invaded the Valley, upon which Sahadeva fled to Kishtwar. His minister, Ramachandra, with the help of his protégé, Shah Mir, a Muslim adventurer from Swat, defeated the forces of Dulchu, consolidated his hold over the Valley and became the king. In this, he was helped by Rinchin, a Buddhist fugitive prince from Tibet.

However, Rinchin got converted to Islam (he wanted to be a Hindu, but Pandits refused to accept him), rose in revolt against Ramachandra and became the first Muslim king of the Valley and took the title of Sultan Sadruddin. He courted and married Kota Rani, the daughter of Ramachandra, who was previously the queen of Sahadeva. Shah Mir became his minister. Kota Rani turned out to be an able woman. However, Rinchin could rule for only three years. He was killed by Udyanadeva, Sahadeva's brother, who married Kota Rani. He had to flee Kashmir when his kingdom was attacked by Achala. Kota Rani organised resistance and killed Achala. When Udyanadeva returned, he remained a nominal king. After his death Kota Rani assumed power. This time Shah Mir revolted against her. She, however, chose to stab herself to death rather than surrender. Thus, the long line of Hindu rule came to an end in Kashmir.

Till the advent of Islam, Kashmir was a flourishing centre of culture. Yuan Chwang, a Chinese traveller, recorded in A.D. 631 that the people of the Valley loved learning and were highly cultured. In the eleventh century, Al Biruni observed that the land was "the high school of Hindu science". The Valley showed remarkable development in such disciplines as medicine, astrology and astronomy.

There is no doubt that the Pandit community made a great contribution to the study and development of Vedic literature. According to Walter Lawrence, the Kashmiri language is Prakrit of the pure original Sanskrit. But Dr. Grierson (*Linguistic Survey of India*, Vol. VIII, Part II), is of the view that Kashmiri is a non-Sanskritic language of the Dardic group. With the imposition of Urdu as the official language and adoption of Persian script to write Kashmiri (it was written originally in the Sharda form of Devanagri), the language lost primacy in the state.

Kashmir can boast of a long line of great writers and thinkers. Among them were Lalluta, Sankuka, Bhatta, Udbhatta, Kshemendra and Kuntala. Anandavardhana, in his *Dhvanyaloka*, propounds *dhvani* as the soul of poetry, a unique idea in the science of poetics. This theory found the support of Abhinavagupta, a great poet, critic, philosopher and saint of Kashmir.

In drama, poetry and criticism, Kashmir produced a number of eminent authors. Among them are Bilhana, Mankha, Somadeva (author of *Kathasaritsagara*). In history, we have Kalhana, Jonaraja, Srivara, Prajyabhatta and Suka. In medicine, Kashmir was responsible two outstanding exponents, namely, Dridhabala and Udbhatta. A number of scholars from the plains made Kashmir the main theatre of their activities. Among them mention may be made of Nagarjuna, Asvaghosha, Vasubandhu and Dharmatrata.

By the thirteenth century, Islam had made a considerable impact throughout North India. Large numbers of Kashmiris had accepted Islam under the influence of Sufi saints. The synthesis of Arabic and Persian cultures produced a new order of Sufis called "Rishis", who had a powerful influence on the minds and the way of life of Kashmiris. These "Rishis" preached religious tolerance – a far cry from what we hear from the latest exponents of Islam. The founder of this order was Sheikh Nur-ud-Din. (His mausoleum at Chrar-e-Sharief was destroyed in May 1995 by a section of the militants in league with foreign mercenaries.)

About the "Rishis", Abul Fazl said that they were the most respected among Kashmiris. They were not fettered by traditions, were true believers in God, and were tolerant of other faiths. He further writes: "They plant the roads with fruit trees to furnish the travellers with refreshment; they abstain from flesh and have no intercourse with the other sex." There were 2000 "Rishis" in the Valley, which explains how Islam was able to convert the Pandits. The "Rishis" also made a significant impact on art and literature. It is a little known fact that Kashmiris have made an important contribution to Persian language and literature. Kashmir was called "little Iran" in those days.

Religious Extremism

With the advent of Islam, Sufis began playing a significant part in the early conversion of Hindus. This was followed by a large influx of Syeds from Central Asia and Persia in the wake of the invasion by Timur. The Syeds were supposed to be descendants of the Prophet. As they became oppressive they were thrown out by Malik Tazi Butt. But many Syeds remained in the Valley.

Muslim rule began well, but gradually became more and more oppressive. Shah Mir's regime was short. He was succeeded by his grandson Shihab-ud-Din (A.D. 1354-1373), and he by his brother Qutub-ud-Din (A.D. 1373-1389). It was during his regime that the Sufi saint Shah Hamadani came to Kashmir with his large following. He enforced a stricter Islam among the converts. Islamic zeal rose to fanatical heights under the next ruler Sultan Sikandar (A.D. 1389-1413), who earned the title of *But-Shikan* (Destroyer of Idols). He demolished most of the Hindu temples and even tried to pull down the great Martand temple. He banned drinking, gambling, dancing, and playing of musical instruments as unIslamic. Hindus were subjected to *jazia* (a kind of religious tax) and forbidden to apply *tilak* on their foreheads.

Historical records show that the Sultan and his chief minister Malik Saif-ud-Din, who was himself a first generation convert to Islam, threw all the sacred books of the Hindus into the Dal Lake – a great loss indeed. A relentless campaign for conversion of Hindus to Islam was launched by Saif-ud-Din (his name was Suha Bhatta before his conversion). After this the Valley acquired a Muslim majority. His son, Sultan Ali Shah, was also a fanatic and did much to either convert the Hindus to Islam or drive them out of the Valley. Anyway, it is believed that only 11 families of the Pandits remained in the Valley at the end of the fourteenth century! However, the next Sultan, Zain-ul-Abidin (A.D. 1420-1470) was a benevolent man who tried to give Kashmir an impartial regime. His rule was followed by a century of intrigues and conspiracies among the Muslim clergy and nobles. The period also saw a steady decline in the economic life of the people.

In 1540, a general of the Mughal Emperor Humayun, Mirza Haider Dughlat, entered the Valley with just 400 soldiers and established Mughal rule. He met with no resistance, which shows the mental and physical paralysis of the people. After his death in 1551, anarchy again threatened the Valley. This time some nobles of the Valley approached Emperor Akbar and requested him to annex Kashmir to the Mughal empire. Akbar first visited Kashmir in 1589. The Mughals gave Kashmir not only peace but also an opportunity to improve its economic life. Kashmir became the hub of Central Asian trade. Akbar visited the Valley again in 1598 and 1601. But it was during the regimes of Jehangir and Shah Jehan that Kashmir flourished. However, under Aurangzeb, there was again a reversal. In a period of 49 years, Kashmir saw 14 governors. Under Governor Iftikhar Khan, the Hindus came under severe oppression, which compelled them to complain to the ninth Sikh Guru, Teg Bahadur. The Guru told them to inform the Mughal rulers that if they could convert Teg Bahadur, they would all voluntarily embrace Islam. This infuriated the Mughal emperor which led to the Guru's martyrdom.

With the decline of the Mughals, Kashmir again became a hotbed of intrigues and conspiracies. Some local Muslim leaders, therefore, decided to invite foreign intervention – this time of Ahmed Shah Abdali, the Afghan ruler. He sent a strong force in 1753 under Abdul Khan Isk Aquasi, who established direct Afghan rule over Kashmir. Afghan rule lasted 67 years, but it was perhaps the most barbarous that Kashmir ever saw. The Afghans looted Kashmir systematically. Lal Khan Khattak and Faquir Ullah became notorious for their oppression. They were cruel to both Hindus and Muslims, but more to Hindus. Life for the Hindus became so unbearable under some Afghan governors that a Pandit nobleman approached Maharaja Ranjit Singh for help. Ranjit Singh had made unsuccessful attempts to annex Kashmir before 1814. This time the Sikh forces under Dewan Chand defeated Jabba Khan on 15 July 1819 and entered Srinagar.

Of Afghan rule, Lawrence has said: "It must have been an intense relief to all classes in Kashmir to see the downfall of the evil rule of the Pathans and to none was the relief greater than to the peasants, who had been cruelly fleeced by the religious sirdars of Kabul" (p. 159).

Sikh Rule

Sikh rule lasted only 27 years. It saw frequent changes of governors, reflecting the inherent instability of the Sikh regime. In fact, ten governors were appointed by the Lahore Court during this period. The Sikhs had no understanding of the geographical significance of Kashmir. Except for the rule of Kirpa Ram, Sikh rule was distinguished neither for good administration nor for development. The Sikhs did not have much empathy for the population of Kashmir either, nor did they have any idea of the importance of the region for the long-term defence of India's North-West. With the death of Maharaja Ranjit Singh in 1839, instability spread throughout his kingdom.

A few more details of this period are necessary to set the stage for the momentous events that took place later. The British had already established their sway over the rest of India, except in Punjab and the North-West, and were waiting for the Sikh empire to fall. And fall it did after Ranjit Singh, for he had no able successors. In fact, as the Lahore Court was ridden with intrigues and conspiracies, the British thought that the Dogras led by Gulab Singh would be more useful to them. Lord Hardinge, viceroy, informed the Queen of England before the Treaty of Amritsar that it was necessary "to weaken the Sikh state by making arrangements by which Cashmere may be added to the possession of Gulab Singh". The seven years after Ranjit Singh's death saw a bitter struggle for power at the Lahore Court. The Sikhs became weaker as a result, and their troops turned restive and ill-disciplined.

Gulab Singh, the Dogra chieftain of the principality of Jammu, was at one time in the employ of Ranjit Singh. He did not go to the aid of the Sikhs in the Anglo-Sikh war of 1845 because the Sikh Court was not favourably disposed towards him. In fact, the nobles were keen to wipe out the influence of Gulab Singh and his brothers on the Sikh Court. But the British were keen to secure the friendship and support of Gulab Singh, no doubt the shrewdest general of his time. To bring Punjab and North-West India under its domain, Britain offered to make Gulab Singh king of Jammu (Jammu then owed allegiance to the Lahore Court). The Lahore Court had done everything to humiliate Gulab Singh – even to deny him the principality of Jammu.

Under the Treaty of Lahore (9 March 1846), the Sikhs ceded certain territories, including Kashmir, to Britain as they had failed to pay Rs. 1.5 crore as compensation. Gulab Singh grabbed the opportunity, and offered to pay Rs. 75 lakhs as compensation for the Valley and some other territories. On 16 March 1846, he signed the Treaty of Amritsar, under which he got these territories "forever in independent possession". Britain recognised him as an independent king, and freed him from allegiance to the Lahore Court. The British saw in Gulab Singh an answer to Sikh militancy. Being a Rajput and a leader of the Dogras, a war-like people, they thought he could be of help against both the Sikhs and the Afghans. However, Lal Singh, prime minister of the Lahore Court, instructed Sheikh Iman-ud-Din, Ranjit Singh's last governor in the Valley, not to hand over the Valley to Gulab Singh. As a result, Britain and Gulab Singh had to force the issue. This strengthened Gulab's hands. By 1850, Gulab Singh became the master not only of Jammu and Kashmir, but also of Ladakh, Baltistan and Gilgit. The states of Hunza, Nagar and Ishkuman, adjacent to Chinese Sinkiang, were added later by his son, Ranbir Singh.

The Dogra dynasty lasted for a little more than a hundred years — Gulab Singh (1846-1857), Ranbir Singh (1857-1885), Pratap Singh (1885-1925), and Hari Singh (1925-1952). According to Y.P. Chathley: "The top as well as junior administrative positions in the state had been occupied mostly by Dogras and Kashmiri Pandits under the Hindu Dogra rulers. The Kashmiri Pandits had a preference for education and government jobs. Most of them possessed landed estates and *jagirs*. Kashmiri Muslims, on the other hand, were mostly cultivators and tenants, and a small section among them was involved in domestic industries such as weaving, shawl making, etc." However, as we will see later, the Dogra rulers did not have the foresight to ensure that their territory, which was an area of great strategic importance for the future of India, remained with India. At a crucial moment in India's history, they were found wanting in adequately responding to the changing needs of the situation and the overall national interests. In 1951, the Dogra dynasty came to an end.

The history of the Dogras under Hari Singh and British interest in the region, as also the developments in Jammu and Ladakh from 1947 onwards, will be resumed in later chapters.

2

Ethnic Profiles:
Some Observations

The people of the Valley constitute a racial mix – Aryan, Mongol, Afghan, Persian and others. The Pandits are of Aryan stock and are considered non-martial. The Gujjars and the Bakerwals are nomadic and are mostly Muslims. The Gujjars are tall, and could have come from the Caspian region. The Dogras are Rajputs, having greater affinity to the people of Punjab. Although a mountain people, the Kashmiris are not given to drink. Perhaps Islam imposed abstinence when it entered the Valley. Finally, the people of Ladakh are mostly of Tibetan origin.

The Pandits of Kashmir evoke our admiration. They are known for their intelligence. Yet they have brought upon themselves the contempt of both foreigners and fellow Indians. And now, by migrating to other parts of India *en masse*, in the wake of the terrorist onslaught, they have exposed their weaknesses and their inability to protect their interests. Their kin in India, holding the highest positions of the land, also failed to come to their rescue at a crucial moment. That the Pandits had a fund of goodwill in India is a fact. If they want to recover it, they must now return to their homeland and fight for their lost rights. Panun Kashmir, the main organisation of Kashmiri Pandits, will be judged by how it manages to get the Pandits back into Kashmir.

Kashmir had very few spells of peace after the Muslim advent. Frequent invasions, tyranny and oppression have been the lot of the Kashmiris. Such factors, however, did not rouse them to action, but made them accept their vicissitudes. They had succumbed to fatalism. It is this easy adaptability which explains the incidence of mass conversion of the Pandits to Islam, which ultimately made them highly vulnerable. They became a minority in their own homeland. Even in the face of this adversity, the Pandits did not stir themselves to defend their interests. In fact, when the Muslims offered to reconvert themselves to Hinduism during the reign of Ranbir Singh, the orthodox Pandits opposed this move, which shows how prone to myopia they can be.

C.E. Tyndale Biscoe, a pioneer of public education in Kashmir, after a long stay in the Valley, has recorded in his book *Kashmir in Sunlight and Shade*: "I must say that an ordinary Kashmiri, such as I have known for thirty years, is a coward, a man with no self-respect and deceitful to a degree." The Chinese pilgrim, Hieun Tsang, held the same view. And Syed Tassadeque Hussain in his book *Reflections on Kashmiri Politics* states that the Pandit would sacrifice everything to attain his objective, namely, his self-preservation. He goes on to say: "While in India, it was the lowest strata of society which willingly escaped to Islam to avoid caste disabilities, in Kashmir it was the high caste Brahmins that converted to Islam unwillingly to escape Afghan tyranny."

Since conversion was not voluntary most of the time, the converts retained much of their Hindu past. However, they could not have retained it in the face of zealous mullahs and the contempt of the other Pandits for the converts. Hussain believes that it was state power which led to forced conversions, for he argues: "Otherwise, Persian and Pathan Saints and Sufis, who spoke a different language and belonged to a different culture, would not have made such a deep impact on the Valley of Kashmir." Similar efforts on the part of European Christian missionaries on the Brahmins of Madurai (Tamil Nadu) had hardly any effect, although the former made a determined effort to convert the latter over a long period of time. In fact, there is no parallel instance anywhere in India.

Although reduced to an abject state under Sultan Sikandar, the Pandits failed to throw up a leadership capable of meeting the challenge. Here was a society with no built-in defence mechanism. Instead, it developed a survival instinct, marked by servility and sycophancy. In their instinct for personal survival, the Pandits even sacrificed the interest of their community. Thus, they continued to serve and please their rulers. Did this policy help them in any way? No. They can clearly see today where it has landed them. The community must address itself to these inherent weaknesses if its members want to go back to their homeland.

I have gone into this matter in some detail, not to cause any hurt to the Pandits, but to make them conscious of their weaknesses. Even today, the Kashmiri Pandits, who are scattered all over India, but predominantly in Jammu and Delhi, find it difficult to unite even over very genuine issues. Adversity has not forced them to forge a new destiny, but only to find new causes to divide themselves.

In 1950, Kashmiri Pandits passed a resolution eschewing politics and aligning themselves with Sheikh Abdullah's party, the National Conference. However, they never occupied a position in the executive committee of this party. P.L. Handoo, an MP, was merely a special invitee to the meetings of the committee.

Strangely, the Pandits were the first to oppose the entry of "foreigners" (i.e., the Punjabis) into the Valley after partition. They were afraid of losing their jobs. This shows how narrow and time-serving their aims were. If Punjabis had settled down in large numbers, the Pandits would not have had to face their present plight. But, then, their immediate problems were, for them, more important than the long-term security of the community. That short-sighted policy has made them pay a heavy price. And they were also clamouring for the protection of "*Kashmiriat*" without knowing that it meant nothing to the majority Muslim community. Before the twentieth century, Hindus and Muslims were more integrated in the Valley. In appearance and habits, they were not much different. They used to live in close proximity, unlike Hindus and Muslims in many other parts of India (Ernest Neve in *Beyond the Pir Panjal*). The ghetto was not so common in Kashmir. Both had places of common worship. During birth, death and marriage Hindus and Muslims followed common customs. It is said that economic competition is at the root of conflict. This is a facile argument. We have heard such arguments from "experts" on Punjab. And yet Punjab had the highest per capita income and it used to lure thousands of skilled and unskilled labourers from other parts of India to both agriculture and industry. Economic hardship does not lead to the demand for secession. In that case, Kerala, with a high rate of unemployment, should have been the first to ask for independence. But its people remain highly integrated with the rest of the country and are highly patriotic.

Other factors need to be considered in this context. Over the centuries, there was a division of work between Pandits and Muslims. As the Pandits mastered the language of their rulers (Persian, for example) they got petty jobs with the government at the behest of the ruling class. But the Muslims confined themselves to agriculture, crafts and trade. With the advent of the British, the Pandits took to English education. The Muslims, on the other hand, refused to learn English and remained backward. As a result, they lost not only job opportunities but also opportunities in industry and commerce. This led to jealousy and hard feelings, which were unwarranted, for the Pandits did not snatch away the jobs of the Muslims. And yet the Muslims occupied most of the jobs in the state service, although only a small proportion among them was literate. Even in recent years, there has been less competition from Muslims for the well-paid higher jobs because highly educated Muslims are still rare.

No doubt, Muslims hated the Pandits because the latter were closely identified with the excesses of the Dogra regime. Nevertheless, since Indian independence (in August 1947), and the accession of Jammu and Kashmir to India, huge investments have been made in the state, and a substantial number of families, both Hindu and Muslim, have become extremely wealthy. Their ostentatious lifestyle has been the envy of the new generation, whose members are finding it difficult even to secure low-paid jobs. They are therefore easily lured towards terrorism – a path which promises easy wealth. To their economic grievance is added the call of religion, which blares out from every mosque. Fundamentalist propaganda and *madrasa* (religious school) education seek to convert every Muslim into a bigot.

Of the Muslims of the Valley, as he saw them during the last decade of the nineteenth century, Walter Lawrence observed: "The Sunni Mussalmans do not strike [one] as zealous or earnest in the profession of their faith, and except in their quarrels with the Shias, they are free from all forms of fanaticism ... they do not keep Friday as a day of rest, and very few Kashmiris make the pilgrimage to Mecca, though the journey is now easy, and does not cost more than Rs. 340. In 1892, twenty-one Kashmiris went to Mecca and this was an unusually large number." He also came to the conclusion that Kashmiri Sunnis were Hindus at heart and "Mussalmans" only in name. Fundamentalism has, however, now infected most of the Muslims; whereas not long ago, a Muslim passing in front of a Hindu temple used to bow in reverence. But no more. Fundamentalism seeks to wipe out all memory of the Muslims' Hindu past.

The Kashmiri Muslims are highly emotional. They are not known for steadfastness. Their loyalty can shift from day to day. They once made Sheikh Abdullah a hero; today his mausoleum has to be protected from vandals. Bakshi Ghulam Mohammad, the Sheikh's successor, was hated, yet when he became chief minister he became the new hero. When the Sheikh was in prison, he was forgotten, but the moment he came out, tens of thousands came on to the streets shouting slogans in his support. Again, when the Sheikh was re-arrested, out went the crowds to hail Bakshi. Those who are at the helm of Kashmir affairs in New Delhi must understand the psychology of the Kashmiri. He is a worshipper of the current gods and fads. At the moment he is for the militants. If the militants appear beaten, the Kashmiri will shift his loyalty to other entities.

The present upsurge of communalism among Muslims shows that a great regression has taken place in their psyche. With constant propaganda from Pakistan dinned into their ears, the Jamaat-i-Islami laying down the rules of conduct and the terrorists enforcing them, the Muslims can hardly have an independent voice. Of course, the British were partly responsible for this situation, for they sowed the seeds of communalism by institutionalising communal differences: for example, through the introduction of separate electorates, communal representation in the services, etc. These policies created vested interests for the perpetuation of communal differences and communal claims and an apparent justification for the communal outlook of the people.

The Kashmiri politician is adroit at speaking in different voices. Thus, a familiar charge is that the Sheikh could be a communalist in the Valley, a communist in Jammu and a nationalist in New Delhi. The former governor of J&K, Jagmohan, has written in his book *My Frozen Turbulence in Kashmir*: "The Kashmiri politicians were adept in speaking with two voices. They could be secular as well as communal, democratic as well as dictatorial, accessionist as well as pro-Pakistan. The underlying motivation was not principles but power – power for the person and for the coterie around. If the Central leaders allowed the Kashmiri leaders to rule the State in whatever manner they liked, whether or not it was in the interest of the country as a whole or even in the interest of the State, they swore by principles of democracy, socialism and secularism, and accession to India was declared as final. If, on the other hand, any question was raised in regard to exercise of authority, or any personal ambition was checked, accession became temporary and issues of autonomy, or identity and of the personality of Kashmir were raised, and communal feelings roused."

Ali Mohammad Sagar, once a minister in the Farooq Abdullah government, admitted not long ago that in 1989 about 60 per cent of the police jobs went to Muslims, whose population strength was 65 per cent. In other jobs, they had a share of 55 per cent. But these figures need to be seen in the light of their low literacy level. In short, Muslims had been enjoying a disproportionate share of the jobs. And yet they continued to accuse the Pandits of stealing their jobs. As for Central Government jobs, the Pandits enjoy a larger share because they have relatively higher education. In any case, Central jobs are acquired through competition. And Muslim youth are reluctant to leave the Valley in search of jobs elsewhere.

With the growth of fundamentalism in the Valley, it was clear that the fate of the Pandits was sealed, for no fundamentalist Muslim will agree to co-exist with communities of other faiths. The presence of an orthodox educated Brahmin community was a constant challenge to these fundamentalists, who saw in them a major obstacle to the establishment of "Nizam-e-Mustafa" (Islamic rule) in Kashmir, whatever that means. Yet, at no point of time in the history of Islam have Muslims been able to establish any such ideal rule anywhere in the world. Even today, some Muslim societies remain steeped in ignorance and are unable to catch up with the rest of the world.

In Kashmir, the fundamentalists have been trying to wean away the converts from their past and this process has been going on for centuries. So, what the Pandit thinks are the greatest achievements of his Kashmiri ancestors are anathema to the converts. They produce feelings of guilt in them. To talk of a common culture, a "Kashmiriat", is to live in a make-believe world in these circumstances, for there is little that is held in equal esteem by both. On the other hand, what brings pride to the fundamentalists are the achievements of Islam. In Kashmir itself there is little to show. So they shift their sights to Iran, Spain, and Baghdad. They want to be a part of the pan-Islamic culture.

Such a phenomenon itself is a great irony, for most Muslims of the Valley have had a history of respecting other faiths. The rich tradition of Sufism along with the cult of Rishis had provided for a healthy and multilayered religious homogeneity at the ground level even as the Muslim rulers during the last few centuries had been strongly opposed to this trend. In fact, the feeling of animosity which we see today in the valley and which appears to be influenced by religion at the person-to-person level has largely got mixed up with economics. From the first two decades of this century onwards, the economic differences between the Pandits and Muslims were highlighted in communal terms. It is equally interesting to note that while the political awakening in India must be ascribed mainly to Hindus, especially in the princely states, in Jammu and Kashmir the lead was taken by Muslims. The Hindus were reluctant supporters. This development revealed its consequences later, for Kashmiri politics came to be dominated by Muslims. No wonder, politics in the Valley began to be centred around Muslims versus non-Muslims and the seeds of political awakening yielded utterly bitter communal fruits.

3

Seeds of Political Awakening

By no means did the Dogras distinguish themselves as rulers. But they did help to bring the Valley into modernity and made it look more beautiful. The northern territories, which they added to their domain, were of great strategic importance. Not all Dogra rulers showed such awareness. For instance, Gulab Singh had lost Gilgit in 1859 after a revolt by the Muslims of the region. Ranbir Singh, however, reconquered it in 1860.

The northern areas of Kashmir became vital to the British after the 1917 October Revolution in Russia. Writes Colonel Algernn Durand in his book, *The Making of a Frontier*: "Gilgit is a poor Valley situated on the far side of the Indus at the extreme verge of Kashmir. Why, it has been asked, should it be worth our while to interfere there? The answer is, of course, Russia. She has advanced practically to the Hindukush; it is necessary to see that she does not cross it." Unfortunately, our own leaders failed to see the importance of the area for India, in peace or war, which is why we allowed the area to be lost. But Pakistan realised its importance as it had a common border with the North-West Frontier Province where the Pakhtuns were not reconciled to the creation of Pakistan.

With increasing British determination to control the frontier policy of the state, the Dogra kings lost interest in the region, though they kept a nominal hold on it. When Ranbir Singh came to power, he was conscious of the importance of these frontier regions, and sent out two probe missions into Central Asia. But these were perhaps the last forays by the Dogras on the other side of the Hindukush.

The state of Jammu and Kashmir was perhaps the first in the country to introduce modern education. A mission school, the first to introduce a university syllabus, came up way back in 1881. English began to replace Persian and Urdu. In 1886, a state school followed the course set by the mission school and turned out a large number of matriculates. It was Dr. A. Mitra who raised the status of the state school, introducing English teaching and imparting instructions according to university curriculum (P.N.K. Bamzai, *History of Kashmir*). Till then, many of the jobs, which needed a knowledge of English, were filled by Punjabis, who had acquired their English education in Lahore. This had given rise to a conflict between "outsiders" and educated local young men. As the "outsiders" started calling themselves "*mulkis*", there arose a need to define who was a real state subject. It is in this kind of opposition to "outsiders" that we must see the cause for the state's isolation from the mainstream of Indian life and the demand for Article 370. Instead of putting an end to this distinction in 1947, the Central leaders legitimised these practices.

In 1905, a college was opened in Srinagar with the help of Annie Besant, and another in Jammu in 1908. The Pandits took advantage of these institutions, while the Muslims kept away from them. However, when the Muslims realised their backwardness and were eager to take advantage of English education, the Pandits had already monopolised these institutions. This created a great deal of frustration among the Muslims.

It was Raja Pratap Singh who undertook the modernisation of Jammu and Kashmir. He linked Kashmir to Punjab, introduced teaching of sciences, ensured proper care of forests, set up one of the first hydropower stations of the country and developed Gulmarg and Pahalgam as new tourist resorts.

Raja Hari Singh, who came to power in 1926, continued the work of beautification of the Valley. In fact, he was closely connected with the administration of the state from 1921 itself. He devoted his attention to agriculture to prevent recurrent famines, made primary education compulsory for boys in the cities of Jammu and Srinagar and made the marriage of boys and girls below the age of 18 and 14, respectively, a penal offence. He also passed rules to reserve state jobs only for state subjects. However, what he began well was soon lost due to the profligacy of his life in later years.

Hari Singh had a weakness for carnal pleasure and for the luxuries of life and this brought him under the influence of his courtiers. The British knew about his weakness and were not slow in exploiting it. G.E.C. Wakefield, one of his trusted ministers, gained ascendancy. Hari Singh did not know what forces were at work in his state or in India, not to speak of the world. When he sought pleasures abroad or was away from the Valley, he entrusted the task of administration to Wakefield, who, following the then British policy, set the Muslims against the Hindus.

Although brought up in the English tradition, Hari Singh was a nationalist. His speech at the London Round Table Conference in 1929 in favour of Indian aspirations brought him under a cloud. Hari Singh declared at the conference: "As Indians and loyal to the land whence they derived their birth and infant nurture, the Princes stood as solidly as the rest of their countrymen for India's enjoyment of a position of honour and equality in the British Commonwealth of Nations." It was after this speech that the British agent in Srinagar kept him under strict watch. This agent also instigated the Muslims against Dogra rule.

Hari Singh was biased in favour of the Dogras and this angered the Pandits as he inducted more and more of the former into the state administration. A stage came when the Hindus occupied almost all the jobs. Moreover, Hari Singh decided to shift his capital to Jammu, thereby reducing the importance of the Valley. The loss of political importance meant, to the Muslims and the Pandits, the loss of their means of livelihood. As we shall see, the army was mainly manned by Rajput Dogras (Hindus and Muslims). The Valley people were considered non-martial.

When necessary, the Maharaja looked for Gurkhas and Sikhs for his army.

Disgusted by these policies of the Maharaja, Sir Albion Bannerjee, the prime minister, resigned in March 1929. His observations on Kashmir made a great impact on the state's educated community. He wrote in his book *Kashmir: Retrospect and Prospect*: "Jammu and Kashmir State is labouring under many disadvantages. The large Muhammadan population, absolutely poor and illiterate, is practically governed like dumb-driven cattle. There is no contact between the Government and the people, no suitable opportunity for representing grievances and the administrative machinery itself requires overhauling from top to bottom to bring it up to modern conditions of efficiency. It has at present little or no sympathy with the people's wants and grievances" (p. 39).

On the other hand, the case of the upper class Muslims was different. The Britishers soon discovered the utility of the Muslim aristocracy to perpetuate their rule in India. Sir John Stratchy, an able British administrator, wrote in 1874: "The existence, side by side, of these (Hindu and Muslim) hostile creeds is one of the strong points in our political position in India. The better classes of Mohammedans are a source of strength to us and not of weakness. They constitute a comparatively small but an energetic minority of the population, whose political interests are identical with ours" (quoted in U.K. Zutshi, *Political Awakening in Kashmir*, p.158). The British followed this policy in letter and spirit till the anti-British Muslim agitation in connection with the Khilafat movement in the 1930s brought about a setback.

With the pampering of the Muslim aristocracy came historical consciousness among Muslims, followed by a communal outlook. Unfortunately, the Dogras were ignorant of the nuances of the British policy. The Valley was the first to see the dawn of political awakening. Jammu lagged behind because the Dogras did not want to embarrass their Dogra ruler. This was a tragedy because the Valley, being more vocal, began to lead the rest of the state. It does so even today. Again, the Dogras have failed to assert themselves.

The Maharaja alone was not to be blamed fully for the backwardness of the Muslims. The British were also responsible. The latter were not in favour of higher education in a frontier area, making it susceptible to foreign ideas. They did not want publication of newspapers, which could spread anti-British sentiments. They were not even in favour of social and religious organisations. Every educated Indian visiting the state was suspect and was screened or watched by the state police. All these factors explain the slow growth of political awakening in the state.

Jammu was closer to Punjab, and its population was in contact with the educated Punjabi people. Before partition, many Jammu students went to Lahore for higher education. This was true of the Valley, too. In spite of the repression, new ideas spread, and people became aware of the freedom struggle in India under the leadership of Gandhiji. Students began to take part in demonstrations inspired by Lala Lajpat Rai. By the late 1920s, the young men of the state were ready to join their compatriots in India to advance the cause of freedom. When Gandhiji was arrested during the Salt Satyagraha, there was a spontaneous hartal in Jammu, Srinagar and some other towns.

Muslim awakening began early enough. The Viceroy, Lord Rufus Daniel Isaacs Reading (1921-26), who perfected the policy of "divide and rule", visited the state in 1924. The Srinagar Muslims organised a demonstration on this occasion and submitted a memorandum about their grievances against Dogra rule. They called for land reforms so that Muslim tillers could become proprietors of Hindu lands. But these ominous developments were ignored by the ruling Dogra dynasty.

The Muslim students of the Valley usually went to Aligarh Muslim University for higher education. They came back with a new spirit of pan-Islamism, and became members of study and discussion groups. In this, they had the support of the British, particularly of Wakefield. The immediate development of this awakening was the 1931 social explosion.

The eye of this storm was in Lahore, where the Muslim press, supported by the Anglo-Indian press, began a chorus of denunciation of the Maharaja and his rule. They claimed that he was deliberately suppressing the Muslims; that the Muslims were denied education and jobs; that the Hindus dominated everything; and that Islam was in danger in the state.

In 1930 the Muslim Conference held its annual session in Lahore which was attended by a few Muslims from Jammu and the Valley. (Lahore, now in Pakistan, continues to influence life in the Valley even today; see Chapter 15.) Early in March 1932 the old Mirwaiz, the chief preacher of Srinagar, died, and his son Yusuf Shah became the new Mirwaiz. Yusuf Shah was a young man inspired by pan-Islamism. He encouraged young men to address Friday prayer meetings. One of these young men was Sheikh Mohammad Abdullah, a product of Aligarh Muslim University with a Master's degree in science. Sheikh Abdullah was under the influence of the "Aligarh spirit". On his return from Aligarh Muslim University, he had taken up a teaching job in Kashmir. Unfortunately, he was dismissed from this job for disobedience. Naturally, he held a grievance against the administration of Maharaja Hari Singh. He and a few other educated young men thus laid the foundation of the Muslim Conference.

The Jammu and Kashmir Muslim Conference was the first political organisation to be set up (i.e., in October 1932) with Sheikh Abdullah as its president. A religiopolitical movement of the Muslims, its main aim was to ensure the welfare of the community. It was inspired by the Political Department of the British administration in India. The British Residency in Srinagar was the local patron of this organisation. Its ultimate aim was to set up an Islamic order in the Valley.

The activities of the Muslim Conference in the Valley created an explosive situation. All that was needed was a spark to ignite the tinder. This spark was provided by the arrest of a Muslim cook. In the agitation that followed, 21 persons lost their lives and many were wounded. Muslim crowds paraded the streets, displaying the bodies of the dead and denouncing the Dogras. A dangerous communal confrontation was in the offing. The crowds turned against the Hindus. Hindu shops were looted and there was violence against Hindus all over the Valley. The Maharaja reacted sharply, and many hundreds were arrested. Also, the police resorted to firing. The date 13 July 1931 remains a landmark in the history of Kashmir, for it was on this day that there was an uprising against the Maharaja (that it turned against Hindus is another matter). The Maharaja appointed a committee to go into the deaths by firing, but the Muslims refused to cooperate. The British tried to appoint an Englishman to hold an enquiry, but the Maharaja refused to accept the suggestion, and dismissed the British minister Wakefield. He appointed Raja Hari Kishan Kaul as the new prime minister, who invited the Muslim leaders for talks. On 26 August the Muslims called off their agitation and the Maharaja released all the prisoners.

Although there was a temporary lull, the All-India Kashmir Committee in Lahore kept up the agitation against the Maharaja. This encouraged the Sheikh to break the truce and start a new wave of agitation. He was arrested on 24 September 1931. The demonstrations which followed his arrest were ruthlessly suppressed. There were large-scale arrests, public flogging and firings in a number of towns. This time the Government of India itself intervened, fearing that there might be an all-India agitation against the Maharaja. It called on the Maharaja to abolish the various measures instituted against the Muslims – ban on cow slaughter, prohibition on *khutba* (religious discourses), stoppage of *azaan* (call to prayer), etc. A British officer was to hold an enquiry into Muslim grievances and demands, and a European ICS officer was to be appointed as prime minister. The Maharaja accepted the demands.

Now the agitation shifted to Jammu, where, with the support of the Ahrar Party of Punjab, the Muslims went on a rampage. British troops had to be called in to quell the riots. This was what the British were waiting for. Now they were in a position to dictate terms to the Maharaja. The British Government forced the Maharaja to constitute a commission under Sir B.J. Glancy of the Foreign and Political Department. This commission, set up on 12 November 1931, made a number of recommendations regarding employment, landholdings, etc., which were favourable to the Muslims. In March 1933, the British imposed a prime minister of their choice (Colonel E.J.D. Colvin) and also three British ICS cadres in charge of home, revenue and police. With the advent of a largely British administration, the Muslims withdrew their agitation. But the British prime minister of the state acted according to his own wishes ignoring the Glancy Commission recommendations. This infuriated the Muslims, who started an agitation in 1934, which was ruthlessly suppressed by the prime minister. British officers did not permit any agitators from outside to visit the state. This changed the attitude of Sheikh Abdullah and others belonging to the Muslim Conference. They now realised that the Muslims and Hindus must stand together if they were to secure any advantage from the British who were opposed to any political agitation in the border areas.

Eventually, the Maharaja appointed a Constitutional Reforms Commission, again under Glancy, which recommended the setting up of a legislative assembly, elected on a limited franchise, and with limited powers. Real power remained with the Maharaja.

Under the Glancy Commission recommendations, the Muslims gained several concessions. The Maharaja agreed to set up a Praja Sabha in which the Muslims got substantial representation. The Muslims also got preferential treatment in the state administration with regard to employment. In 1934, the Maharaja issued a regulation, known as Regulation I, which promised to associate the subjects in legislation and administration. These gains gave a boost to Sheikh Abdullah's standing among the Muslims and spread the influence of the Muslim Conference to other regions of the state. The Sheikh was hailed as "Sher-e-Kashmir" (Lion of Kashmir).

In the 1934 election, the Muslim Conference won 19 seats out of the 21 allotted to the Muslims. In 1932, newspapers were allowed to be published. After Colonel Colvin relinquished his post as prime minister, the Maharaja appointed Sir Gopalaswamy Ayyangar to this post. Sir Gopalaswamy was a liberal, and, therefore, allowed the growth of a healthy political movement.

On 8 May 1936, the Muslim Conference held a "Responsible Government Day", in which Hindus, Muslims and Sikhs participated at the initiative of Sheikh Abdullah.

The movement for reforms now spread to other segments of the population. In 1937, the state saw the growth of the workers' movement, which was led by Bakshi Ghulam Mohammad and G.M. Sadiq. At the sixth annual session of the Muslim Conference, on 26 March 1938, the Sheikh declared: "We must end communalism by ceasing to think in terms of Muslims and non-Muslims when discussing our political problems... and we must open our doors to all such Hindus and Sikhs, who like ourselves believe in the freedom of their country from the shackles of an irresponsible rule" (quoted in P.N.K. Bamzai, *A History of Kashmir*).

On 28 June 1938, the Working Committee of the Muslim Conference met at Srinagar and passed a resolution after much debate, recommending that the doors of the Muslim Conference be thrown open to all people "irrespective of their caste, creed or religion". In 1939, the General Council of the Muslim Conference accepted the recommendation, and thus came into existence the National Conference.

However, in spite of these momentous changes, the forces of communalism were not dead. There was already widespread opposition to the change, and the fundamentalists kept alive the Muslim Conference, which was later to receive support from the Muslim League and Mohammad Ali Jinnah.

In the meantime, the struggle for Indian independence was gaining ground. More and more people from the princely states began to join the mainstream of this struggle under the leadership of the Indian National Congress.

As a consequence, the All-India State Peoples' Conference was born in 1927. It called for the integration of the national and state struggles. Unfortunately, the Congress was not united on this issue. Gandhiji felt that the Congress should not interfere in the affairs of Indian princely states and should not offer direct support to the movements of the people of such states in their struggle against their rulers. Perhaps Gandhiji did not want to create new enemies in the country. This was his attitude towards the Indian trading community too. Jawaharlal Nehru, however, opposed this view and called for the integration of the two movements. This was, of course, in keeping with his view that all anti-imperialist and anti-feudal forces should join on a global scale to make a success of their struggle. Gandhiji opposed this grand strategy. The Congress reconciled the two positions and declared that it stood for full responsible government and the guarantee of civil liberty in the princely states. It deplored the backward condition of these states, the lack of freedom and the suppression of civil liberty in many of them. But, the Congress remained silent on the future of the 560-odd hereditary princes. This was a tactical stand, which explains why the Congress frowned on Sheikh Abdullah's "Quit Kashmir" call against the Maharaja.

However, the Muslim League under Jinnah's guidance took the safer line of not antagonising the princes. So, it never identified itself with the peoples of the princely states and their struggles. The League declared that, constitutionally and otherwise, the Indian princes were sovereign. Jinnah's immediate aim was to secure the support of Muslim rulers in India for his demand for a separate country for Muslims, namely, Pakistan. These developments did not fail to influence the evolution of Kashmir. Sheikh Abdullah said at the first meeting of the National Conference in September 1939: "For the last nine years, I have been nourishing a keen desire that all the people of Jammu and Kashmir State should form one organisation and become one unified force, and discard all discords and differences" (cited in Ghulam Hasan Khan, *Freedom Movement in Kashmir*, p.127). But this shift in his attitude did not bring about any marked change in those who were opposed to him. Nor did it make the National Conference a democratic organisation. Yes, by creating the National Conference, the Sheikh freed himself from the clutches of the mullahs, especially Moulvi Yusuf Shah, who chose to remain with the Muslim Conference.

The foregoing change did not, however, make the National Conference a secular party. The Sheikh's politics continued to veer around the mosques and Islam. He continued to address the Friday prayer meetings because a crowd was always available. Naturally, the Pandits did not attend these meetings. In fact, Kashmir politics was always based on the mosque and the Quran. The mosques of Kashmir, therefore, continue to be in the grip of various political parties and groups. (This reminds us of Sikh politics, which is influenced by the gurdwaras.) The mullahs naturally dominated such a society.

The Muslims of Jammu and Mirpur-Poonch-Muzaffarabad areas, however, refused to fall in line with the Sheikh's ideas. Only the Valley Muslims supported him. However, the leadership of the Muslim Conference now passed into the hands of leaders of the Punjabi-speaking areas of the state, such as Chaudhri Ghulam Abbas and Sardar Mohammad Ibrahim, who were opposed to the Sheikh. In 1939, Nehru presided over the All-India State Peoples' Conference in Ludhiana. Here, he declared the support of the Indian National Congress for the demand for self-government.

In 1939, yet another important development took place – the Maharaja promulgated the state's Constitution, making further concessions to the people.

The new leadership of the Muslim Conference, which was already in touch with Jinnah's Muslim League, made its organisation a part of the League. (The leaders left the National Conference to revive the Muslim Conference in 1941.) Thus, the League emerged as a foe of Sheikh Abdullah. The Muslim Conference not only subscribed to the League's demand for Pakistan, but also wanted Jammu and Kashmir to become a part of it. But its leaders knew that Mehr Chand Mahajan, the prime minister, was opposed to Pakistan. Therefore, they sought to achieve their objective by force. They failed to seize J&K and had to flee to Pakistan before the state's accession to India. Some changed their loyalty. There were many supporters of the Muslim Conference in the state administration. They were given shelter by Abdullah. These political leaders and the administrative cadres formed the backbone of the new organisations – the Plebiscite Front and the Political Conference – when Abdullah's fortunes began to sink. Some of them joined the Jamaat-i-Islami, a fanatic pro-Pakistan fundamentalist organisation in the 1950s.

Opposition to the formation of the National Conference did not deter Sheikh Abdullah, for he was now in favour of moving close to the Indian National Congress and to the movements of the people of the princely states. He wanted their support, as also the sympathy of the Indian media in his struggle against the Maharaja. Moreover, the Congress had earlier come to power even in Muslim-majority provinces such as the North-West Frontier Province (NWFP), while the Muslim League did badly in the elections all over India, including Punjab (it got only one seat out of the 90 seats won by Muslims). This was an eye-opener to the Sheikh. So, in 1939, the National Conference was set up, which threw open its doors to Hindus and others. But the Sheikh was not popular in Jammu. The Dogras refused to join the National Conference. But the Sheikh knew that power would always remain with the Muslims in the Valley and with those who had their loyalty. That is why the Sheikh never moved out of the ambit of his mosque politics. He took up Muslim issues at the meetings addressed by him and never gave the Muslim Conference an exclusive field, although he stopped his denunciations of Dogra rule and focussed his ire against "feudal" elements.

However, as already mentioned, the National Conference was by no means secular. In 1941, its members (all Muslims) in the Praja Sabha resigned *en masse* as they opposed the introduction of the Devnagari script in addition to the Persian (Urdu) script. This was not even compulsory. The National Conference justified its stand by saying that this would create a "Pakistan" in the field of education. But the NC had no qualms while imposing Urdu on Ladakh.

At this stage, we must pause and take a look at the activities of the communists in Jammu and Kashmir. The Sheikh was by no means a communist, not even a socialist, but he was accommodative to a number of educated young men of the National Conference who were sympathetic to communism. A number of communists had taken shelter in the state when the British began to persecute them for branding the Second World War as imperialist. (Later, the same communists were to call it the Great Patriotic War when Hitler attacked the Soviet Union.) The Sheikh had little differences with the communists. They both denounced the feudal system and were in favour of self-determination. Both these aspects suited his purpose. What is more, they were for an independent Kashmir linked to the

USSR. It was because of their influence that Srinagar's central square came to be called Lal Chowk (Red Square).

Jinnah visited Kashmir in 1944. The National Conference received him by declaring: "We Kashmiris today receive you as a prominent Indian despite ideological differences we have with you." But Jinnah had come to widen these differences. He told a meeting of the Muslim Conference: "Muslims have one platform, one Kalma, one God. I would request the Muslims to come under the banner of the Muslim Conference and fight for their rights" (cited in G.H. Khan, *op. cit.*, p.132). He branded the National Conference a "band of gangsters". The Sheikh had personally welcomed him to the Valley and had private talks with him. But when Jinnah told him to wind up the National Conference and charged him with double-talk, he was furious and asked his National Conference workers to boycott further engagements of Jinnah. Jinnah was compelled to leave the state.

The same year the Hindu Mahasabha leader, V.D. Savarkar, also visited Kashmir to woo the Hindus and, when he tried to explain his views, the president of the Yuvak Sabha, Pandit S.N. Fotedar, told him that Kashmiri Hindus believed in communal amity.

These two instances reveal that the two communities were engaged in a process of coming together after the conflicts of the 1930s. This process continued for a number of years.

"New Kashmir", a 1944 manifesto, largely the handiwork of communists, issued by the Sheikh, gave him the aura of a socialist. It raised the slogan of "land to the tiller" because land in Jammu and Kashmir belonged to Hindu landlords. For the same reason, the Sheikh never agreed to pay any compensation to the landlords when he abolished landlordism. In the rest of India, landlords were given compensation. In an introduction to his booklet, the Sheikh praised the USSR and socialism. This pleased Jawaharlal Nehru, for in the Congress Party, there were few who could appreciate socialism. The point is that the Sheikh was as far away from socialism as Mao was from Marxism. These 'isms' provided convenient masks for them. The Sheikh was never a socialist. However, the communists attached themselves to him as "advisers".

The manifesto, submitted to the Jammu and Kashmir Government, declared that the state must take into account the global and national context in order to determine its own future. Sheikh Abdullah was seriously thinking of joining the cabinet at this stage. But B.N. Rau, the then prime minister, resigned, giving place to Ramachandra Kak (in June 1945), a Kashmiri Pandit who was not friendly towards the Sheikh. Soon Kak came into conflict with the National Conference representative in his cabinet, who resigned in protest on 16 March 1946. As the Maharaja took the side of Kak in this dispute, the Sheikh launched the "Quit Kashmir" movement in May 1946 in order to bring the rule of the Dogras to an end. The Indian communists went wild with joy over the Sheikh's demand, although it embarrassed the Indian National Congress.

In 1945, the National Conference held a session at Sopore. There was a simultaneous meeting of the Standing Committee of the All-India State Peoples' Conference under the presidentship of Nehru. Maulana Azad and Khan Abdul Ghaffar Khan were also present. In 1946, when the Cabinet Mission visited India, his communist friends asked the Sheikh to make a direct approach to the Mission on the future of Kashmir. In a memorandum, Abdullah called for an end to Dogra rule. He was arrested on 20 May 1946. Interestingly, on that very day, he was elected president of the All-India State Peoples' Conference, which raised his status to that of a national leader.

Jinnah labelled the "Quit Kashmir" call as an agitation by a few malcontents, who were out to create anarchic conditions in the state. Such observations convinced the Sheikh that he had no future in Pakistan.

Nehru rushed to the state but his entry was prohibited. He was arrested on 10 June. He was, however, released as he was wanted back in Delhi by Gandhiji. He could never forgive the Maharaja or his prime minister for this slight. This insult rankled in him for a long time, complicating the Kashmir issue. The Sheikh understood these weaknesses of his hero, and took full advantage of them. When the entry ban was lifted later, Nehru visited the state and met the Sheikh on 24 July. However, the

Sheikh was tried and sentenced to three years' imprisonment and the National Conference was banned.

During his visit to Kashmir, Nehru did meet the representatives of the Sanatan Dharam Yuvak Sabha, who called on him to apprise him of the situation in Kashmir. They told him that the Sheikh was no nationalist, but only a communalist. They warned him that the future of Hindus in the Valley was dark. Perhaps Nehru might have agreed with them, but he told them that there was no alternative to the Sheikh.

The creation of the National Conference did not bring any advantage to the Sheikh. On the contrary, he lost many Muslims to the Muslim Conference, and did not gain many Hindus. So, in 1945, he was seriously thinking of giving up his nationalist stance to revert to his communal plank. He wrote a letter in this connection to the Working Committee of the Muslim Conference, in which he confessed that the National Conference wished to merge with the Muslim Conference. His game to establish himself as the supreme leader of the Muslims, however, was exposed when his letter was made public to Hindu leaders of the National Conference. The idea to wind up the National Conference was, therefore, dropped.

On 5 March 1948, the Maharaja made a proclamation to establish a popular government. He had already appointed the Sheikh as emergency administrator earlier. On the basis of the new proclamation, he converted the emergency administration into a popular interim government. He also entrusted it with certain powers and duties so that it could evolve into a fully democratic government. In the meantime, there was a growing demand for a constitutional head of state, which forced the Maharaja to entrust all his powers and functions to his son, Yuvaraj Karan Singh. On 25 November 1949, Karan Singh made a proclamation in which he declared that the Indian Constitution to be adopted by the Constituent Assembly (it came into force on 26 January 1950) would govern the constitutional relationship between his state and the Indian Union. He also declared that the provisions of the Indian Constitution would supersede and abrogate all provisions in the state's laws and regulations which were inconsistent with the Union Constitution.

4

Pakistan Strikes

Meanwhile, Pakistan made its presence felt. Its economic blockade of Jammu and Kashmir was a success. This factor encouraged it to try and seize the state by force. Pakistan, therefore, let loose tribesmen, as also its soldiers in mufti, on the people of the state, who least suspected this perfidy. On 4 September 1947 Major General H.L. Scott, the commander of the state forces, reported the presence of raiders. The state's Dogra forces failed to stem the tide of the raiders. The Muslim police and army personnel under the command of Dogra officers began to desert their posts or turned their weapons against their own comrades. Throughout September the raids continued. The state administration protested to the Pakistan Government repeatedly, but there was no response.

These raids soon took on alarming proportions with the influx of Pakistan's regular forces and the stream of exservicemen, especially from the Punjabi-speaking areas of the state. It was perhaps Pakistan's calculation that the Valley and the northern territories, including Ladakh, would be cut off during the winter months preventing any assistance from India. By blocking the supply of petrol, Pakistan hoped to halt the movement of the state police and the army. It was almost conceived as a *fait accompli*. As Pakistan had expected, the state police and troops were paralysed. The local administration of Srinagar was in turmoil. It did not know how the police and the army would behave in case the raiders reached Srinagar.

Obviously, nobody had the answer to this question. There was total unpreparedness.

One may well ask: How come that these fearful possibilities were not anticipated by those who were in authority, by those who were in favour of joining India and by those who were likely to suffer the most from a takeover by the raiders? Neither the Maharaja and his court nor the Indian authorities knew how to respond to the situation. The worst part of the tragedy was the paralysis of the police and the army. The Pandits are not known to have taken any initiative to face this unprecedented situation. In any case, they were not members of either the police or the army.

As for the National Conference, it forked out the excuse that its leaders were in jail. This situation gave the pro-Pakistan Muslim Conference a free hand to organise itself against the state administration. Yet that administration, which was manned by Pandits, failed to see the need to release the National Conference leaders promptly or to suppress the Muslim Conference activities. The Punjabi-speaking Muslims were the first to revolt against the Maharaja. In June 1947, they ran a no-tax campaign in Poonch, which spread to other regions. Soon they attempted to hoist the Pakistani flag and celebrate Pakistan Day. The Muslim League, which was well established in most areas, played an active part in fanning the revolt. The release of Sheikh Abdullah on 29 September 1947, and the appointment of Mehr Chand Mahajan as the prime minister, however, improved matters slightly. Mahajan was known to be pro-India and, though old, was a capable administrator. Pakistan had not anticipated these developments.

By 22 October the infiltration became a full-scale invasion when a large force entered Muzaffarabad and began looting the town. These raiders were led by Major-General Akbar Khan under the pseudonym "General Tariq". At Uri, Brigadier Rajinder Singh of the state army put up a heroic fight, but was killed. Maqbool Sherwani of the National Conference met a similar fate while resisting the raiders. Even the Sheikh was not sure whether he could trust his own National Conference followers. He sent his family to Indore and he himself slipped away to New Delhi.

The Hindu administrators cannot be exonerated. They failed to anticipate the impending conflagration, although they were aware of the holocaust in Punjab and the North-West Frontier Province. Only when the Mahora power plant was destroyed by the raiders on 24 October and the entire region was plunged into darkness did the Maharaja and his court, and the population of Srinagar, realise the gravity of the situation. Even at this stage the Maharaja was in two minds about accession to India!

The British played a nefarious role in the tribal invasion. They wanted the state to accede to Pakistan. Sir Francis Mudie, the governor of West Punjab, a Tory, gave all-out support to the tribals. The US and British press called the raiders "liberators". Jinnah reappointed Sir George Cunningham as governor of North-West Frontier Province. Both Lord Louis Mountbatten and his adviser, Lord Ismay, backed this request of Jinnah. It is believed that Cunningham played a crucial role in organising the raiders from the tribal belt.

Much has been written about the heroic role of the Sheikh and the National Conference in those momentous days. Whether the National Conference cadres fought against the raiders is even today a hotly debated subject. (In any case, the raiders never entered the Srinagar area.)

By the end of October 1947, the Maharaja was facing his doom. The state army was either decimated or in disarray. It was at this juncture that he made a frantic appeal for help to the Government of India. And on 25 October Sheikh Abdullah flew to New Delhi.

The raiders met with no opposition anywhere. The northern areas were lost because the people revolted against the Srinagar regime. What was more, these areas became inaccessible to Indian troops and military supplies could not be maintained. The British garrison there, as was expected, played a traitorous role. The Gilgit Scouts, raised by the British, especially for security reasons, were more than willing to serve the cause of Pakistan. In fact, the commandant of the Scouts, Major Douglas Brown, raised the Pakistan flag in the Scout lines. Pakistan was thus able to occupy the entire northern area and threaten Ladakh. Its forces captured Kargil and advanced towards Leh, taking Zojila

Pass on the way. It was the bravery of an army officer and a pilot that saved Leh. But the entire Hindu refugee population of Askaria fort was put to the sword. By August 1948, all northern areas were occupied by Pakistan. India wrote the loss off without a whimper. Yet, over Aksai Chin, "where not a blade of grass grows", we fought a war with China!

The raiders were now at the outskirts of the Valley. They had captured Muzaffarabad. Radio Pakistan announced the formation of a provisional government of the state under Sardar Ibrahim. Jinnah was expected to make a triumphal entry into Srinagar. At last the Maharaja decided to accede to India and called for military assistance. This was accepted by Mountbatten on 26 October 1947.

The Indian Defence Committee had met on 25 October but both Mountbatten and the service chiefs opposed action against the raiders. They pleaded that, in the absence of a proper road, and due to the existence of bad terrain, the losses could be too great. In any case, Mountbatten tried to delay the process of decision so that the raiders could create a *fait accompli*. The Sheikh's appeal must have, therefore, been effective, for it turned the decision against Mountbatten's advice. On the morning of 27 October a small contingent of Indian infantry was flown to Srinagar airport. The plane landed at 10 a.m. carrying the I Battalion of the Sikh regiment led by Colonel D.R. Rai. The Maharaja appointed the Sheikh the chief emergency officer. Rai and his troops died in a heroic attempt to stem the raiders at Baramula. They managed to slow down the onward march of the raiders. This 'breathing space' helped India because, in the meantime, the airlift was going on non-stop.

When Jinnah came to know of the state's accession to India and of the entry of the Indian army into Kashmir, his first reaction was to order the Pakistan army to invade Kashmir. However, the British commander refused to obey without permission from the commander-in-chief, General Claude Auchinleck. In these circumstances, Mountbatten wanted Nehru to accompany him to Pakistan to meet Jinnah. But Sardar Patel put a stop to this mischief by telling Nehru not to go. In the event, Mountbatten went to Pakistan with Lord Ismay. In view of what had happened, Jinnah put up plans for ceasefire and plebiscite. These plans were to be carried out under the two governors-general. It was then that Mountbatten proposed a plebiscite under UN auspices. Jinnah did not accept it. He insisted that both India and Pakistan should have equal status in Kashmir. This was not possible since a legal accession to India had taken place. The Mountbatten mission was thus a failure. Pakistan, for its party claimed that the accession was a fraud.

However, on his return to Delhi on 1 November 1947, Mountbatten is reported to have persuaded Nehru to make a commitment on plebiscite under UN auspices. Hence, in his broadcast on the very next day, Nehru declared: "We are prepared, when peace and law and order have been established, to have a referendum held under international auspices like the United Nations."

Pakistan rejected Nehru's plebiscite offer too. Liaquat Ali Khan, the prime minister of Pakistan, declared that the accession of the state to India posed a threat to Pakistan. He wanted the state to accede to Pakistan not through a plebiscite, but as a matter of course.

During the crucial meeting on accession, the Sheikh did not participate but sat in a room adjoining the conference hall (see Chapter 5). When he heard the details of the Pakistani raid, he was almost frantic and wanted the accession to take place immediately so that India could rush assistance. He urged Nehru to accept the Instrument of Accession brought by Mehr Chand Mahajan and even opposed the "reference to the people" suggested by Mountbatten, stating that he represented the people of the Valley as head of the National Conference.

By 8 November the tide turned against Pakistan. By 16 November the Valley was cleared of the raiders, and Uri was retaken. This created a new fear among Pakistan leaders that they might lose all. They, therefore, accepted a referendum under UN auspices. They were hoping that the Western powers would come to their help. Liaquat Ali now proposed the withdrawal of the forces of both countries and setting up of an impartial administration under the UN to conduct a plebiscite. To this proposal, Nehru replied that the Kashmir administration was impartial enough to hold a referendum. This view was not acceptable to Liaquat Ali, who declared that he had no faith in the Sheikh, who was merely "a quisling and a paid agent".

Negotiations between India and Pakistan continued for achieving a peaceful settlement, but with no practical results. According to Alan Campbell-Johnson (*Mission with Mountbatten*), it was Mountbatten who "injected the suggestion that the United Nations Organisation might be called upon to fill the third party role". In the meantime, Lord Clement Attlee, the prime minister of Britain, also wrote to Nehru (no doubt on Mountbatten's request) asking him to refer the matter to the UN. India decided to refer the issue to the United Nations on 1 January 1948.

General Thimmayya was for the advance of the Indian army till the entire territory was retaken, but Nehru was keen to improve his image as a peacemaker in view of the Asian Relations Conference he had called. This was why Nehru took the matter to the UN without his cabinet's approval and perhaps against the advice of the Mahatma. According to Louis Fischer (*Life of Mahatma Gandhi*, p.97): "He [Gandhi] regretted the fact that Nehru had submitted the dispute to the UN. He told Horace Alexander, the British Pacifist, that at the UN, considerations of international 'power politics' rather than merit would determine the attitude of countries towards the Kashmir issue." This was exactly what happened. Instead of dealing with India's complaint, the Security Council members became entangled in power politics. Eventually, ceasefire came into force on 1 January 1949 and in July 1949, India and Pakistan signed an agreement in Karachi, under which the ceasefire line was defined. This time it lasted till 1965.

5

The Question of Accession

The "Mountbatten Plan" for the transfer of power from Britain to India was announced on 3 June 1947. Bakshi Ghulam Mohammad and G.M. Sadiq, two of the prominent leaders of the National Conference, were at Lahore at that time. They had gone there to contact the Muslim League to bring about a *rapprochement* between Jinnah and the Sheikh.

The Muslim League hoped that Jammu and Kashmir would accede to Pakistan. This is clear from what Sadiq has disclosed. According to him, he was deputed by the National Conference to approach the Pakistan Government at the highest level to seek recognition of the democratic rights of the Kashmiri people for self-determination. The NC wanted Pakistan to abide by whatever decision the people took. Sadiq met the prime minister of Pakistan, Liaquat Ali Khan, on 7 November 1947, as also some other ministers. But these meetings produced no positive result. According to him, the Pakistani leaders were unwilling to subject the Kashmir issue to a referendum. They were willing to allow an election only if the Sheikh gave a solemn pledge that the National Conference would solidly back accession to Pakistan. This condition was not acceptable to the National Conference (reported in *Dawn*, Karachi, 17 November 1947). It is clear from this that Pakistan was afraid that the people of the state would vote as the Sheikh wanted them to. And it was known that the Sheikh was in favour of India. Historians should note this point that Pakistan was not ready for an election at that point of time. Having given up that opportunity, Pakistan has no right to resurrect an election option at a time suitable to it.

The Sheikh himself met two representatives of the Muslim League, who asked him to join Pakistan. But the Sheikh was then reported to have been indecisive. They asked him to visit Lahore and have direct talks with Jinnah. Although he accepted the invitation, he could not make it because he had to attend a meeting of the All-India State Peoples' Conference. The question naturally arises: Was Nehru aware of these developments?

The Hindus of Jammu were not in favour of Sheikh Abdullah, for his anti-Dogra utterances had naturally alienated them. So they set up a new party in November 1947 – the Praja Parishad – to represent their views and aspirations at a time when the raiders, unleashed by Pakistan, were already occupying a large part of both Kashmir and Jammu. The Sheikh did not want Ladakh too to turn against him. He, therefore, persuaded Kushak Bakula, Head Lama of the Spituk Gompa, to join the National Conference, and made him a minister of state in his government in charge of Ladakh affairs. This move was made to win over the Buddhists.

The Jammu and Kashmir state had a Muslim majority before partition. Under the terms of partition, it was for the Maharaja to decide whether to join India or Pakistan. It is not known what precisely was in his mind. Authors of Kashmir's history hold different opinions on this issue. There is no doubt that his prime minister, Ramachandra Kak, was in favour of independence. So was the spiritual mentor of the Maharaja, Raj Guru Swami Sant Dev. But independence was not an option open to the princes, although with the lapse of paramountcy they were supposed to have become independent. The Congress had opposed such a course. The option was to join India or Pakistan. The Maharaja had not considered the option of joining Pakistan. He would have known that it would have been easy for Pakistan to oust him by stirring up a revolt against him. As for India, he was not without anxieties. Nehru continued to be hostile to him and was bound to put the Sheikh in charge of the state government. This would mean accepting daily humiliation at the hands of the Sheikh.

He was not prepared for such an eventuality. He offered to sign a Standstill Agreement in the hope of gaining time. This offer served no purpose. In any case, he could not have joined India before 18 August 1947 as the future of Gurdaspur (in Punjab) was to be decided only on that date. Gurdaspur, a Muslim-majority area, was given to India as a link with Jammu and Kashmir. But this is a matter on which no authoritative statement is available. If Gurdaspur had gone to Pakistan, then India would have lost Pathankot – the only link between east Punjab and Jammu. It has been authoritatively stated that Sir Cyril Radcliffe (the chairman of the Boundary Commission) was not thinking of Kashmir but of the division of waters when he demarcated the boundary of the region. But the intriguing question is: did the Congress agree to give away Lahore (a Hindu-majority area) in lieu of Gurdaspur? If so, the whole Kashmir question will appear in a new light.

It is interesting to recall here the role of Radcliffe as recounted by Lord Louis Mountbatten to Larry Collins and Dominique Lapierre (*Mountbatten and Independent India*). According to Mountbatten: if the Radcliffe award did not give Gurdaspur and two *tehsils* to India, perhaps Jammu and Kashmir could not have joined India. As Mountbatten put it: "... Radcliffe let us in for an awful lot of trouble by making it possible for them (Jammu and Kashmir people) to accede to India. If he hadn't made that award, the Maharaja would really have had no option but to join Pakistan." Mountbatten also admits: "It's a terrible thing to say it, but it might have been a solution."

Mountbatten apparently never discussed the matter with Radcliffe. It appears that he felt sorry for not having decided in advance the strategy to be followed. He says: "It never occurred to me that he (Radcliffe) would be influenced by this question of Kashmir having to accede." We do not know the precise background of the Radcliffe award. He was probably influenced by the flow of rivers and distribution of waters. However, in Pakistan there was a hue and cry that the Radcliffe award had been influenced by Mountbatten. Mountbatten's own reply was as follows: "That I, as Viceroy, had brought improper pressure to bear on Radcliffe on behalf of my future dominion, as

Governor General designate of India, to open up this route to make it possible for them to join us. I am sure Radcliffe had no notion of the consequences."

This is a subject worth deeper study, for if Nehru and Sardar Patel were not all that committed to possess Kashmir, as stated by Mountbatten, then the Radcliffe award needs further explanation. By the way, Patel was already dead when Mountbatten gave the interview.

Mountbatten wanted the Maharaja to accede to Pakistan (*Time Only to Look Forward: Speeches of Rear Admiral the Earl Mountbatten of Burma*, London, 1949-56). But Mountbatten failed to persuade him. There were also other pressures on the Maharaja, to act one way or the other, from his British friends, who wanted him to declare independence, and from other princes who wanted him to set a precedent for them (for example, Hyderabad, Travancore) by declaring independence. It was perhaps under the influence of these pressures that the option of independence suggested itself to him. Prime Minister Kak was enthusiastic. He had personal interests. He could have continued as prime minister -- a vital consideration. Another factor could be that he was genuinely afraid of handing over power to the Sheikh. This is what Kak told Professor Balraj Madhok (a former president of the erstwhile Jana Sangh): "I too am a Kashmiri. I know Sheikh Abdullah too well. His antecedents and present politics if studied realistically cannot warrant any other conclusion" (cited in Balraj Madhok *Kashmir: Centre of New Alignments*). In short, in Kak's eyes, the Sheikh was unreliable. Time has proved him right and Nehru wrong. Nehru knew little of the man he was dealing with and he put his implicit faith in him. He went out of his way to make the Sheikh the vice-president of the All-India State Peoples' Conference. This step must have inflated the Sheikh's ego. But Kak could not explain how Kashmir, a small landlocked region, could ever become independent, when India and Pakistan were not prepared to reconcile themselves to Kashmir's independence. In any case, did he think that Pakistan would let him rob it of this precious territory? Perhaps Kak wanted Jammu and Kashmir to remain independent for some years before joining India? But, in that case, he neither prepared the ground in Kashmir for this step nor did he take the Indian leaders into confidence. Strange Maharaja and strange prime minister!

Under the Indian Independence Act, a state could accede to either of the dominions by executing an Instrument of Accession by the ruler. On doing so, the state became an integral part of that dominion. A state could also enter into a Standstill Agreement with either dominion in order to prevent the disruption of services such as transit and communications, post and telegraph, and customs, between 17 June 1947, when the Act came into force, and 15 August 1947, the deadline. The Congress made it clear that the termination of paramountcy did not mean automatic independence of the states. It did so because states such as Hyderabad and Travancore were thinking of independence. In fact, on 14 June the Congress passed a strong resolution against the balkanisation of India.

According to a number of authors, the Maharaja would have perhaps signed the Instrument of Accession earlier, if there were no conditions attached to it, allowing the Indian army to reach the state before events took a serious turn. But Nehru insisted that the Maharaja hand over power to Sheikh Abdullah before the Instrument of Accession could be signed. This was not acceptable to the Maharaja, which led to unnecessary delay, confusion and tension. The delay cost India dearly.

Gandhiji visited the state in the first week of August 1947, and pleaded for the Sheikh's release. He is also supposed to have called for the dismissal of Kak. (Kak was eventually dismissed on 10 August 1947.) On 12 August the Maharaja offered to sign a Standstill Agreement with both India and Pakistan "on all matters... pending settlement of details and formal execution of fresh agreements". Pakistan signed the Standstill Agreement, but India wanted the Maharaja or his representative to visit Delhi for "negotiating" this Agreement.

The dismissal of Kak gave Pakistan advance warning that India was preparing to force the hand of the Maharaja to accede to India. Some historians contend that if Maharaja Hari Singh had signed the Instrument of Accession before 15 August, the fanatic pro-Pakistan elements in Jammu and Kashmir would have fled the state and gone to Pakistan as did the pro-Pakistan Muslims from other parts of India. The issue of accession, in that case, would have been closed, for there would have been no Muslim majority in Jammu and Kashmir. It would have been permissible in such a situation to rehabilitate the Hindu refugees, who were moving into India, in Jammu and Kashmir, a safer area. Jammu and the northern areas could have absorbed a few million refugees. But these options were not availed of.

In an address to the East India Association on his return to the UK, Mountbatten revealed: "I spent four days with him (Maharaja) in July 1947, and on every one of these four days, I persisted with the same advice. 'Ascertain the will of your people by any means and join whichever Dominion your people wish to join by August 13, this year'. He did not do that, and what happened can be seen. Had he acceded to Pakistan before August 14, the future Government of India had allowed me to give His Highness an assurance that no objection would be raised by them" (Michael Breacher, *The Struggle for Kashmir*, p. 76). And who represented this "future Government of India"?

The role of Mountbatten has never been clear. There is evidence to show that he was a true imperialist, working out the partition of India in the interest of Anglo-Americans, and that his real sympathies were with Pakistan. His detailed interview to Larry Collins and Dominique Lapierre (*Mountbatten and Independent India*) reveals certain facts, which no writer on Kashmir can ignore. Mountbatten describes the Maharaja of Kashmir as an "old friend", and "quite a pleasant social person". He further states that "he had, of course, perversions" (not stated) and "was a very weak personality". Mountbatten claims that he told Hari Singh: "I have come with full authority from the present government of the future Dominion of India (basically Sardar Patel, but he had got the agreement of Nehru). I've come to tell you that if you decide to accede to Pakistan, they'll think it a natural thing to do, because the majority of your population are Muslims. It'll not only cause no ill-feeling, but they'll give you all the support and help they can."

Did the Sardar give any such assurance? It is extremely doubtful. We need more authentic verification to believe Mountbatten.

Mountbatten discloses that it appeared to both him and Hari Singh that Kashmir's accession to Pakistan would be the wisest course. If, however, Hari Singh decided to join India, Mountbatten would arrange to send up one or two Indian infantry divisions to prevent interference from Pakistan. If he had given this assurance, it is difficult to understand why Hari Singh did not seize this option, for this could have guaranteed his security as also that of the Hindus in his state. But was he thinking along these lines in July 1947 when Mountbatten visited Kashmir to meet him?

Mountbatten claims that he told Hari Singh that if he did not want to take the decision, he could "consult his people either by a plebiscite or, if time did not permit, by a show of hands". He says Nehru agreed to the plebiscite option.

Mountbatten also claims that he spoke to Jinnah and got a similar assurance from him that Hari Singh would be welcome in Pakistan if he (Hari Singh) decided to join that dominion. This shows how little thought had gone into the complex issue of partition. If the purpose of partition was to create a purely Muslim state, then the question of minorities left in each dominion had apparently never been a subject of discussion.

According to Mountbatten, he did not think that Kashmir would be viable as an independent state. He thought that it was more likely to become a battlefield for the two contending forces – India and Pakistan. But Hari Singh, who toyed with the idea of independence, refused to meet Mountbatten on the last day under the pretext of illness.

The reaction to the attack on J & K by Pakistani tribesmen in October 1947 was equally confused. Here is Mountbatten's statement on what he told Nehru: "This is a very serious situation. Let us look at it, let's face it. Kashmir is an independent place. We have no right to go in its defence...whether Pakistan is helping or not is quite immaterial, but we've got to face the tribesmen. We've got to stop that. You cannot intervene at the request of the Maharaja unless in fact he accedes." It is amazing how a soldier could talk in this manner. He wanted to face the tribesmen without entering Kashmir. It is even more surprising how Nehru could accept all these utterances. Here was an instance of total paralysis of a whole nation and its government.

When the Maharaja signed the Instrument of Accession, Mountbatten introduced a proviso: "I'll only countersign it on condition you (Nehru) offer a plebiscite." Nehru agreed with only one stipulation, according to Mountbatten, that the tribesmen should be withdrawn to create peaceful conditions for the plebiscite. The tribesmen were never withdrawn.

It is interesting to recall here what Mountbatten told the Pakistani prime minister, Liaquat Ali: "All you've got to do is pull out (the tribesmen). Have a plebiscite, and you'll win. You'll get it [J&K] again. By refusing to pull out the tribesmen, you are playing into Nehru's hands. He's already got himself into trouble with his followers for risking a plebiscite on my account."

From the foregoing statement three things are clear: one, it was Mountbatten who was the real author of the idea of plebiscite; two, he was hoping that the people of J & K would opt for Pakistan; and three, he knew virtually nothing of the popularity of Sheikh Abdullah, though, at another place, Mountbatten conceded that the Sheikh could turn the plebiscite in favour of India. But his own desire lay elsewhere. Mountbatten confessed: "I must tell you honestly, I wanted Kashmir to join Pakistan. For one simple reason, it made Pakistan more viable." Mountbatten thought that East Pakistan would not stay with Pakistan: "I was always convinced East Pakistan would never work. But West Pakistan was something else. I wanted it to work, I wanted it to be viable. After all I was responsible for it. I wanted Kashmir with them."

Now the questions that arise in this context are as follows: Was it a mere wish on the part of Mountbatten? Or did he work actively to bring about what he desired? These questions have never been gone into by Indian historians.

Mountbatten claims that the rescue operation (in October 1947 to drive out the invading raiders from Pakistan) was all his handiwork as chairman of the Defence Committee. It is difficult to accept his claim. Of course, his statement could be an afterthought. He had time to revise his earlier stories. But interestingly, his main concern in sending Indian troops to

Srinagar was to save the large number of British officers and their wives stranded there: "We had to get there, because if we didn't I should be held responsible for the slaughter, which will undoubtedly occur to the British retired colonels there and their wives." (Yet, as the reader will notice, he later dismisses this fear in his letter to General Claude Auchinleck). I am sure the thought of the 1857 Sepoy Mutiny and the massacre of British men and women must have been in Mountbatten's mind. He was not thinking of the Maharaja and his Hindu subjects at this time, which was what was uppermost in the minds of the Indian leaders.

And what was the reaction of General Auchinleck, the commander-in-chief? This is what he told Mountbatten: "Srinagar is the Chelmsford of India. All the British officers retired from the Indian army are up there. They'll have their throats slit by these tribesmen, because they're British. You'll have the massacre of several hundred British officers and their wives on your hands."

To this, Mountbatten's reply was: "My dear fellow, this is the penalty of this job." So, he was ready to sacrifice the Britishers by postponing the airlift of Indian troops to the morning. Auchinleck wanted the operation to proceed in the night itself. The only reason for delaying the airlift was to give time to the raiders to occupy Srinagar.

From Mountbatten's procrastination, it was clear that he had his own reasons for delaying the operation. For example, when a decision was taken to send in the troops, Mountbatten opposed it: "You cannot do it until Kashmir is a part of India. You can only do it, therefore, if he (Hari Singh) accedes. If he doesn't, I shall have to advise you, you are not entitled to send troops in."

To pick up our story, as Pakistan was convinced that the Maharaja was going to sign the Instrument of Accession with India, it tried, at first, to use pressure tactics and, later, force. As Jammu and Kashmir regions were more closely linked to the Punjab for essential supplies (Jammu with Sialkot by rail and road, and Srinagar with Rawalpindi by road), Pakistan imposed an economic blockade and cut off supplies of a number of items, including petrol and kerosene, to paralyse life in J & K.

On 22 October 1947, Pakistan unleashed the raiders. The Maharaja appealed to India for help. On 25 October the Defence Committee met in Delhi, presided over by Mountbatten. The raiders were just 35 miles from Srinagar. The urgency was apparent. Yet India was hesitant. It was in favour of accession before taking any military action. This was the correct constitutional position. But who was insisting on this "correct" constitutional position? Mountbatten?

V.P. Menon, secretary to the Government of India, was sent immediately to Srinagar to make an on-the-spot study of the situation. He advised the Maharaja to leave Srinagar and go to Jammu so as to remain out of danger. His capture would have otherwise frustrated the process of accession to India. In the meantime, the situation which Srinagar was facing turned grave. There was the lurking fear that the raiders, if they entered the city, would butcher the entire Pandit community. So the main concern of the Maharaja and his prime minister was to somehow save the Hindus. On the evening of 25 October it was decided that Mehr Chand Mahajan should fly to Delhi if he could manage to get a plane, or go to Pakistan to surrender so that the Hindus could be saved. Menon reached Srinagar at this critical moment. The Maharaja expressed his desire to accede to India. On 26 October he prepared a letter for Mountbatten.

Mehr Chand Mahajan flew with Menon to Delhi. He held a meeting with Nehru and Sardar Patel to apprise them of the grave danger the Hindus faced. Mahajan told them that he had instructions to go to Pakistan to make a surrender offer if New Delhi was not responsive. It is reported that Nehru was angry and upset over Mahajan's remarks. He told Mahajan, "to go away", at which Mahajan got up to leave, when the Sardar detained him saying: "Of course, Mahajan, you are not going to Pakistan." According to Mahajan (*Looking Back*, p. 152), a piece of paper was then passed on to Nehru, on reading which Nehru exclaimed: "Sheikh sahib also says the same thing." The Sheikh was sitting in the adjacent room listening to the discussion. As per Mahajan, the Sheikh asked Nehru to expedite military assistance.

The Sheikh was sincere about accession at this stage, though he never failed to hedge his statements. At a press conference on 18 June 1948, in New Delhi, he said: "We, the people of Jammu and Kashmir, have thrown our lot with the Indian people, not in heat of passion or a moment of despair, but by deliberate choice" (*The Hindustan Times*, 19 June 1948). Later, he told the UN Security Council: "We realised that Pakistan would not allow us any time, that we had either to suffer the fate of our kith and kin of Muzaffarabad, Baramula . . . and other towns and villages, or to seek help from some outside authority. Under the circumstances, both the Maharaja and the people of Kashmir requested the Government of India to accept our accession" (quoted in P.B. Gajendragadkar, *Kashmir: Retrospect and Prospect*).

In his reply to the Maharaja, Mountbatten stated: "My Government have decided to accept the accession of Kashmir State to the Dominion of India." However, he added: "Consistent with the policy that in the case of any State when the issue of accession has been the subject of dispute, the question of accession should be decided in accordance with the wishes of the people of the State, it is my Government's wish that as soon as law and order have been restored in Kashmir and her soil cleared of the invader, the question of the State's accession should be settled by reference to the people" (cited in V.P. Menon, *The Story of the Integration of the Indian States*, p. 112).

Menon flew to Jammu with the Instrument of Accession. (The Maharaja had dashed to Jammu from Srinagar overnight, and was sleeping when·Menon went to see him.) He woke up the Maharaja, who signed the Instrument. The Maharaja also prepared a letter for Mountbatten, in which he stated that it was his intention to set up an interim government and instal Abdullah in a responsible position so that he, along with Prime Minister Mahajan, could meet the emergency. In his letter, he did not mention any reference to the people.

On 2 November 1947, Nehru declared in a broadcast: "We have decided that the fate of Kashmir is ultimately to be decided by the people. That pledge we have given and the Maharaja has supported it, not only to the people of Kashmir but to the world. We will not, and cannot, back out of it. We are prepared, when peace and law and order have been established, to have a referendum held under international auspices like the United Nations. We want it to be a fair and just reference to the people, and we shall accept their verdict" (quoted by V.P. Menon, *op. cit.,* p. 117).

The idea of plebiscite had, however, been held by the Sheikh for a long time – only its specific application changed with the times. He was already familiar with the concept of self-determination proposed by his communist friends.

So, after launching the "Quit Kashmir" movement, he asserted: "Sovereignty is not the birthright of the ruler. Every man, woman and child will shout 'Quit Kashmir'. The Kashmir nation has expressed its will. I ask for a plebiscite on this question" (*The Tribune,* Lahore, 26 May 1946).

Nehru did not mind a plebiscite based on any other issue but religion. In an interview to Taya Zinkin, the *Guardian* correspondent in India, on 30 June 1950, he said that he would not agree to a plebiscite so long as Pakistan held a part of the Valley because the people there were "timorous". He went on to say that "if the Kashmiris want a plebiscite to be fought on economic and not, mind you, religious grounds, they can have it. But I shall never allow, so long as I live, a plebiscite over cow's urine and all that. It would undo the whole of communal harmony" (Taya Zinkin, *Reporting India,* p. 206).

The death of Sardar Patel on 15 December 1950 was a great setback to India. He would have been a source of not only strength, but also of sound advice. After his death, Kashmir affairs came under Nehru in every way and no interference from any quarter was permitted. The death of the Sardar also emboldened the Sheikh to place before Nehru the demand for Article 370 – the first separatist demand of the Kashmir Muslims.

Sheikh Abdullah was interested only in the Valley, not in Jammu and Ladakh. He knew that only in the Valley was he supreme. He had the least interest in the Hindus of Jammu. These aspects come out clearly in his autobiography *Aatish-i-Chinar*. Sheikh Abdullah took over as chief emergency officer of the state on 31 October 1947. He continued in that office till 25 March 1948, when he became the prime minister of the state. He inducted Bakshi Ghulam Mohammad, G.M. Sadiq, Mirza Afzal Beg, Shyam Lal Saraf, Girdhari Lal Dogra, Sardar Budh Singh and Colonel Pir Mohammad Khan as members of his cabinet.

Under the Instrument of Accession, the Government of India had jurisdiction over the state of Jammu and Kashmir in respect of defence, external affairs and communications. However, all the provisions relating to the Constitution of the states in Part B contained in Article 238 were not applied to the state of Jammu and Kashmir. Instead, a separate and distinct provision was made with regard to these matters in Article 370. This was a political decision, and was directly related to the commitment of the Government of India to consult the people of the state before drawing up the Constitution of J & K. Article 370 restricted the powers of the Indian Parliament to make laws for the state. This blocked the integration of the state with the rest of India, for the State Assembly could reject any law made by the Indian Parliament in the interest of the whole nation.

Article 370 has generated a lot of heat in discussions on Kashmir. What is needed is more light. The demand for autonomy is not the issue. The issue is separatism – the desire to be separate for its own sake. This cannot be accepted, and if Article 370 is promoting separatism, it must go. There is also a case for strengthening links with the Centre and for equal development of all areas. That is why we have a uniform civil service for the whole country. But in Jammu and Kashmir, from the times of Sheikh Abdullah, there has been resistance to the appointment of Central cadres. This resistance has helped Kashmir politicians to promote their separatist designs. Such a state of affairs can no more be tolerated. J&K must have a dedicated civil service, which, while guarding the autonomy of the state, should put a stop to the separatist politics of its leaders.

The Constitution of the state, framed in the 1950s, has effectively cut it off from the mainstream of Indian life and development. Under the constitutional provisions introduced by the Maharaja in 1927, on persistent demand by the people of the Valley, no outsider can purchase land and immovable property in the state. The Kashmiri agitation for protection began as early as 1891. The first measure to give partial protection was introduced in 1912. There is no doubt that such a provision might have helped the Kashmiris then but now it has become the major stumbling block to Kashmir's development. Unfortunately, a number of other states such as Assam, Nagaland, Manipur, Andhra Pradesh, Mizoram, Arunachal Pradesh and Goa have similar provisions. One hopes that the people of these states will realise early that such provisions will only condemn them to backwardness on a permanent basis. In a world where globalisation of the economy is seen as the solution to backwardness, such provisions will help no one.

As regards Articles of the Indian Constitution not valid to Jammu and Kashmir, it was left to the President of India to decide whether they should be made applicable or not. But even such a decision was to be made in consultation with the state. This is stipulated in Article 370. It was under the powers conferred on him by Article 370 that the President issued the Constitution (Application to Jammu and Kashmir) Order in 1950. This order made specific the areas of competency of the Indian Parliament to make laws for Jammu and Kashmir.

The state's Constituent Assembly, which was convened on 31 October 1951, elected Yuvaraj Karan Singh as Sadr-i-Riyasat. Thus, unlike in other states, the governor of Jammu and Kashmir was elected by the Assembly. This procedure was recognised by the Government of India by issuing a Presidential Declaration, under Article 370, on 15 November 1952.

6

The Mind and Moods of Sheikh Abdullah

I t did not take long for Sheikh Abdullah to reveal his true colours. As the constitutional future of the state came up for discussion, he asked for a special status for Kashmir to "protect its Muslim character". Among the demands were a separate Constitution and a separate flag. He wanted for himself the title of "prime minister". Nehru granted all these demands and more. He even assured him that all these special provisions would be enshrined in the new Article 370 of the Constitution of India. That partition was the result of Muslim separatism was conveniently forgotten.

No wonder, the Sheikh was in a triumphant mood. He called for elections to form a Constituent Assembly which could then draw up the state's Constitution. But then, he was given to extremes. He wanted all the 72 members of the Assembly "elected" unopposed and he wanted all of them from his own party. So, he engineered the defeat of the only two opposition candidates from the Jammu region. Thus, he established his reputation as the uncrowned king of Kashmir.

One-party rule brought about the alienation of the Jammu population, which started an agitation under the leadership of Pandit Prem Nath Dogra. The people of Jammu (mostly Hindus) wanted full accession of the state to the Indian Union without any reservations. They opposed the "special" status that Sheikh

83

Abdullah was seeking. Dogra, therefore, raised the slogan: *"Ek Vidhan, Ek Pradhan, Ek Nishan"* (One Constitution, One Prime Minister, One Flag). Dogra's party, the Praja Parishad, called for the extension of all constitutional provisions to the state of Jammu and Kashmir. Sheikh Abdullah was furious, and unleashed his full force against the agitators. As a result, about 40 Parishad activists were killed. Sheikh Abdullah got away with it by branding the Parishad a "communal" organisation, although it had a large Muslim membership.

The Sheikh's assertion of independence came out early enough. The agent general of India, Kanwar Dalip Singh, informed the Government of India of the dangerous independent tendencies of the Sheikh, but he was told not to interfere. He resigned in disgust.

The Sheikh was no respecter of opposition. So he ran into trouble even with Muslims who were opposed to him. As more and more Muslims began to leave his party, he was compelled to alter his strategy. He began to put the blame for the state's difficulties on the Centre. He claimed that the problems of the state arose not due to his misrule, but because of accession to the Indian Union.

Soon, he had a good cause to justify his accusations. The Jana Sangh was on the warpath against the Sheikh. Dr. S.P. Mookerjee, its president, wanted to know whether there could be a republic (meaning Jammu and Kashmir) within the Indian Republic and warned that Kashmir would be lost the way it was going (*The Hindustan Times*, 27 June 1952). Dr. Mookerjee had entered the state without a permit. He was arrested and incarcerated. His unfortunate death, while in detention, created convulsions in India, and the Sheikh came under severe criticism in Jammu and the rest of India. Consequently, he became more critical of the accession of the state to India.

This turn of events was the situation least expected, for the Sheikh was viewed as a symbol of secularism. The situation upset even National Conference leaders such as Bakshi Ghulam Mohammad, G.M. Sadiq, D.P. Dhar and others. Central leaders tried to reason with the Sheikh, particularly Maulana Abul Kalam Azad, whom the Sheikh is reported to have insulted.

It was at this time that the Sheikh began to meet American representatives such as Ambassador Loy Henderson and presidential candidate Adlai Stevenson. Such meetings infuriated his friends in the Indian communist movement, who thought that he was selling himself to the imperialists. There was a demand that he should step down. But nothing daunted the Sheikh. He continued his attacks on the Central Government and refused to meet Nehru. Perhaps, the Sheikh overplayed his hand. He thought that Nehru would succumb under pressure. Instead, this time, there was pressure on Nehru to drop the man and instal some other National Conference leader. Nehru accepted the new course reluctantly.

The Sheikh had been nursing the idea of an independent Kashmir. In 1949, he told Michael Davidson, a correspondent of the London *Observer* and the *Scotsman*: "Accession to either side cannot bring peace. We want to live in friendship with both the Dominions. Perhaps a middle path between them with economic cooperation with each will be the only way of doing it. However, an independent Kashmir must be guaranteed not only by India and Pakistan, but also by Great Britain, the US and other members of the UN" (cited in *Observer*, 7 March 1953). He was not interested in the Punjabi-speaking areas or the Pathans of Gilgit. "Let them join Pakistan", he said in an interview to Montreal's *Daily Star* (6 May 1949). Perhaps he was thinking only of ethnic Kashmiris. Whether or not the Pandits had a place in his scheme is not known.

Sheikh Abdullah went abroad in 1949. The Western media, which used to spite him, was deferential to him this time. In April 1952, the Sheikh spoke against the growth of communalism in India and the application of the Indian Constitution *in toto* to Kashmir. In what emerges as a clear declaration of support for Kashmir's independence, the London *Times* reported on 12 May 1952 : "Sheikh [Abdullah] has made it clear that he is as much opposed to domination by India as to subjugation by Pakistan. He claims sovereign authority for the Kashmir constituent assembly without limitation by the Constitution of the

Indian Union.... This line has a strong appeal to Kashmiris on both sides of the ceasefire line." Obviously, the Sheikh had gone too far.

A memorandum submitted by three cabinet colleagues of the Sheikh on 7 August 1953 alleged that he had resorted to arbitrary measures in running the administration; disregarded the wishes of his cabinet colleagues; denied freedom to legislative members to express themselves; encouraged factionalism; failed to implement development programmes; promoted corruption, nepotism, inefficiency and wanton waste of public funds; caused discontent in the administration; accentuated political uncertainty with serious adverse consequences to economic growth; caused unemployment to grow, tourism to decline and so on. "You have thus arbitrarily sought to precipitate a rupture in the relationship of the State with India", the memorandum charged. The memorandum also accused Mirza Afzal Beg of following communal policies and the Sheikh of encouraging Beg.

Neither Nehru nor the opposition leaders in India understood what was really happening in the Valley. While Nehru saw a "deeper significance" than the constitutional link in India's relations with the Valley, Dr. Ram Manohar Lohia hoped that the Valley people would continue to put their faith in the one-nation theory.

Bakshi Ghulam Mohammad, who succeeded the Sheikh in the latter half of 1953, began his career as a salesman in one of the Khadi Bhandars of Srinagar. But he had been in politics for a long time and knew the ropes. He provided a reasonably good administration and carried out pioneering developmental activities. He released all political prisoners, abolished the levy on peasants, made education free up to the university level, and introduced food subsidy. He also began the planning process in the state and sought Central assistance.

Bakshi Ghulam Mohammad was a shrewd politician. He was not averse to blackmailing the Centre. Thus, he would get more Central assistance, and, at the same time, buy the silence of the opposition. To him goes the credit of constructing the Banihal tunnel on the Jammu-Srinagar highway, the first all-weather route to Srinagar. But with development came corruption and the Bakshi regime became notorious. He and his family were deeply involved in unsavoury activities.

Bakshi Ghulam Mohammad was arbitrary and authoritarian. He created a secret police to nab those who were opposed to India and a voluntary force to deal with the opposition. Bakshi developed a cadre of workers sworn to loyalty, who were to become powerful gangsters called "Gogas". A relative of Bakshi, i.e., Bakshi Abdul Rashid, a gangster who was called "Khrushchev", was installed as general secretary of the National Conference. He had no education, but was made an MP. All these factors led to rampant corruption and lawlessness. The Centre knew about all these developments but looked the other way. It is this permissiveness for which the country is paying today. But worse was to follow. Although Bakshi was one of the most reliable leaders in Kashmir, and known for his total dedication to accession, the Centre did not stir when anti-Indian forces joined hands to defeat him in the elections.

The year 1953 witnessed a crisis in the state. Some disgruntled elements floated a new political party – the Political Conference – in June with Ghulam Mohi-ud-Din Karra (a cousin of G.M. Sadiq) as president and Raghu Nath Vaishnavi as vice-president. The main objective of the party was to join Pakistan. Mohammad Shafi Qureshi, a former Union minister, was one of its activists. In its very first public meeting, it announced its objective. But this party did not last long, for feuds broke out over the control of illicit funds received from Pakistan.

In the meantime, the followers of the Sheikh were getting restive. Mirza Afzal Beg organised a new party – the Plebiscite Front – in 1954 with the obvious intention of embarrassing the Centre by asking for a plebiscite. This party had the blessing of the Sheikh.

In January 1957, the Sheikh was released, but he did not change his stand against the Centre. He called on the people for a social boycott of those who were pro-India or members of national political parties. This call had serious consequences for pro-Bakshi and pro-Sadiq groups. In October 1957, G.M. Sadiq, Mir Qasim and Dogra resigned from Bakshi's cabinet, thereby precipitating a crisis. They formed a new party called the

Democratic National Conference. It was, of course, pro-India, and advocated a leftist programme. However, the Sheikh dubbed it a party of "Indian agents" and its leaders as enemies of Kashmir. He was again arrested and charged with sedition against the state.

The Democratic National Conference could not make an impact in the Valley and was wound up in 1959. Its leaders went back to Bakshi at Nehru's suggestion. In 1963, Bakshi was asked to resign under the Kamraj Plan. He put his own man, Shamsuddin, in power against the advice of Central leaders. But Shamsuddin could not survive for more than three months, for the unrest that resulted in the wake of the loss of the holy relic of Prophet Mohammad from the Hazratbal mosque (in December 1963), in which Bakshi was alleged to have had a hand, swept him and his followers out of power.

It was now the turn of G.M. Sadiq, who at one time was a radical leftist. Sadiq turned out to be a different man once he came to power. He got his own men elected. Although he favoured development of the state, there was little developmental activity. He did nothing to stop the growing anti-India agitation by the Sheikh's followers. Of course, he wanted the state to join the national mainstream, and with this view in mind, he extended the jurisdiction of the Supreme Court to the state and applied several sections of the Indian Constitution to the state. But the most significant step he took was to merge the National Conference with the Indian National Congress. This could have had momentous results. Unfortunately, Sadiq died in December 1971.

Despite all his progressive ideals, Sadiq introduced the communal virus in the educational system by reserving 70 per cent of the seats for Muslims. Again, it was during his regime that a major Hindu-Muslim clash took place, but he took no action against the Muslim instigators. The clash occurred over the conversion of a young Hindu girl after her marriage to a Muslim boy. During this period, many of Sadiq's close friends took the side of the Muslims.

One interesting episode in the man's life shows that the Indian leaders failed him at a crucial moment. That is, when he wanted to ban the Jamaat-i-Islami in the state, Indira Gandhi discouraged him by saying that in that case she would have to ban the RSS, too. Thus, she equated the RSS and the Jamaat – a gross instance of ignorance of what the Jamaat stood for. Sadiq then suggested simultaneous ban of both organisations. Indira said no. If she had agreed she could have nipped this evil in the bud.

Development of democracy in Jammu and Kashmir was not the concern of the Centre. It took no interest in this matter. Elections in J&K were invariably rigged and the 1967 elections were no different. Some eminent persons like C.D. Deshmukh, M.C. Setalvad and others were forced to protest. They doubted the fairness of the elections. But the Centre was indifferent to all such appeals.

The Sheikh never wanted an opposition in the Valley. The first political party to open a branch there was the PSP (Praja Socialist Party), which was headed by Balraj Puri. But soon the *goondas* of the National Conference beat up the leaders of the PSP, including its national chairman Asoka Mehta. Other attempts to form a secular opposition party in the Valley met with a similar fate, states Balraj Puri in an article entitled "Secular Crown on Fire: The Kashmir Problem".

Mir Qasim, who succeeded Sadiq, was not committed to socialism, nor was he a good administrator. He spoke of secularism, but encouraged fundamentalism. During his regime, the Jamaat grew rapidly.

In the 1972 elections, the Jamaat won five seats in the Legislature with Qasim's support, an ominous development. For its part, the Congress won 57 of the 74 seats. In 1972 negotiations began with the Sheikh and his lieutenants, which led to the Kashmir Accord, under which the Sheikh was brought back to power in February 1975. Mir Qasim stepped down to make way for him. Nevertheless, the Congress refused to elect the Sheikh as leader. This was a tactical mistake, although the Sheikh was averse to a Congress connection. However, the Congress offered him support in the Assembly. The Sheikh was opposed to the merger of the National Conference and the Congress. He had begun to work for their separation. The

Congress' refusal to join the cabinet suited Sheikh Abdullah admirably. He was free from constraints. But Indira Gandhi was unhappy. She did not trust the National Conference, which she considered a regional party. That is why she was in favour of a strong Congress presence in the state.

The Sheikh was not happy with the Kashmir Accord he had arrived at with Indira Gandhi, but he could not assert himself, for India was supreme in the region, having humbled Pakistan again in the 1971 war, which resulted in the creation of Bangladesh. India's victory was so decisive that 90,000 Pakistani soldiers had surrendered to the Indian army. The break-up of Pakistan into two was a blow to all Muslim fundamentalists in the Valley and in the rest of the country, for they used to believe that religion was the unifying force. The emergence of Bangladesh, the exposure of Pakistan's atrocities against Bengali Muslims, the close friendship of Mujibur Rahman, the prime minister of Bangladesh, with Indira Gandhi – all these factors must have had a humbling effect on the Sheikh.

However, the Sheikh was not a man given to introspection. He was merely biding his time. He continued to be critical of the Centre and was in conflict with the Congress party in the state. He cut off food subsidies to turn the people against the Centre. As before, he continued to speak in two voices: he would say one thing in Srinagar and another in New Delhi. In early 1975 the growth of opposition to Indira Gandhi in India led by Jayaprakash Narayan helped him in his plans.

Under the Shimla Agreement of 1972 negotiated between Indira Gandhi and Zulfiqar Ali Bhutto, it was decided that the "line of control" resulting from the ceasefire of 17 December 1971 should be respected by both sides without prejudice to the recognised position of either side. Neither side should seek to alter it unilaterally, irrespective of mutual differences and legal interpretations. Both sides further undertook to refrain from the threat or use of force in violation of this line. The new line was later referred to as the line of control (LOC). It, in fact, became the *de facto* border between the two nations.

The 1977 J&K state elections are accepted by all as clean and free and fair. The Sheikh refused to·cooperate with the

Congress. In fact, he had already revived the National Conference. However, the Congress had its main rival in the Janata Party. Adopting an unrepentant attitude, the Sheikh called for the opening of the Jhelum Valley road to Rawalpindi and the withdrawal of the Indian army from the state. He was now pitted against the Mirwaiz, who was emerging as a rallying point for the Muslims.

During the 1977-82 period, the Sheikh continued his not-so-friendly stance towards the Centre. He encouraged fundamentalist forces, allowed Friday prayers in offices, banned cinema shows during Friday prayers, and "Islamised" the administration as far as possible. He tried his best to undermine the authority of the Centre in the state, discouraged appointment of IAS (Indian Administrative Service) officers from the Centre and disallowed the work of the income tax authorities. Instead of the state taking over Jamaat schools as he promised, he now encouraged opening of more of them, and foreign money was allowed to flow in liberally to fund fundamentalist organisations.

It is interesting to note what the Janata Party (J&K unit) election manifesto felt about the National Conference in 1977: "The Kashmir nabobs resorted to blackmailing the Central leaders to achieve their personal ends and would raise, at times, the slogan of plebiscite and right of self-determination if the Central leadership slightly tried to resist the fulfilment of their extravagant ambitions. The unprincipled self-seekers had one purpose in mind: to amass wealth, whether coming from indigenous sources or from foreign countries" (Pyare Lal Kaul, *Crisis in Kashmir*, p.143). In fact, the Janata party members ran a campaign against the Sheikh, and the Sheikh came down heavily on them after he won the election. Many of the Janata workers had to flee to refugee camps in the face of the fury of the NC workers. The Sheikh seized the Janata Party headquarters in Srinagar. Not a finger was raised in protest by the Central leaders. All this happened right under Prime Minister Morarji Desai's nose.

The situation did not improve during the V.P. Singh period (December 1989 to November 1990). The Chandra Shekhar interlude (December 1990 to May 1991) was no better.

The Jammu Hindus were a bugbear to the Sheikh, for whenever there was a Pandit agitation in the Valley, the Jammu Hindus would agitate in sympathy. In order to teach them a lesson, the Sheikh established a Muslim Gujjar colony on the outskirts of Jammu city. The idea was to stir up the Gujjars against the Hindus if necessary. The Gujjars were provided all facilities from the state budget.

Ultimately, it was the Resettlement Bill, which the Sheikh introduced in the J&K Assembly on 30 March 1982, that raised a real furore. The Bill sought the permanent return and settlement of Muslims who had migrated to Pakistan or to the area held by Pakistan. They were to be rehabilitated in Jammu. The objective was clear – to bring Jammu under Muslim dominance. But the Sheikh made no such offer to people who had migrated to India.

Governor B.K. Nehru, however, returned the Bill and sought the opinion of the Attorney-General of India. But after the demise of the Sheikh, his son and successor as CM, Farooq Abdullah got the Bill passed. Rabi Ray, Janata Dal leader and former speaker of the Lok Sabha, had described this Bill as "dangerous for the security and integrity of India". The implementation was, however, stopped on a public interest appeal to the Supreme Court. But people who infiltrated into Jammu from PoK (Pakistan-occupied Kashmir) were quietly rehabilitated by the administration. The Sheikh's set attitude came to light in the way refugee property cases were handled. After 30-40 years, the J&K Government began to take over the property occupied by Hindu refugees who came from Pakistan which was held as evacuee property by the custodian.

Similarly, several towns and villages which had anything to do with Hindu culture were renamed in the guise of "modernisation". Such activities continued even after the Sheikh's death.

In short, the Sheikh created the most favourable conditions for fundamentalism to grow. In March 1980 a delegation from Medina University (Saudi Arabia) visited the Valley and received the hospitality of both the Jamaat and the Sheikh. The delegation members spoke publicly of the need for sacrifices to achieve

Islamic objectives. In September 1980, the Amir of the Jamaat of Pakistan-occupied Kashmir visited the Valley and declared that Kashmiris were not a party to the Shimla Agreement. He was asked to leave the country by the Centre. It was during this period that the Sheikh expanded the police force by recruiting Jamaat activists. This factor explains why the police force of the Valley since then has come to be viewed as "undependable". The period also saw hectic activity for building new mosques and renovating old ones. The mood is reflected in the autobiography of the Sheikh himself in which he castigated the Pandits, the Congress and Indian secularism. Incidentally, this book was given the Sahitya Akademi Award!

The ethnic policy then pursued helped the growth of fundamentalism. In the pre-1947 days, the Sunnis, the dominant group in the Valley, constituted half the population. The rest was made up of Hindus and Shias. Even today there are about a million Shias in the state. While the Shias were engaged in handicrafts, the Sunnis were dominant in agriculture but mainly as landless cultivators. The Hindus were either landlords or employees of the state administration. Being a Sunni, Sheikh Abdullah has often been accused of being partial to his sect. He introduced land reforms the moment he came to power in 1947 and denied compensation to Hindu landlords.

The Sheikh was not only partial to the Sunnis, but he was also a proud Kashmiri. He had a hand in shaping the ethnic identity of the Kashmiris, now referred to as *Kashmiriat*. This identity has little to do with their ancient culture. His objective was to isolate the Kashmiri Muslims from other Muslims. In this process he had employed four different means: isolated the Jammu Muslims (mostly Punjabi-speaking and pro-Pakistan); prevailed upon Nehru not to cross Uri during the advance of the Indian army (for beyond Uri lay regions where the Muslims were anti-Sheikh); denied refugee status to non-Muslims who migrated from PoK to the Valley (they were forcibly marched off to Jammu from the Valley); and resented secularisation of the Kashmiri Muslim society. It may also be recalled that the Sheikh was even ready to rehabilitate Muslims from Central Asia in the Valley, but not the Hindu refugees from Punjab. In the early 1950s, the Sheikh invited 5000 Kazakh Muslims to settle in the Valley. Again, in the late 1950s, when the Dalai Lama fled Tibet, the Sheikh invited the Tibetan Muslims to come and settle in Kashmir. But he refused to allow a single Tibetan Buddhist refugee to settle in the Valley, not even in Ladakh.

The Sheikh died in September 1982. But before his death he made his son, Dr. Farooq Abdullah, the president of the National Conference, and asked the Kashmiris to place their trust in him, for, he said, his son would accomplish what he had not been able to.

It was Nehru who had built up Sheikh Abdullah. It is a kind of poetic justice, therefore, that he denounced the Sheikh before his death. B.N. Mullik, head of the Intelligence Bureau, wrote: "Suddenly to our utter surprise, Pt. Nehru started talking bitterly against Sheikh Abdullah's communalism (at a Cabinet Committee meeting). He traced the Sheikh's history from 1930 onwards and mentioned how he had started his career with the Muslim Conference, which was an out and out communal organisation. He said that as a result of pressures from outside and seeing developments of the State people's movement in the rest of India and for purely tactical reasons and probably on the advice of some of his more liberal followers, the Sheikh had converted the Muslim Conference to give it a non-communal appearance. At this time, Pt. Nehru suddenly looked at me and enquired whether I had not come across some information of possible British connivance in that movement (Muslim Conference). I replied in the affirmative".

Mullik further wrote: "He continued his talk against the Sheikh and mentioned all his communal activities throughout the period he had acted as the National Conference leader. It was the Pakistan aggression which had mellowed him a little for a short time, because the tribesmen had committed gruesome atrocities on the Muslim population in the Valley. But as soon as he became the Prime Minister, he came out in his true colours, praised Bakshi and Sadiq for their completely non-communal outlook.... Pandit Nehru said that all the trouble in Kashmir was due to the Sheikh's communal outlook and it was he who was not allowing the State to settle down to peace and stability"

(B.N. Mullik, *My Years with Nehru*, p. 134). And let us not forget that when the Sheikh applied for a passport to go abroad, he mentioned his nationality as "Kashmiri", not Indian. Consequently, historians must look afresh at the Sheikh's connection with Jinnah and other Muslim League leaders.

7

The 1965 Flare-up

I shall now make a quick survey of the Kashmir scene, Pakistan's involvement in the US military alliances and the 1965 war between India and Pakistan.

In the early 1950s, Dr. Frank Graham's mission was a failure (see Chapter 14 for details). He, however, suggested bilateral negotiations between India and Pakistan. He put forward a proposal for a meeting between Nehru and Khwaja Nazimuddin, prime minister of Pakistan, but the latter was dismissed for his opposition to Pakistan's entry into military alliances. Hopes were again raised when Mohammad Ali Bogra became the prime minister in 1954. He and Nehru did work out a formula for a plebiscite, but it did not find favour with either the Pentagon or the Pakistani leaders.

It was at this time that reports of US military aid to Pakistan began to appear in the media. Nehru warned that the proposal to demilitarise Kashmir would become a farce if Pakistan received military assistance. On 22 February 1954, Mohammad Ali announced US aid to Pakistan under the terms of the US Security Act. President Dwight Eisenhower assured Nehru that US arms would not be used against India. (But on 10 April 1953, Chou-En-lai, the Chinese premier, told Associated Press of Pakistan that Pakistan had assured him that it had joined the Western military alliance to augment its military power against India.) Nehru made it clear that US military aid to Pakistan had altered the basis of the discussion in regard to the quantum of forces to be maintained in Jammu and Kashmir.

Nevertheless, on 15 May 1955, Indo-Pak discussions were resumed, wherein it was decided to resolve other bilateral issues. The topic of Kashmir, however, came up in the UN Security Council in 1957. The Indian minister of defence, V.K. Krishna Menon, made a powerful presentation of the Indian case. On 21 February 1957 the Security Council appointed Gunnar Jarring, the Swedish representative in the Council, as a mediator. In his report of 29 April 1957, he declared that India was not ready to implement the UN Security Council resolution unless Pakistan first carried out its part of the obligations. He acknowledged that since 1947 vast changes had taken place in power relations in West and South Asia. The US and Britain managed to send Dr. Graham back to the subcontinent, but his mission was again a failure.

In 1960, the Pakistan President Ayub Khan visited New Delhi, but his talks proved futile. In 1962, again, Pakistan tried to bring up the subject in the Security Council, although it was now planning a military solution to the Kashmir problem.

In the meantime, radical changes had been taking place in Jammu and Kashmir. The state had made considerable progress. Land reforms had been carried out. Canals and roads had been constructed. More than 70,000 tourists visited the Valley in 1961. Education had been made free up to the graduate level. New schools and colleges had been opened. The student figure at the primary level had gone up from 65,000 in 1954 to 197,000 in 1961. In 1948 there were 52 high schools; the number went up to 262 by 1961. There were 89 hospitals in 1947; by 1961 there were 449. Life expectancy rose from 30 to 41 years.

Between 1952 and 1962, there were three general elections to the State Assembly.

During the 1962 Chinese aggression on India, the West tried to force India to come to terms with Pakistan on Kashmir. The West did not like Pakistan's closeness to China and wanted it to sever this relation. But Pakistan's price was Kashmir. Certain prominent public figures such as Averell Harriman of the USA and Duncan Sandys of the UK tried their best to pressurise India. On 27 December 1962, Zulfiqar Ali Bhutto, foreign minister of Pakistan, and Sardar Swaran Singh, his counterpart in India, met at Rawalpindi, but could make no progress. In 1964, Pakistan again raised the Kashmir issue in the Security Council, charging that India was going ahead with the integration of Kashmir.

By early 1965, war clouds began to gather on the horizon. Sheikh Abdullah was in an ugly mood. In March 1965, the Government of India issued passports to the Sheikh and Mirza Afzal Beg to visit Mecca. They took this opportunity to attend the Afro-Asian Conference, which was being held at Algiers. At London, they broke journey to address a press conference, but they said not a word about the Chinese aggression of 1962. At Algiers, the Sheikh met Chou-En-lai. This was an unpardonable offence in view of the acrimonious nature of India-China relations. India cancelled his passport and ordered him to return. Pakistan offered him a passport, which he refused. On their return, he and Beg were arrested. Riots and civil disobedience resulted. By August 1965, war broke out between India and Pakistan in which both the USA and China played significant roles.

In counterpoint, India's move to develop closer relations with the USSR had begun immediately after independence. By 1955, both Indian and Soviet leaders had made their historic visits: Nehru to the USSR and Nikita Khrushchev to India, thus cementing a relationship that was to have far-reaching global significance. On his visit to India, Khrushchev, on his own initiative, went to Kashmir to underline the new global reality, and declared that "the question of Kashmir as one of the constituent states of the Republic of India has already been decided by the people of Kashmir.... Facts show that the population of Kashmir do not wish that Kashmir becomes a toy in the hands of imperialist forces" (M.S. Rajan, *India in World Affairs, 1954-56*, p. 319).

It did not take Pakistani strategists long to realise that a linkage with China was more advantageous than an alliance with the USA, for while the USA could not be an "enemy" of India, China was already one, having a number of disputes with India.

At the same time, only the USA could provide Pakistan with modern weapons. These twin strategic needs ultimately shaped Pakistan's policies. But Pakistan had a border problem with China (it has a 2000-mile border in the Hunza region). On 23 October 1959, three years before the India-China war, Ayub Khan made a statement that any Chinese intrusion into Pakistan along this common border would be repelled. But these hostile perceptions soon changed with the India-China war in the offing. Pakistan could, obviously, perceive that a settlement of its border with China would lead to Chinese recognition of its claim to the Jammu and Kashmir state. In any case, the region was a "disputed" territory, which was to be settled through a plebiscite as per UN resolutions, and, thus, Pakistan could not lose much. So, it gave away 2000 sq. miles of Kashmir territory to China.

The war of 1965 between India and Pakistan was the direct result of massive US military assistance to Pakistan. Had it not been for such assistance from 1953 onwards, Pakistan would not have taken the plunge, because the results were by no means certain.

China openly came out on the side of Pakistan. This was inevitable after the 1962 war between India and China, when Pakistan had taken the side of China. Geopolitical calculations were decisive factors in the Chinese outlook. That is why Nehru's policy of friendship (*Hindi-Chini Bhai Bhai*) never worked. Nor did Nehru's Tibetan policy produce a favourable response from China. In population, resources and size, India posed a long-term problem to China. This is so even today. That is why China was bound to support and encourage India's neighbours (Pakistan, Bangladesh, Burma, etc.) in their hostility towards India. China is unlikely to give up this policy on its own. Only tactics can change. Similarly, it is more useful for the USA to have a strong Pakistan as an ally to keep the Middle East under its control. In turn, Pakistan finds its friendship with the USA as a means to checkmate India. Only a very powerful India can change the calculations of both the USA and Pakistan. The tragedy of India lay in the fact that, in the 1960s, it was blissfully unaware of the insidious roles of the various actors.

Nehru had passed away on 27 May 1964. Lal Bahadur Shastri assumed office as prime minister shortly. Pakistan was under the wrong impression that Shastri was a weak man and India would enter a period of instability.

As a result of acquiring the latest weapons from the USA, Pakistan developed a false sense of invincibility. The débâcle suffered by India against China also encouraged Pakistan in its aggressive designs. Consequently, Pakistan launched a military campaign, codenamed "Operation Gibraltar", which essentially involved a renewed effort to seize Kashmir by force. Pakistan, however, tested India's preparedness in the Kutch region first. India's response turned out to be weak. Instead of an effective befitting reply, India agreed to ceasefire and arbitration by a third party. This emboldened the Pakistan military regime to attack Kashmir. From early 1965, Pakistan began a massive infiltration of its soldiers into Kashmir. During this process, it followed Chinese guerrilla tactics. Coming in groups of two's and three's the infiltrators were to take up strategic positions so as to create anarchy, and bring about a total breakdown of the administrative machinery in Jammu and Kashmir. The infiltration went on till August, when they were discovered. The objective was to capture or destroy airports, police posts and bridges, as also manufacturing facilities. But the people of Kashmir reported these infiltrators to local police stations, and they were soon rounded up. Perhaps Pakistan had hoped for cooperation from the people. As in 1947, Pakistan failed to get any help, although in 1965 the Plebiscite Front had exhorted the people to side with Pakistan.

Lal Bahadur Shastri's reaction was prompt and decisive. India retaliated with determination. And when India's strategists thought that there was need to open a second front to humble Pakistan, Shastri did not wobble as Nehru did in 1947. He gave his full support. Pakistan did not expect this action.

In his Foreword to Air Marshal Asghar Khan's book *The First Round: India-Pakistan War 1965*, Altaf Gauhar reveals that Pakistan first mounted the guerrilla operation (Operation Gibraltar) on 5 August and then followed it up with an open military attack on Kashmir on 3 September. This time, the Indian response was quick and effective. This explains why the UN Security Council resolution called for the withdrawal of all armed personnel to the positions held by them before 5 August. Both the Anglo-Americans and Chinese backed Pakistan.

Eventually, the UN called for a ceasefire at 12.30 hours on 22 October 1965. Thus, it was a short war, but very destructive. Pakistan's war machine was crippled. It was at this juncture that the USSR offered its good offices to both parties to bring about peace. This led to the Tashkent Agreement of 10 January 1966 between President Ayub Khan and Prime Minister Lal Bahadur Shastri.

As before, Pakistan denied any responsibility for the war. This time, too, its leaders had miscalculated. They thought that the Valley Muslims would rise against India. They did not.

The 1965 war exploded some common myths such as that Pakistan was better armed and that it could take on the might of India. This was not so. The Tashkent Declaration, which raised high hopes, expressed the firm resolve of both countries to restore normal and peaceful relations, not to have recourse to war and to settle disputes peacefully. It also spelt out the various steps to restore normalcy in their relations. But the "Tashkent spirit" did not last long.

8

The Growth of Militancy

Exhorting Muslims to heroism, the poet Mohammad Iqbal asserts: "*Allah ke sheron ko aati nahin rubahi*" (Allah's lions know no cowardice). This was no Sufi saint showing the path of love. Was Iqbal a fundamentalist who was suggesting the path of violence and the use of the sword? Maulana Wahiduddin Khan, a respected Muslim scholar and a sane voice today, says that by setting up the imaginary lion as an ideal, Muslims have opted for the path of conflict and confrontation on the mistaken premise that this is what is meant by bravery and that what they are doing amounts to a jehad (*The Times of India*, 17 May 1995). Perhaps militancy in a section of Muslims draws on these wild poetic imageries.

Militancy in Kashmir began with the Plebiscite Front, set up in August, 1955 by Mirza Afzal Beg on the Sheikh's instigation. The Front worked among the young, and turned their frustrations against India. Soon, it linked its fortune with the fundamentalist forces such as the Jamaat-e-Islami. And it fully exploited the emotional outbursts of the people in 1964, when the holy relic of Prophet Mohammad disappeared from the Hazratbal mosque. This event also stirred up the mullahs, who were rather dormant. Since then, they have occupied the centrestage in Kashmir. But all these developments arise from the fact that there was a pro-Pak group in Jammu and Kashmir after partition.

Naturally, the first concern of the pro-Pak forces was the release of the Sheikh. Next came the demand for plebiscite. The Holy Relic Action Committee received support not only from PoK but also from Pakistan. Islamabad was preparing for a new aggression on Kashmir. By 1965, the moderate forces in the Valley were replaced by the hawks. The release of Sheikh Abdullah and his re-arrest following his scandalous attacks on India gave a new boost to these violent forces.

The unrest in Kashmir offered a golden opportunity to Pakistan to make another bid to seize the Valley. With this objective in view, Pakistan set up training camps in PoK and West Punjab. Volunteers were recruited from the Pakistan army as also from PoK, and trained and despatched to the Valley to be ready to act as guerrillas. They were to provide leadership to the militant groups in the Valley. But, as mentioned earlier, the Kashmiris were not ready for an uprising. However, the guerrillas began their depredations – sabotage and ambushes. Bridges were blown up and police stations were attacked. On 8 August 1965, the *Voice of Kashmir* announced the setting up of a Kashmiri Revolutionary Council to wage a war of liberation against "Indian oppression".

The war of 1965 left a nucleus of militancy among the youth of the Valley. Many of them learnt how to handle weapons. Thus, the war did not dampen the spirit of the rebels. On the contrary, organisations such as the Plebiscite Front became more militant. There were attempts to steal weapons from government armouries.

Soon enough, the Kashmir Liberation Front (KLF), under the leadership of Mohammad Maqbool Butt, appeared. In 1967 a number of teachers, who formed the core of the KLF, were arrested. Butt too was arrested for the murder of Amar Chand Pandit, for which he was eventually hanged at Delhi's Tihar Jail on 11 February 1984. However, militancy gained ground. In 1971, a large-scale plot of subversion was unearthed. Al Fateh, a militant outfit, formed in 1968 with Pakistan's help, was behind it. This organisation, a close ally of the Plebiscite Front, was responsible for many murders, kidnappings and bank robberies. In January 1971, about 350 Plebiscite Front workers were detained. Mass arrests of Al Fateh cadres were ordered. It was at this time that an Indian Airlines plane *Ganga* was hijacked to Lahore. Z.A. Bhutto visited the airport and embraced the hijackers, declaring "no power on earth can stifle the Kashmiris' struggle for liberation". The two hijackers demanded the release of 36 members of the KLF in Indian custody, and were given a hero's welcome in Lahore.

The war of December 1971 was a traumatic event for Pakistan, for with its dismemberment and the emergence of Bangladesh as an independent country, the two-nation theory was in tatters. This development came as a setback to the fundamentalist and militant forces in Kashmir. However, with the advent of General Zia-ul-Haq in Pakistan, these forces got a new lease of life.

Zulfiqar Ali Bhutto had always done his worst to stir up his people against India. In fact, he burnt with a fierce hatred of this country. In 1965 (he was the foreign minister then) he took a personal interest in instigating the infiltration of Pak forces into Jammu and Kashmir. Indeed, he played a major role in the 1965 Indo-Pak war. His vituperation against India in the Security Council forced Sardar Swaran Singh to walk out of the Council. Such was the intemperance of the man that he exclaimed: "The dogs have gone home!" And yet when this man came to India in 1972 for negotiating the Shimla Agreement along with his daughter, Benazir, they were objects of endless adoration in the Indian media. The pro-Pak elements in this country almost went wild with joy. Such are the idiocies that one has to live with in this country. As for Indira Gandhi, she proved to be a novice before Bhutto, the past-master in deception. In this context, the well-known political commentator, Ajit Bhattacharjea, writes: "Yet, this was the man that Indira Gandhi and her advisers chose to believe when he pleaded *'aap mujh par bharosa keejiye'* (trust me) at the Shimla Summit in June 1972." He goes on: "The failure to exploit the victory won by India's armed forces to secure Pak recognition of the Line of Control in Jammu and Kashmir as an international border is perhaps the greatest diplomatic blunder in our history since independence." Thus, our rulers messed up not only the domestic life of the state of Jammu and Kashmir, but also the negotiations with Pakistan. In no way has the situation improved since then.

General Zia-ul-Haq, who felt the humiliation of the 1971 Pak defeat bitterly, had sworn to take revenge on India. He wanted to pay India in the same coin by engineering its dismemberment. And he was able to make an attempt at no great expense to Pakistan, for he used US funds that were flowing into the Afghan war through Pakistan for financing yet another proxy war, this time in Kashmir and Punjab. Arif Nizami, editor of *The Nation*, wrote on 21 May 1990, that Pakistan's ruling party "credits Zia with laying the foundations for the present uprising" in Kashmir.

According to Selig Harrison of the Carneigie Foundation (*The Washington Post*, 23 April 1990): "Pakistani stimulation of the Punjab insurgency goes back to the beginnings of the Zia-ul-Haq regime in 1978. By 1984, the Pakistan army's Field Intelligence Unit was helping to organise the Liberation Front in the Indian-held Kashmir Valley. By 1988, the Inter-Services Intelligence (ISI) Directorate in Islamabad had begun to set up training camps in Pakistan-held Azad Kashmir, manned by retired Pakistan army officers."

Yet, Indian leaders thought of winning the friendship of General Zia-ul-Haq by inviting him to witness a cricket match in India! General Zia had come to Jaipur to watch the cricket match on Rajiv Gandhi's invitation. Just before emplaning for Islamabad, according to Zia's son Ejaz-ul-Haq, who became an opposition leader in Pakistan's National Assembly, Zia had taken Rajiv Gandhi aside and informed him that Pakistan had the same weapon (meaning atom bomb) as India. He claims that this statement made Rajiv Gandhi understand the situation (*The Times of India*, 31 August 1994). Did he ? One wonders, for at least in Kashmir there was no policy response from the Indian side.

Pakistan has been constantly asserting that it has nothing to do with the insurgency and that it had not provided any assistance to the militants, which is a brazen lie. There is any amount of evidence to prove that Pakistan has been organising the training of the militants and arming them. Nizami, wrote on 13 June 1990, that "the Gates Mission (Robert Gates who became the CIA chief) has confirmed that the information (regarding Pakistan's running of 31 training camps for the Kashmiri militants) was supplied by Pakistani officials" (*The Nation*).

It was not that there was no opposition to the policy of proxy war sponsored by Zia-ul-Haq and followed by his successors. Already Pakistan's proxy war in Afghanistan had cost that country heavily. Five million refugees were tearing up the country with their violence, gun running, narcotic trade, and drug distribution. And, in addition, there were a few million drug addicts among the young. *Al Ahram*, an Egyptian daily, reported on 8 April 1993 : "In a warning cry against the increasing sway of terrorists in Pakistan, the Pakistan Minister of State for Economic Affairs, Asaf Ali, tendered his resignation and accused the government that Pakistan has now become a haven of the terrorists."

The daily added: "The abundance of weapons and absence of control in the border area also have led to complaints, particularly from the USA and Egypt, that the region is a breeding ground for radical Islamic terrorists."

I am quoting different sources on this issue, for there is an impression in the Indian press that the insurgency is spontaneous and that it is a mass uprising of the people against the Central Government. This impression is no doubt the result of disinformation. But it speaks poorly about our media which tends to support Pakistan, when there is a mass of evidence to show that the present imbroglio is the result of a well-planned conspiracy hatched by the ISI of Pakistan.

When Benazir Bhutto became the prime minister of Pakistan on 2 December 1988, she seemed inclined against the proxy war in Punjab and Kashmir. But President Ishaq Khan and the Pak army had the final say in these matters. In fact, the army and the ISI had already drawn up detailed plans to give training facilities to Kashmiri youth and to arm them. Benazir had assumed power on the tacit understanding that she would not interfere with Pakistan's Afghan and nuclear policies. Later, the army top brass compelled her to accept the new Kashmir policy.

The only concession they made was to transfer ISI's director-general Hamid Gul on 25 May 1980. Lieutenant-General (retired) Shamsur Rehman Kallu was appointed in his place.

Pakistan has been making persistent efforts to promote disaffection against India since 1947, particularly after 1972. In 1973, a book was discovered in a Srinagar college library with a drawing of Prophet Mohammad and Gabriel, the angel (Islam prohibits the depiction of the Prophet in any manner). This was a children's book of knowledge by Arthur Meo, brought in perhaps in 1911 by a missionary school, which later found its way to this library. Yet, in Kashmir, there were violent agitations against India for having "imported" this book. That the book came into the country during the colonial period made no difference to the militants. There were attacks on churches (one of them was torched), and many people died in the agitation. This shows how irrational these militant outfits could be and how inept and worthless the administration was. The Centre was a supine observer of all these happenings.

When Syed Mir Qasim became the chief minister, he depended on the fundamentalists for political support. Although he arrested a number of these young men, he let them off on the pleas of their parents. It is this leniency which later turned them into hardcore killers.

Al Fateh, a Pak-funded organisation consisting of criminal elements, broke up into two at this stage – perhaps under Pak inspiration – one faction turning against the Sheikh. However, after the Mirza Beg-G. Parthasarathy accord (Kashmir Accord of 1975), the group against the Sheikh was wound up, and Qasim made way for him. A new youth organisation, Jamaat-e-Tulba, was founded by Azam Inquilabi (alias Mohammad Artaf Khan) which went on to play a destructive role.

The 1977 general election was fair, but it revealed that pro-Pakistan groups existed in the Valley. But this fact made no difference to the state authorities who were not prepared to curb the activities of such groups.

The number of separatist outfits increased when Dr. Farooq Abdullah came to power on the death of his father in September 1982. During the 1983 election, the Congress and the National

Conference were rivals. Indira Gandhi visited the Valley in mid-1983 and addressed a massive crowd in Iqbal Park (which shows that the Congress was still popular). This meeting was marred by one unsavoury incident – when she rose to speak, she was facing a number of nude young men (this shows how inefficient and indifferent the administration was). Soon after, the state Congress office was attacked and torched. (In 1977 the NC workers did the same to the Janata Party office.)

In the 1977 Assembly election, the Congress and the Janata were routed by the National Conference in the Valley. In 1983, however, the Congress won two seats in the Valley and 38 went to the National Conference. But in Jammu, the Congress won 23 of the 32 seats against six won by the NC.

In July 1984 the Farooq Abdullah ministry was toppled by the Congress by engineering a defection in the ranks of the National Conference. The Congress put G.M. Shah, brother-in-law of Farooq, on the seat, although there was little to choose between their policies. It was during Shah's regime that the hijacking of an Airbus took place, the work of Sikh terrorists. This incident brought to light a secret which was related by Indira Gandhi to Khem Lata Wakhlu, minister of state for tourism, in the Shah cabinet.

According to Khem Lata, Indira Gandhi told her during one of her official visits to New Delhi that there was a Pakistani in that hijacked flight and that he had been in Srinagar to meet Dr. Abdullah. He was seen off at Srinagar airport by two ministers of Dr. Abdullah (Anil Maheshwari, *Crescent over Kashmir: Politics of Mullaism*).

The imposition of the Shah regime on the state was perhaps the last straw as far as the people were concerned. This is what the militants exploited. In February 1986, riots broke out at Anantnag against the Pandits – a small community in that area. There was unprecedented violence, as also loot, arson and destruction of temples. The local administration, including the police, remained indifferent. No one came to the rescue of the Pandits. Such a reaction produced a shock wave among them. This is what set them off on their Diaspora. However, no action was taken against the Anantnag administration.

After the withdrawal of Congress support to Shah, he resigned on 7 March 1986, and president's rule was imposed. (Jagmohan took over as governor.) Under the Rajiv-Farooq accord, Dr. Abdullah was brought back to power in November 1986, with Congress support. However, he could not control the militants. In fact, militancy gained ground even as he tried to win the militants over. New elections were ordered in March 1987. These were rigged heavily both by the Congress and the National Conference. Against them were ranged the combine under the Muslim United Front (MUF) led by Maulana Abbas Ansari, supported by the Jamaat and its military wing. Of the 75 seats, the NC won 40, the Congress 25, the MUF four, the BJP (Bharatiya Janata Party) two and independents four.

Farooq was back in power, but this time he had to face hostile crowds. He tried to overcome this problem, as was his wont, by spouting vituperations against the Centre. But the killings went on unabated. Governor Jagmohan wrote to both the president and the prime minister of the seriousness of the situation. But there was no response.

According to Hashim Qureshi, once a leading figure in the Jammu and Kashmir Liberation Front (JKLF) (now residing in Amsterdam, and who had successfully hijacked a plane to Pakistan), the ISI wanted him to recruit young Kashmiris for training in Pakistan. He refused to be an agent of Pakistan as his objective was the independence of Kashmir. He was, therefore, thrown out of Pakistan. ISI next turned its attention to Amanullah Khan, whose views on the future of Kashmir were not yet clear. He informed the press that his experience told him that the JKLF would not be able to secure international support on the issue of accession even among the friends of Pakistan. It is clear from this statement that without Pakistan's support, he was not sure of achieving anything.

The emergence of the Muslim United Front, an alliance of fundamentalists and pro-Pak elements, is significant, for it threw up the real challenge of Pakistan's ISI to the Indian authorities. This political outfit of the Jamaat which was backed by militants needed only an alibi for mounting an all-out attack on Indian positions. Such an opportunity arose during the 1987 election, when Dr. Abdullah resorted to large-scale rigging and other malpractices to defeat MUF candidates. It is interesting to note here that the young men who used to work for Dr. Abdullah were now working for the MUF, and they were enraged over the defeat of their candidates. They were determined not to let Dr. Abdullah enjoy his power.

The return of the Janata Party to power at the Centre in December 1989, with its pro-Muslim vote bank politics, had the worst possible impact on the Valley. The appointment of Jagmohan as governor was perhaps well meant, but he could not have cleaned up the Augean stables without the full support of the Centre. Although V.P. Singh (the prime minister), a confused man at the best of times, was supportive to begin with, Srinagar politicians were able to poison the minds of the Central leaders once they knew that Jagmohan meant business. They ultimately persuaded V.P. Singh to appoint George Fernandes as minister of Kashmir affairs over the head of the governor. Neither V.P. Singh nor Fernandes was able to see the consequences of this action. Soon, the minister and the governor were not on talking terms. While Jagmohan was promoting the pro-India elements in the Valley, the minister's actions indirectly helped the anti-national elements. What was worse, while the governor wanted to apprehend the criminal elements, Fernandes gave them protection. Kashmir had never witnessed such anarchy.

Mention must be made here of the all-party initiative in going to Srinagar in March 1990. The performance of Rajiv Gandhi at Srinagar shocked the nation. In this context, two excerpts deserve to be reproduced here. One is a report in *The Statesman* of 9 March 1990, which ran as follows: "Touché, Rajiv Gandhi. First, you create the mess. Then, you and your allies try to be martyrs.... Your feigned concern for Devi Lal's position as Deputy Prime Minister and the lack of courtesy supposedly shown by the Governor, only confirm doubts that your insistence on all-party initiative in Kashmir is nothing short of gimmickry ... when will you grow up, Gandhi? Or, alternatively why don't you suggest to the present PM, his Deputy and his

Home Minister to make a gift of the Valley to any one of your choice." Devi Lal himself denied any slight on the part of the governor.

The second is a news item in *The Hindustan Times*, 11 March 1990. On 10 March 1990 Saifuddin Choudhary and Biplab Dasgupta (CPM), M. Farooqi and A.S. Malhotra (CPI) and Jaswant Singh and Kedar Nath Sahni (BJP), who were part of the all-party initiative, made a joint statement: "Rajiv Gandhi broke the consensus and briefed the press on issues discussed confidentially at the meeting. He frustrated one of the main objectives of the visit, that is, to demonstrate the common national concern, cutting across political boundaries. We deplore such attitude on his part."

I have reproduced these two excerpts to show how matters of great moment in Kashmir were being handled by the political leadership of the country, particularly by the leadership of the Congress, which was then out of power. There was no statesmanship, no effort at finding a solution. The performance of Rajiv Gandhi directly encouraged the militants' intransigence with all the consequences that followed.

The threats of the militants began with the call on women to observe purdah and not to visit cinema halls, and Hindu women were urged to wear the *tika* (the dot on the forehead) to identify them. Village Muslim women hardly wore purdah in Kashmir and even in urban towns the practice had almost been given up. There is still no unanimity among the militants on these codes. For example, the Dukhtaran-i-Millat, a women's fundamentalist outfit, came out with an elaborate code of conduct for women. But other militant outfits spoke against this code.

There was continuous provocation of the Hindus through the use of posters, asking them to either quit or get converted to Islam. These "poster wars" continued for a long time. Then there were repeated attacks on temples. Many of them were torched. And there were idol thefts.

For almost six months, the Kashmiris could not understand what was happening in their land. Of course, the Indian leaders were in no way better informed. All the three prime ministers – Rajiv Gandhi, V.P. Singh and Chandra Shekhar – were living in a fool's paradise. While Rajiv Gandhi had confabulated with Zia-ul-Haq on cricket, Chandra Shekhar had negiotated the release of kidnapped Kashmiris through Pakistan's mediation! In the meantime, Dr. Farooq Abdullah went on assuring the Centre that there were only a couple of hundred "misguided" young men in the insurgency outfit.

The Kashmir police and the Central paramilitary forces had warned both the Kashmir administration and the Centre that without additional reinforcements it would be difficult to stop the infiltration of militants and that once the militants crossed over to the border villages it would be impossible to identify them. Yet, there was no response. The mischief of Pakistan could have been nipped in the bud.

Today, there are more than one hundred militant outfits in the Valley. They are, in a way, rivals for achieving maximum influence, but they unite to protect themselves against the Indian armed forces. Apart from such well-known outfits as Al Fateh, there are Al Jihad, Al Maqbool, Muqqadas Jang, Hizb-e-Islam, Allah Tigers, Al Khomeini, Al Faran, etc. The state police has been completely infiltrated. In any case, the Sheikh, during his time itself, had filled the police with Jamaat volunteers. In the Valley, cops and terrorists co-exist because, in most cases, they know each other. This immunity from police prosecution is an important factor. In Punjab, no judge dared pass a sentence against the terrorists out of fear. In the Valley, no cop will dare arrest a militant.

The Pakistani intelligence agency (ISI) emasculated the JKLF and simultaneously formed the Hizb-ul-Mujahideen, a party of pro-Pak religious fanatics. From then on terrorism became a "jehad" and Amanullah's secular approach, reflected in the JKLF philosophy, became a casualty.

Perhaps it was the calculation of the ISI that the assassination of Rajiv Gandhi in May 1991 would lead to chaos in India and that the nation would fail to throw up a leader who could contain the various fissiparous tendencies. In any case, this agency thought that the event would offer the most propitious time for abetting an insurgency in Kashmir.

Militant depredations increased rapidly because the Janata interregnum had kept the focus of attention on New Delhi rather than elsewhere. So terrorists in Punjab and Kashmir had a free run. And, in December 1989, Mufti Mohammad Sayeed started from a weak position as Union home minister because he had to make a deal with the militants to get his daughter, Dr. Rubaiya, released from the kidnappers.

When five militants were released in return for Dr. Rubaiya, there was illumination as well as jubilation throughout the Valley. The Central power just stood by watching helplessly. But worse was to follow. When Nahida Imtiaz, daughter of Professor Saifuddin Soz, MP, was kidnapped, the Indian Prime Minister Chandra Shekhar literally begged Nawaz Sharief, prime minister of Pakistan, to get the girl released. That incident showed who was in power in the Valley. No prime minister of India had gone through such humiliation. All these events took place without a challenge from the law enforcement forces.

The militants had literally taken over Srinagar. Their writ ran all over the Valley. Thus they demanded closure of liquor shops. To frighten the still honest policemen, many police personnel were gunned down in December 1989. On 13 February 1990, Lassa Kaul, director of the Srinagar Centre of Doordarshan, was shot dead. On 25 March, Mir Mustafa, a liberal independent legislator, was shot dead. On 6 April, H.L. Khera, general manager of the HMT (Hindustan Machine Tools) factory, was taken hostage. Professor Mushir-ul-Haq, vice-chancellor of Kashmir University, was kidnapped and shot on 10 April. The militants' objective was to create awe and fear. In this they succeeded, for by selectively killing a few Pandits, they were able to frighten the entire Pandit community, which fled the Valley.

There is no doubt that the militants are divided on the issue of the future of Kashmir. The JKLF is for independence. Most others are for accession to Pakistan. Obviously, those in favour of Pakistan are getting funds not only through ISI sources, but also from fundamentalist forces in other Islamic countries, particularly the Gulf. These funds offer the real attraction to the militants. ISI had been trying to unite the pro-Pak elements. The fact that it has failed to do so shows that their declared objectives are not a passion with the militant outfits. By keeping their identities separate, they can continue to receive foreign funds.

In matters of communication, the militants are well provided. There is a clandestine radio functioning in PoK run by the ISI. And there is an excellent disinformation outfit in the Valley. In order to forge the unity of the militant outfits, ISI sponsored an outfit called Tehrik-e-Hurriat-e-Kashmir in 1990. Azam Inquilabi was placed as its chief.

From September 1989 onwards, when terrorism raised its ugly head in the state, attention has been focussed on the JKLF which professed to be secular and was fighting for independence. When Tika Lal Taploo, an eminent Pandit, was murdered, JKLF branded him as an Indian agent. The Pandits did not take the hint. Only when the selective killings increased did they understand that they were the targets.

On 21 January 1990, when the army began its house-to-house search, hysterical mobs roamed the city throughout the night shouting slogans and threatening the Pandits. Khem Lata Wakhlu writes in her book: "Hardly anyone in Kashmir slept on the night of January 21...hysterical screaming spewed out of hundreds of mosques. Anti-India slogans rent the air, coupled with Allah-o-Akbar and Nizam-e-Mustafa.... People owing allegiance to secular political parties were terrified to see the massive spectacle and were afraid that they might be the first victims of the onslaught of people in anger. It looked as if everybody was hell-bent on killing those who swore by Indian secularism.... Government officers, who may have controlled the situation, were scared to their bones."

From December 1989 onwards, Kashmiri Pandits started receiving threatening letters, asking them to quit the Valley. But Chief Minister Farooq Abdullah did nothing to check the terror tactics. The attacks on Pandits at Anantnag and later the indiscriminate killing of members of this community at Habba Kadal in Srinagar forced them to migrate. Panic gripped them and they left in haste leaving everything behind.

On 14 April 1990, the terrorists issued a warning that the Pandits should leave the Valley within 48 hours. If they dared to return, the punishment would be death, they threatened. Today, Farooq says that he is ashamed of the entire episode. Too late for comfort!

Mass exodus of Pandits started from the Valley. Houses of Pandits were burnt and property was looted. There was utter chaos as the state government could do little to control the situation. It instead provided help to the Pandits to flee. The Central Government watched silently and did nothing to strengthen the administration.

Governor Jagmohan then decided to get tough with the militants and it was the firing on the funeral procession of the Mirwaiz on 21 May 1990, by the CRPF (Central Reserve Police Force) that led to his recall. But the militants were out to provide the gravest provocation to the security forces when they snatched the body of the Mirwaiz and launched the procession. The militants had a clear objective: to inflame the population. They did not know who had killed the Mirwaiz. Yet they put the blame on Jagmohan. Here, too, the objective was clear: they wanted Jagmohan to quit. Then, who are these "innocents" who died in the firing? Surely, those who were participating in the procession were no innocents. They were agitators, out to stir up violence and cause bloodshed.

Jagmohan was viewed as pernicious because he was trying to put a stop to the permissiveness of the Central Government. No one but he dared to ban the Jamaat and seize its *madrasas*. There were more house-to-house searches during his regime, the only way to flush out the militants. Because these searches were proving effective, there was a cry of outrage, and the Central leaders were aghast.

Jagmohan may have been hated, may have been unpopular, and anti-Muslim. But which governor or politician was popular in the Valley? Jagmohan was popular in both Jammu and Ladakh, as also with the Pandit community in the Valley, not to speak of the rest of India, which saw him performing a difficult task with zeal and dedication. Jagmohan was actually sacrificed because of the politics of expediency that the V.P. Singh government preferred to pursue in the Valley. "*Kisi ko bali ka bakhra banana hai*" (somebody has to be made a scapegoat), former Prime Minister V.P. Singh told me during an informal chat during a flight from Goa in 1991.

What we see today in Kashmir is an effort to bring the Valley under the umbrella of pan-Islamism. Already several Islamic contingents from different countries are working in the state. As a consequence, the local militants have been sidelined.

One may not believe in the conflict of civilisations, but is not what is happening in Kashmir a revival of some ancient crusade? Today, there are Islamic soldiers from about six countries fighting against India in Kashmir. Tomorrow more will join this jehad against different countries.

Yossef Bodansky, director of the US Task Force on Terrorism and Unconventional Warfare, believes that militant Islamic forces constitute the principal threat to world peace. The USA is worried over the revival of Islamic radicalism. The Islamic "warriors" do not constitute a large force at present, but the Nazis too were not a large force in the initial part of the 1930s but became extremely powerful in the 1940s. The Organisation of Islamic Countries acts on the orders of the fundamentalists. Interestingly, the Sunnis and Shias seem to have joined hands in this jehad; this has not happened since the Crusades.

Bodansky considers Benazir's party more dangerous in this sense. It is she who has been promoting the strategic alliance with Iran and China.

Bodansky has warned India that if for some reason it decides to quit Kashmir, the state would be grabbed by the Islamists. They have a vital interest in absorbing Kashmir into the hub of the revivalist Islamic bloc, he says. He is also of the view that the Kashmiris can never enjoy independence as they will always have to obey the orders of the fundamentalists. Bodansky also believes that the loss of Kashmir would have serious adverse consequences for India's security.

The Kashmir administration is now under the threat of the militants. Governor Krishna Rao has been forced to depend more and more on this administration because he chose to be in conflict with the security forces. As a result, he has not been able to clean up the administration, which is the only way towards recovery. The revival of police activities is slow in the Valley, where many policemen are Jamaat followers. In Punjab, on the other hand, only a few policemen had "sold" themselves to the dreaded terrorist leader Jarnail Singh Bhindranwale. Terrorists are virtually invisible. Only the police can see them, not the army. That is why the police has a key role to play in anti-terrorism measures. So far, the Centre has not even given thought to this subject. Reviving the Valley police will be a daunting task. Yet the entire police machinery has to be created anew.

It has now been realised that there is need for revamping the administration. The loyalty of a large section of the employees of the state government has already been lost. As for the rest, they dare not assert themselves. Pro-Pak elements are like Trojan horses in the Indian camp. The security forces have to work, willy-nilly, with these enemies of India. They naturally feel demoralised by the brazenness of their treason and the indifference of the Central Government to these developments. Most of these pro-Pak elements contribute to the funds of the militants. It is an open secret that a number of senior officials of the state government signed a petition to the UN against India a few years ago. It is true that we cannot dismiss the whole lot of them. But treason should be punished. Why can't we make examples of a few of them and send the message across?

Union Home Minister S.B. Chavan has said that government officials in Jammu and Kashmir who did not enjoy a good reputation will have to go. But this is unlikely to happen, for behind each official is also his political patron. And yet unless the anti-national and corrupt bureaucrats are weeded out, there is no scope for real improvement in that state.

A great deal is being trumpeted about winning the hearts of the Kashmiris, about the need to restart the political process, and about wooing back the Kashmiris with a generous economic package. It is also being asserted that India must root out the causes of alienation.

No such concern was ever expressed in the case of Tamilians (when they demanded greater autonomy in the 1960s and 1970s) or the people of the north-east. In fact, I do not recall a single visit by our busybodies, the civil rights activists, to these far-flung north-eastern areas to find out the causes of insurgency in that region. Which shows that the people who make frequent visits to Kashmir have nothing beyond a good holiday in their minds.

Today, there are people from Afghanistan, Sudan, Egypt and the Gulf states fighting in Kashmir in the name of Islam. As far back as 30 January 1990, *The Times* (London) published a report from Pakistan that the Hizbul-e-Islamic led by the Afghan leader Gulbuddin Hikmatyar "was one of the main groups which helped in training Kashmiri activists". The Afghan mujahideen are also believed to be the main source of arms for the Kashmiris.

The Harkat-ul-Ansar has emerged as a major international fundamentalist Muslim outfit. According to a document entitled "Patterns of Global Terrorism – 1994", issued by the US State Department, the objective of the Harkat-ul-Ansar (founded in 1993) is to continue the armed struggle against non-believers and anti-Islamic forces. It has several thousand armed members in the "Azad Kashmir" area, many of them veterans of the Afghan war. They have taken part in terrorist operations in Kashmir, Myanmar, Tajikistan and Bosnia.

The militants are not united. In 1993, violent clashes among the militant groups brought into the open the rift among them. And there have been a great number of deaths. Most of these clashes involved outfits such as JKLF, Hizb-ul-Mujahideen, Al Jehad, Ikhwan-ul-Musalmeen, Al Buro and Muslim Mujahideen. During the Hazratbal crisis (October-November 1993), the JKLF and Hizb-ul-Mujahideen clashed over the issue of surrender of the militants holed up inside the shrine. It is the Hizb-ul-Mujahideen which gets money and guidance from Pakistan's ISI.

Pakistan was not pressing the case for plebiscite as much as for self-determination. This is, of course, a tactical policy, for it can be better understood. Pakistan was also blatant in asserting that the Kashmir question is an "unfinished business" of partition. Reported *The News*, a Pakistani journal, on 4 December 1991: "As the right of self-determination and the annexation of Kashmir to Pakistan is a part of the Two-Nation Theory, Pakistan is not complete till Kashmir is annexed to it."

It took a decade to bring insurgency under control in Nagaland and Punjab. In Kashmir it can be done sooner or later. The National Conference leaders state today that the Centre should initiate a dialogue with the militants on the restoration of the pre-1953 status quo. This is sheer blackmail. They are trying to use the militants to get back their power.

The government can get out of this situation if it bombs training camps, pursues the militants into Pak territory or otherwise eliminates them. All these options involve a heavy price. But these options must be weighed against other "softer" options open to our intelligence agencies.

There is no doubt that insurgency is not something that the people can accept forever. It is possible that insurgency itself can be kept going (as in Ireland), but it is not possible to retain the support of the people. Already, the people of the Valley are fed up with the violence and deaths, mostly perpetrated by the Hizb-ul-Mujahideen and other extremist elements. One thing is clear: militants are now on the defensive. The kidnapping of foreign tourists (June-July 1995) shows their sheer desperation. It is a fact that Islamabad and its supporters have had their quota of setbacks. The Pakistan authorities could not get their resolution passed at the UN Human Rights Commission, Geneva, in March 1994, for lack of adequate support, even from Muslim members. The release of Yasin Malik, president of the JKLF, and other key figures showed that the Indian side is not frightened. Malik's bold stand for pluralism, secularism and negotiations has given courage to the moderate elements in the Valley. It is significant that no militant organisation has so far condemned his stand. Even Shabir Shah, another vociferous militant, has been set free and allowed to air his views freely.

Today, what is alarming is the fact that the control of militancy has passed into the hands of foreign mercenaries, who are funded by fundamentalist forces in the Islamic world.

9

The Myth of Poverty

There is a myth that militancy in Kashmir is the direct result of poverty. But in reality it can be broadly attributed to the growing fundamentalism among the youth. And, of course, the external factors are important too.

J&K covers an area of 222,236 sq. km, one of the largest states of India, including 76,114 sq. km under Pak occupation, 5130 sq. km handed over by Pakistan to China, and 39, 605 sq. km illegally occupied by China. The net area with India is 101,387 sq. km. The mountains, which surround the Valley up to an average height of 1800 metres to 5000 metres, have kept Kashmir isolated geographically and economically. Ladakh has the highest habitations in the world. The Kashmir Valley is 134 km in length and 32 km to 40 km in breadth. It is a veritable amphitheatre surrounded by snow-bound mountains, traversed by the navigable river Jhelum. The population of the state in 1981 was 5,987,389, which included 3,164,660 males and 2,822,729 females. These figures exclude PoK and Chinese-occupied areas. The density of population, at 59 persons per sq. km, is one of the lowest in India. During 1971-81, the population grew at 28.71 per cent, as compared to 29.65 per cent during the preceding decade. Jammu had 1,802,000 Hindus, 804,637 Muslims, 100,164 Sikhs, 1141 Buddhists and 7778 Christians. Kashmir had 124,078 Hindus, 2,976,932 Muslims, 33,117 Sikhs, 189 Buddhists and 466 Christians, while Ladakh had 5338 Hindus, 61,882 Muslims, 334 Sikhs, 68,376 Buddhists and 237 Christians.

Surrounded by high mountains, with no easy access to any part of the world, the economy of the Valley was restricted to growing fruits and manufacturing wool, silk and handicrafts. The absence of good roads and a transport system made matters worse. For long, much of the transportation was done by boats. The products of the Valley went by a footpath through the Banihal Pass to Jammu, where merchants from other parts of India came to buy them.

Not all rulers of Kashmir were distinguished for their concern for the economic development of the Valley. Regular famines killed thousands. Yet nothing was done to link Kashmir to the rest of India by a proper road. The first effort in this direction was made by the Mughals. But the construction of a proper highway from Rawalpindi to Srinagar had to wait till the British came on the scene. But, to the British, this highway had more military significance, for they wanted to prevent the expansion of the Tsarist empire into India. This situation, however, led to the neglect of the footpath across the Banihal Pass till 1920, when the British improved it to a cart road. When the state acceded to India, the first task was to reconstruct the cart road and convert it into an all-weather road with a tunnel across the Banihal Pass. This marks the shortest route to the rest of India.

Although not well endowed with minerals, Kashmir has a viable economy. Apart from a variety of orchard, forest and horticultural produce (apples, apricots, cherries, plums, walnuts, almonds, timber, etc.), it is the most attractive tourist centre in India, and has a highly developed handicraft industry.

Kashmir's trade was mostly with India. In 1945-46, the total value of fruits exported to India was Rs. 104.5 lakh, of which about 14 per cent went to the area that now comprises Pakistan. As for tourism, the Valley earned a revenue of Rs. 200 lakh in 1944-45, of which Rs. 20 lakh came from the Pakistan area. These figures show that the Kashmiris stand to benefit greatly from being part of India. The silk industry has, of late, made rapid strides and this is true of the shawl industry too. Since 1947, tourism has developed rapidly with the assistance of the Central Government. In 1953, foreign tourists numbered 21,381, but by 1961 the figure had risen to 92,455. In 1963, the figure had risen up to more than one lakh. And it had been rising steadily till militancy first stemmed foreign tourist traffic and later domestic tourism.

Jammu had a legitimate grievance of "neglect" because of the dominance of the administration by Kashmiris. The state had registered all-round development in every sphere of activity till 1989, when terrorism, secessionism and Muslim fundamentalism began to disrupt the process. As things stand today, tourist traffic, both Indian and foreign, which is the main source of revenue, has almost been halted. Crafts too have been hit, but the various fairs organised by the Centre all over the country have helped provide livelihood to many. Industry, which is nascent, has given job security to workers. Jammu is better placed with regard to industry.

As against this background, what is the picture in PoK? There, basic rights are still denied and development has been totally neglected. Many young men have left PoK for jobs either in Pakistan or abroad. The 2.5 million people of PoK have resented Pakistani occupation, but they have no way to express dissent. The per capita income of PoK remains much lower than that in J&K. The People's National Party of PoK lamented: "Our country is under subjugation at present. Unemployment has assumed serious proportions. Corruption is rampant. Our country is full of hatred and fanaticism."

The Muslim Conference, the first party founded in J&K, has a dominant voice in PoK and it has become a party of contractors with vast forest and mining interests. Those who oppose the PoK regime are summarily dismissed from service. In the last 40 years and more, PoK has seen little industrial development. A textile spinning mill and a vegetable oil unit have been set up at Mirpuri, and a wool-weaving mill and a match factory at Muzaffarabad. Only in three districts have industrial units come up. In contrast, there were 720 registered factories in J&K in 1985-86 and about 17,000 registered small-scale units. Industrial estates have been set up at all district headquarters.

As far as unemployment is concerned the Legislative Assembly was told (in August 1989) that there were only 69,099 educated unemployed youth in all the 14 districts. Of these 23,191, i.e., 34 per cent, belonged to Jammu. As against this there were 26,784 educated unemployed in six districts of the Kashmir region – Srinagar, Badgam, Anantnag, Pulwama, Baramula and Kupwara. In spite of their professions of "brotherhood", the fundamentalists have ignored the claims of the backward communities such as the Gujjars and Bakerwals. The Gujjars constitute 7.6 per cent of the population (about 25 lakh) of the state. Although a Gujjar Development Board exists, it has achieved nothing, its funds having been misused by Kashmiri-speaking politicians. The Gujjar herdsmen have prevented the intrusion of Pak spies and soldiers, a point in their favour.

Compared to Bihar or eastern UP, J&K is relatively prosperous. The terrorists and fundamentalists ignore this fact conveniently. If Kashmir has not done better, it is because of Muslim fundamentalism, which has frightened away potential investors and traders, and disrupted production. In any case, the Kashmiri politician does not want "Indians" investing in Kashmir. What is more, the state Constitution prevents ownership of landed property in Kashmir by "Indians". As long as the Kashmiris insist on this provision, they will not be able to attract private investment from outside. And they are forcing the Jammu and Ladakh people also to suffer. They have no right to do this. The militants forget that tourism and federal subsidy on food and education bring in a net inflow of wealth into Kashmir from the rest of the country. Not surprisingly, 16 states of the country have a per capita income less than that of Kashmir.

It is a fact that the Valley cannot be viable unless there is a flourishing tourist trade. But tourism cannot flourish when there is violence, when society is highly bigoted and intolerant. There was one honest way to prosperity for the Kashmiris and that was by linking their fortune with India. This course they have never sincerely followed. If they think that Pakistan can provide resources and markets, they are sadly mistaken. Nor can they look to other Islamic countries for help. The economic future of the Valley lies with India. Kashmiris would do well to understand that militancy has already forced Indian traders to look for other sources of supply; for example, of fruit.

The people of the Valley, engaged in tourism, trade, handicrafts development and horticulture have done well during the last several years. However, they have been badly affected by the militancy. Unlike the Punjabi, the Kashmiri is more often a craftsman. Peace is more vital to him than to the Punjabi farmer. As for the educated Kashmiri, he has always depended on government jobs. There is no scope for expansion here. Kashmir must increase industrial employment. Unfortunately, investment for job creation is not taking place in the Valley. As a result, the state of Jammu and Kashmir lags behind other states of India.

It is not that the state's economy is not viable. Tourism alone is contributing substantially, and out of this contribution a major proportion is spent on the Valley. Little goes to Jammu and Ladakh. This is an aspect of unequal development of the economy that needs considerable attention. The Centre must help develop tourist resorts in both Jammu and Ladakh to the maximum potential. Otherwise, this will remain a permanent grievance.

The Buddhists have longstanding grievances against the state administration, dominated by the Valley Muslims. They claim that money meant for Ladakh is regularly transferred to the Valley and that no major project has been undertaken in Ladakh in the past three decades. The Stakna power project took 25 years to complete, which shows the lack of interest in the Ladakh region. And it took the Srinagar administration 47 years to decide to set up degree colleges in Leh. But what should surprise anyone most of all is the total indifference of the Central Government (I include the Parliament too) to uniform development of all regions.

Similarly, the state used to earn Rs. 800 crore from the export of fruit and handicrafts to the rest of India before militancy began. However, there is much greater potential. Now that Himachal Pradesh and the rest of the Himalayan states have become strong competitors in this field, there is need to examine the viability of fruit cultivation in Jammu and Kashmir. The one fruit-processing plant in Kashmir had to be closed for long periods because of militancy. Such closure has driven the farmers to desperation.

The per capita income in the Valley has been of a relatively high order. As for unemployment of the youth, which is partly the fault of the educational system, it is not an insuperable problem. The Kashmiri youth must take greater interest in tourism and tourism-related activities all over India, as also organise the export of fruit and other horticultural products. Why should they allow middlemen from other states to take over this business? Packaging, trading and transport – all these can be handled by Kashmiris. At present, the jobs go to people from other states. These are matters of planning. And why have they not tried out new products for export? For example, flowers.

The leaders of the Valley must understand that both Jammu and Ladakh want full economic integration of their regions with the rest of India so that they can take full advantage of the Indian economy. The Valley people have no right to stop them. From the economic point of view, each region is a distinct entity. That is why each region must have a separate economic council to look after its interests. And there must be an apex development council in which each region will have equal say. If the Valley leaders and people do not want full integration, it is up to them. But they should realise the consequences. The world's economy is getting "globalised" today. The Kashmiris should know this trend. What is more, even if they wish to, they cannot stop these global processes. Wisdom lies in taking advantage of these changes.

The politicians of the Valley, who still speak of the "neglect" by the Centre, should understand that it is they who have blocked all prospects for development. They do not want full political or economic integration of the state with India. But they insist on full economic benefits. These are contradictory stands.

It is true the Muslims in India have not benefited uniformly from development. But, then, development itself has not been uniform in India. There are many pockets of indigence and affluence. The intellectuals of Kashmir must understand this fact and find ways to derive the best advantage under the circumstances.

It is time we explained to the Kashmiri leaders that greater autonomy, which they are seeking, will go against their economic interests, for the more autonomous the state becomes the less attractive it will become to investors. Investors want a uniform playing ground with the same rules and benefits. Kashmiri leaders must also understand that no autarchy is possible in today's world and that, if they want to take advantage of the global opportunities, they must be in line with global trends. Even Central projects have been adversely affected by the restrictions imposed by the Jammu and Kashmir state. Projects relating to power, railways and other areas need heavy investment and long-term gestation. And yet the Centre has carried out a number of power projects, including the hydroprojects at Salal, Lower Jhelum, Upper Sind, Lower Sind, and Dulhasty, in order to give a boost to development. A highway was built to Kishtwar through the Sinthan pass (2743 ft), which is said to be an engineering marvel. And more ambitious projects are being proposed. If after all this the militants think that India will surrender these benefits to Pakistan, they must be living in a fool's paradise.

The construction of a railway track from Pathankot to Jammu and its further extension to Udhampur are now nearly complete. There is a plan to extend the railway line to Srinagar, a project which will cost Rs. 1500 crore and mark the final integration of the state with India. Kashmir's climate is suitable for the pharmaceutical and electronic industry. Undertakings such as the HMT watch factory were doing well. The militants have, however, disrupted their functioning. A modern airport has been constructed at Srinagar to promote tourism and also export. A network of canals has been constructed for irrigation in the rather arid zones of the state.

Article 370 crops up regularly in day-to-day discussions on Kashmir. Yet its implications are not properly understood. This Article prevents economic integration of the state with India and also free movement of capital. A private party expects economic freedom. India, which was earlier virtually closed to foreign investment, is now opening up. But Kashmir politicians want to close the doors there. Again, Kashmir lacks industrial labour; but the present laws prevent labour movement. Private sector investors are fed up with these restrictions. They want to close down their units and quit. The Cadbury plant in Sopore set up to manufacture fruit juice and jams, which was one of the first MNCs to come up there, was sold to the state in 1987. It is now running at a regular loss. Can the Kashmiri politicians invite investment when those who are already there want to run away?

As for jobs, most of the government vacanies are filled through the UPSC (Union Public Service Commission), which entail tests and interviews. No exceptions can be made here. The same is true of the private sector companies – they too have their own tests. The special considerations given to "backwards" under the Mandal Commission recommendations do not apply to the Muslims, but the economic criteria can be applied to them.

Instead of freeing the economy as India is doing, the Kashmiri politicians want to impose new restrictions. For example, they have been demanding that the flow of bank deposits to and fro must be regulated. While flow inwards is welcome they want to put a stop to the flow of funds outwards. Such interference with the normal functioning of an economy cannot be permitted.

The Valley politicians allege that the state's share of the public sector investment, which runs into about Rs. 100,000 crore, is only 0.03 per cent. We do not have authentic figures. But these politicians do not want to admit that even the public sector is unwilling to invest in the state as a result of various restrictive laws. In any case, have these politicians been demanding from the Union Planning Commission a better share of the public sector projects? They have not, for such a demand would lead to an opening up of the Valley to "outsiders". This is the crux of the matter.

They also claim that Kashmir is not getting enough Central grants. It is not known to many Kashmiris that Central grants are made from receipts accruing to the Centre from the state's taxes and duties. Unfortunately, Kashmir contributes little to these funds because the politicians refuse to levy taxes and impose customs duty. Even then the Centre has continued to provide grants to Kashmir.

It has been claimed by politicians like Saifuddin Soz that the ratio of grant to loan is unfavourable to the state. Such politicians know little about these matters. J&K has been getting 70:30 (loan-grant), whereas Himachal Pradesh has been getting 10 per cent in loan and 90 per cent in grant. True, but in Himachal Pradesh no obstructions are placed to collection of taxes and duties, while the Kashmiri politicians tell the people not to pay any tax or duty. You cannot have it both ways.

Of late, Jammu and Kashmir has been declared a "backward state" in order to enable the Centre to provide special funds. Now, 90 per cent of Central assistance will be as grants and 10 per cent as loan. Under this new provision, the state has also been exempted from income tax (it has hardly paid any tax in all these years). In fact, Jammu and Kashmir is among the prosperous states; there are states in a far worse economic condition.

The Tenth Finance Commission has awarded Jammu and Kashmir double what the Ninth Finance Commission did. In spite of all these special favours, Dr. Farooq Abdullah wants a bigger economic package.

There is a proposal to revive the traditional trade of Ladakh with Tibet and Central Asia, which was broken during the second half of the last century. This is certainly welcome, but its political implications must be well understood by the policy-makers of this country. Yet another proposal is to open the motorable Damchuk road for pilgrimage to Mount Kailash, which would spare pilgrims the month-long arduous trek through the Garhwal mountains. There is also a plan to open a trade mart at Damchuk. All these moves are welcome, and will strengthen Ladakh's links with India.

Over the last few decades, the Centre has invested in the Valley a sum of about a hundred thousand crores in the military sector. In fact, no other state has received so much military funds. Those funds have definitely helped to raise standards of living of the Kashmiris. But neither the figures nor the extent of the impact will be fully known to the country. These are "secrets" which are held back in public interest.

Militancy has played havoc with the state's economy. It has taken a heavy toll of not only human lives but also assets. Disruption of tourism has meant a big loss. The absence of infrastructure support, fall in revenue, and enhanced expenditure on security needs have adversely affected the health of the state. In due course, the administration itself became a victim of militancy. All public institutions have become weaker and, as a result, less effective. But the worst onslaught was on the education system, which was practically taken over by the fundamentalists.

There are, however, visible signs of an economic buoyancy from 1994 onwards. For example, inflow and outflow of goods have markedly picked up.

Agriculture, the mainstay of the economy, has improved. It contributes 42 per cent to the gross domestic product. Productivity of paddy at 40 quintals per hectare is one of the highest in the country. Agriculture has not been badly hit by militancy. In fact, there has been marginal growth. Saffron and *zeera* cultivation in the Valley and in Doda has received a tremendous impetus. Both these items can earn foreign exchange.

About 25 lakh people are engaged in fruit orchards. The emphasis has shifted to walnut, as it has a ready foreign market. Under an Italian assistance programme, the state has taken to olive cultivation.

As regards employment generation, the thrust is on the rural areas. All national programmes are being implemented in the state.

Handicrafts play a major role in the J & K economy. As such the government has been giving considerable backup to infrastructure development, marketing, etc. About 2.25 lakh artisan families depend on handicrafts production and sale. Both production and exports have gone up over the years.

Communication and transport form the core elements for the development programmes in the state. However, militancy has damaged many hundreds of bridges and culverts. Sericulture, for which the state was unique, has been revived. Production of cocoons grew from 6.99 lakh kg in 1990 to 8.23 lakh kg in 1991. But militancy has struck a blow to this trade too.

There is no strong industrial base in the state because of locational disadvantages. Small-scale industries (SSIs) serve as a major source of employment. The number of SSI units grew between 1989 and 1993. Some medium-scale industries had to be closed because of militancy. A new package has been announced by the Centre to boost industrial growth. A number of bridges are expected to be either built or repaired.

J&K has high hydropotential – about 15,000 MW. The state has earmarked 30 per cent of allocations of the Eighth Plan for power development. The installed capacity of power in 1989 was 267.64 MW, which has risen to 360 MW in 1994. The Salal hydroproject and Uri hydel project (480 MW) are expected to go on stream some time in 1996. Two gas turbines of 150 MW have been commissioned in the last two years.

Although tourist traffic has declined, pilgrimage has picked up. The number of pilgrims going to Vaishnodevi rose to 35 lakh in 1992. In 1994, the number was about 45 lakh. About 10 lakh pilgrims visited Shahdara Sharief. Ladakh has been thrown open to tourism. Some facilities for tourism have been created in Jammu.

Lack of rail facilities has meant high cost of inputs. The Jammu-Udhampur line will be ready, hopefully, by 1996. Also, as already stated, the Government of India has approved the extension line from Udhampur to Srinagar at a cost of around Rs. 1500 crore.

In sum, J&K has great potential to develop rapidly, provided the political leadership gives up its games and engages itself seriously in bettering the lot of the people. Corruption at all levels, coupled with lack of political will to generate employment and investment, has prevented the state from reaching the required level of prosperity that is so much within its reach. Central funds have never been a problem, and J&K has always got more than its due. But they have invariably been squandered. Compared to many states of the Union, Kashmir is relatively well off. But the bogy of poverty is raised continuously by politicians to keep the focus away from their own misdeeds and bad governance.

10

Fundamentalism at Play

I t is claimed that Kashmiri Islam is not fundamentalist, that it is rooted in Kashmir's soil, that the Sufis (Rishis) left behind a tradition of tolerance, and so on. It is, in a way, true, that the Sufi tradition has been getting slowly eroded over the last century or so. As a result, the power of local priests has declined. The present generation is largely influenced by the Jamaat school of thought. What still remains – greater freedom for women, absence of triple *talaq* and the one-wife norm – is now under threat from the fundamentalists.

Islamic fundamentalism has been on the rise from the turn of this century. Such a phenomenon, in turn, has raised a number of questions: Do Kashmiri Muslims care more for their Kashmiri identity than for their Islamic identity? Why did they opt for Urdu as the official language? Why did they adopt the Persian script for Kashmiri? Why did they force the Persian dress on Kashmiri women? Could this step be part of the quest for separatism? Seldom do the protagonists of "identity" think that the people of Jammu and Ladakh also have an identity of their own.

Do the Kashmiri Muslims consider themselves "special" because they are Muslims? If so, what about the 120-odd million Muslims in the rest of India?

Professor Saifuddin Soz, MP, and other Kashmiri leaders of his ilk, believe that dilution of Article 370 is the cause for the present alienation. Obviously, Professor Soz and others are opposed to the integration of the Valley with the rest of India.

Asghar Ali Engineer, a Bohra Muslim, believes that if Kashmir goes to Pakistan, it may mean the end of secular nationalism in India (*Secular Crown on Fire: The Kashmir Problem*). He has a point, though it is difficult to believe that the basic outlook of the Hindus, their tradition of tolerance and their continuing quest for truth will change.

In his book, *The Nation That Lost Its Soul*, Sardar Shaukat Hayat Khan, whose family played a major role in the Muslim League and Punjab politics, blamed Liaquat Ali Khan, the first prime minister of Pakistan, for the growth of fundamentalism in Pakistan. This growth, he said, gave Pakistan a direction that Jinnah, the founder of Pakistan, did not want. Towards the end of his life, Jinnah himself gave expression to his deep disappointment and disillusionment. The point of regret is that the present advocates of fundamentalism in Pakistan and Kashmir can hardly visualise the consequences of their actions.

It is competitive communalism which has generated fundamentalism. The Shah Bano case illustrates the point. The Muslim fundamentalists opposed the Supreme Court verdict on Shah Bano and Rajiv Gandhi chose to appease them in order to retain the Muslim vote bank. This single event exposed the dangerous nature of "vote bank" politics of the Congress, although it has practised such politics ever since the 1952 general election. The Shah Bano case revealed more than ever before that the Congress, the main ruling party of India, was vulnerable to various pulls and counterpulls. It needs to be realised that the communal vote bank politics (now there is a new one – the Mandal vote bank) can only be disastrous to the basic soundness of the nation's polity.

Communalism was injected into the Valley by the Jamaat-i-Islami and its front organisations. Arab money helped the Jamaat to organise *madrasas* in large numbers, which spawned a semi-educated new generation of communalised young men. It is these young men who are providing grist to the militants' mill. They have been responsible for the flight of the Pandits from the Valley.

The mullah has always dominated life in the Valley. And the politicians too have built their politics around the mosque. There is no separation of mosque and state in Islam. The Muslims have chosen to keep quiet on this issue although the matter has been under intense debate in Europe for centuries and, of late, in India. But in a diverse society like that in India, religion and politics cannot be mixed. If they are, this would be the surest way to anarchy. No other society in the world is comparable to ours in this respect.

The Jamaat presents Islam as a political ideology. Its founder, Abul Ala Maududi, has asserted that there is no department of life, private or public, not covered by Islam. On the face of it, this is an absurd statement. No religion is a complete guide for the present and future generations. Religions have changed and evolved. Only Islam refuses to change, more so in India. Thus, culture is within the purview of the mullah. As a result, Salman Rushdie is to be shot; Taslima Nasreen is to be killed; women have to wear veils; and music and dance are frowned upon. To the mullah, culture means the traditions of the Bedouin tribes of the times of the Prophet, not the sophistication of the Mughal court.

The Jamaat also believes that Islam is the only true creed, and that all others are false (other creeds, it agrees, also came from God, but only Islam remains pure). There is no scope here for co-existence with other faiths, which must give way to Islam. That is why Muslims have not been able to adjust themselves wherever they are in a minority. Muslim minorities must denounce this dogma before they can be accepted by the communities in which they live. They must accept that other religions also represent the truth.

Maududi believed that God made the social laws. That is why, he insisted, social laws, which have come down through the centuries, must not be changed, however grotesque they might appear in our times. Chopping hands for theft, for instance. In such a society there is no scope for progressive social legislation. There is no scope even for compassion or mercy. It is strange to find these barbarous habits among a people who see their God as the Fountain of Mercy!

Maududi concentrates his ire on secular people as the chief adversary of Islam because, he claims, they drive religion out of public life. The Jamaat continues to promote its opposition to secularism in a country whose Constitution proclaims its faith in secularism! And the Central leaders, who also speak of secularism, like chanting a mantra without any commitment to it, have allowed hundreds of *madrasas* run by the Jamaat in Kashmir to spew out this anti-secular ideology. Although the Jamaat was banned in 1990 by Governor Jagmohan on the basis of clear evidence of its complicity in the insurgency, it always enjoyed total freedom. Such are the absurdities of the Kashmir situation, which is why one despairs for its future. Although the Jamaat is the largest anti-India secessionist organisation, with the largest number of cadres at its command, it has been allowed full control of hundreds of *madrasas*, which were centres of propaganda and secessionist plots, in spite of the ban. No efforts were made to take control of the *madrasas*, to check their textbooks and other propaganda material.

As just stated, the Jamaat was banned in 1990. It now transpires that the authorities did not renew the ban in 1992. So the Jamaat functioned as if there was no ban on it for two years right under the nose of the governor and his advisers!

The Jamaat has taken full advantage of this lapse. It has raised the strength of its cadres by 10,000. And what is worse, the Jamaat cadres now occupy key positions in the education and police departments. This is how we have reached an impasse in J&K. Here is yet another instance of gross appeasement of the Muslims. One partition and the holocaust that followed are not enough to deter these politicians from pursuing the same policies. The President of India is supposed to protect the Constitution, and yet constitutional goals have been trampled upon with impunity in the name of religion.

According to Maududi, secularism creates its own value system and that leads to atheism. This ideology is dangerous because it encourages a militant Islam. Jehad comes easily to it. It encourages the belief that Muslims have an unfinished task – to conquer the rest of the world for Islam. It believes that Muslims can realise their spiritual goals only in an Islamised society. A mixed society is not suitable for this purpose, according to this view. The Jamaat is not fighting for economic and social justice and other such goals of minorities everywhere, but for total power. All other objectives are secondary to Maududi.

Kashmiri Muslims have a nearness to Maududi, for although he was born in Hyderabad, he chose Jammu as the theatre of his activity in 1941. In 1942 the Jamaat started work in the Valley. In those days, it had a free hand in expounding its philosophy, for it called the Dogra ruler "the shadow of God on earth". This accolade was enough for the vain ruler to permit the Jamaat to carry out its activities. After 1947, and the ensuing partition, the Jamaat came under a cloud, and it went into hibernation for some years.

Although the Jamaat in J&K had to take into account the policies of the all-India Muslim bodies and the hopes and aspirations of the Muslims in the rest of India, it had developed an independence of its own and was functioning as a branch of the Pakistani Jamaat. Consequently, the Jamaat members of Jammu and Kashmir did not accept the accession of the state to the Indian Union.

It is interesting to note that Maududi preferred the communal Hindu organisation to the secular Congress. The immediate objective of the Jamaat in Kashmir was to purge the Valley of its Sufi influence. Orthodox Islam had always looked upon Sufism with suspicion. But the Jamaat in the Valley was not in favour of the "adjustments" accepted by its parent body in India in the wake of partition. In order to free itself from the influence of the all-India body, the Kashmir branch severed relations with it in 1953.

The Jamaat was at first opposed to the Sheikh as he was inclined to speak in favour of secularism. It did not appreciate his paying obeisance to the Sufi saints. Besides, the Jamaat did not like the growing popularity of the Sheikh among the Muslims, which stood in the way of its own advance. The arrest of the Sheikh in 1951 gave an opportunity to the Jamaat to build up its strength, but its success came mostly with the organisation of *madrasas* on a large scale using Gulf money. The intolerance of the Jamaat followers can be gauged from the fact that they objected to Vinoba Bhave, the Gandhian reformer, reading the Quran at Sopore. But the Jamaat's stand made no difference to the policies of the Indian National Congress in the Valley, no doubt manned by communalist elements, which, under the leadership of Mir Qasim, patronised the Jamaat to use its youth wing against the activities of the Plebiscite Front, a creation of Mirza Afzal Beg, the chief lieutenant of the Sheikh. This kind of opportunism has flourished in the Valley all the time.

In 1977, the Jamaat launched its student wing, Jamaat-e-Tulba, founded by Ashraf Sahrai. The growing popularity of the Jamaat became evident when it secured five seats in the J&K Assembly in 1972, no doubt with the support of the Congress. This success made the Jamaat bolder. It, therefore, opposed the Sheikh's accord with Indira Gandhi in 1975. For such opposition, the Jamaat had to pay a heavy price – most of its leaders were imprisoned during the Emergency (imposed in June 1975) and Jamaat offices were sealed. However, with the lifting of the Emergency in early 1977, the Jamaat was back in form. This time it began to oppose the emergence of other Muslim organisations like the Plebiscite Front and the Awami Action Committee of Maulvi Farooq. During the 1977 election, it teamed up with the Janata Party and won one seat from Sopore.

Thus, the Central parties, ruling or opposition, were prepared to sup with the devil. However, the 1977 election was a setback to the Jamaat as most of its sponsored candidates flopped at the hustings. During the 1983 elections, when Indira Gandhi ran a communal campaign in Jammu, the Jamaat did so in the Valley.

The Jamaat soon became a serious contender for power. However, it bided its time. It did not challenge the Central authorities, especially on the issue of accession. This gave rise to an extremist wing in the Jamaat under hardliners like Said-ud-din and Ghulam Mohammad Butt. The extremists were naturally supported by Jamaat-e-Tulba, which was led by Tajmul Islam, who eventually fled the country. Jamaat leaders such as Syed Ali Shah Geelani were sympathetic to the extremist cause.

The Jamaat's ambition grew by leaps and bounds. It conducted an international conference, in which several prominent organisations and personalities from Muslim countries participated, including the Imam of the Kaaba. This conference called for the implementation of the UN resolutions on Kashmir. Not a word was said of Pakistan's occupation of a part of Kashmir or its refusal to implement the UN resolutions there. The Jamaat had the support of the Sheikh in calling this conference.

Emboldened by such successes, the Jamaat began the process of Islamisation by stepping up "Islamic" education, organising Islamic courts, etc. It also organised a women's wing called Dukhtaran-i-Millat.

The Jamaat's success, however, provoked other organisations to retaliate. Several mosques were burnt and considerable property belonging to the Jamaat was destroyed. But the biggest setback to the Jamaat was the ban on its activities imposed by Governor Jagmohan. He also took over the Jamaat schools. But nothing is reported to have changed in these schools because their staff remained the same, as also the books, thanks to the secret support the Jamaat received from the administration. Interestingly, all the Jamaat schools were drawing grants-in-aid from the state government. Even in 1989, when terrorism, supported by the Jamaat, grew in intensity the state government gave recognition to 19 new Jamaat schools out of the total 51 recognised that year. The Central authority merely watched these developments.

The disappearance of the holy relic of Prophet Mohammad (in December 1963) was a blessing in disguise for the fundamentalists, for no other event gave such a boost to strident communalism in the Valley. Even today no one knows how the relic disappeared. Yet fundamentalists used the occasion to stir up hatred against the Pandits. Demonstrations by Muslims in the Valley, however, had their repercussions in Jammu against their co-religionists.

The recovery of the relic was a task for the police and intelligence agencies. Yet the Muslim politicians decided to take the fullest advantage of the event. Maulana Mohammad Sayeed Masoodi, who was at one time the general secretary of the NC, set up action committees throughout the state to carry on an agitation against the Centre. This step allowed anti-social elements to take the law into their own hands. The state administration stood by helplessly. Not much study has been done on the growth of terrorism in the state. There is no doubt that at its roots lie the system of Muslim priests, which is peculiar to the state. In Islam there is no provision for hereditary priests. Yet the Mirwaiz has become a hereditary institution in the Valley and this is unique to Kashmir. There is a historical reason for this.

During the long rule of the sultans and the Mughals, who were all foreigners to the Valley, the priests brought by Afghan, Persian and Central Asian military leaders held key positions in the Valley in every field. They were, however, considered interlopers by the Kashmiris. The Kashmiri converts, therefore, took to the Sufi movement. (This movement also came from the same sources, but it was closer to the Kashmiri heart. It produced a new order of priesthood called the "Rishis".) The Mirwaiz tradition is roughly 600 years old. Although a local tradition, it became highly orthodox and pro-Pakistan. The Mirwaiz has not played a constructive role in the state and has not been a stabilising factor. He has changed sides regularly, now supporting the Sheikh and then his enemies. In 1986, a case was registered against Maulvi Farooq for violation of the Foreign Contributions Regulation Act. Although the violation was proved, the state refused to proceed in the matter. During Friday prayers, the Mirwaiz would play the fanatic, but to the press he offered another visage. The Mirwaiz has, however, lost his pre-eminent position. Maulvi Farooq fell victim to Jamaat assassins. The present young Mirwaiz is fully committed to pan-Islamism and is pro-Pakistan.

During the period of the Dogras, the rulers introduced British laws and modernised the customs and traditions of many of the institutions. With that the hold of the mullahs on the Muslim masses was somewhat loosened. The former resented these developments and became supporters of Pakistan. The Mirwaiz tradition had encouraged Kashmiri nationalism and tolerance. Unfortunately, Mirwaiz Maulvi Yusuf Shah (who migrated to Pakistan) and his son Farooq came to preach intolerance, which explains why there is no force today in the Valley which can stand up for a tolerant order. Today, the Jamaat is controlled by descendants of the immigrants from outside the Valley who have little love for the traditions of the Kashmiris. They are opposed to *Kashmiriat*, nationalism, secularism and women's rights. They promote not only the Jamaat, but also its political organisation, the Muslim United Front, and its military wing, the Hizb-ul-Mujahideen. It is clear from the foregoing discussion that there is a clear cleavage between the perceptions and aspirations of those who claim to be descendants of the conquerors and those who were converted. This aspect calls for a deeper study.

The fundamentalist outfits are now threatening, with dire consequences, anyone who chooses to cross their path. Thus, Maulana Wahiduddin Khan, president of the Islamic Centre, is on the hit list of "Ikhwan-ul-Musalmeen", a terrorist outfit in Kashmir, because the Maulana dared to say on TV that carrying of weapons into a mosque is unIslamic. He was, of course, referring to the 1993 Hazratbal episode. The militants announced a reward of Rs. 5 lakhs to the person who would kill the Maulana. The press statement of the organisation also claimed that "a death squad has been despatched to Delhi to accomplish the job of assassinating the Indian scholar" (*The Times of India*, 2 November 1993). All these developments remind one of the unprecedented incarceration of Salman Rushdie and the offer of millions of dollars for his head. Is this the way the world is going to be run? Are we to revert to primitive barbarism? This will silence the very faint voice of protest of the Muslim community in India against the depredations of the fundamentalists in Kashmir. As a result, the Maulana has to be provided round-the-clock security cover. It is ironic that while the fundamentalists want the best publicity for their views, they want to snuff out any view opposed to them.

Professor Mushir-ul-Hasan, pro-vice-chancellor of Jamia Milia University, Delhi, was turned out of the campus by student militants, because he dared to defend the rights of Salman Rushdie to publish his book (*The Satanic Verses*), although Professor Hasan did not approve of what Rushdie had written. He said he was against banning books. He was brutally assaulted by students when he returned to the campus after a committee had exonerated him of all charges. As in every other case, the

Central Government looked the other way, although Jamia is a Central university. The Centre failed to protect the fundamental freedom of the professor to say what he truly believed. Thus, for three years, the professor was denied his right to teach. The government of this country is expected to protect the values of its people, but being cowardly, it has left the task to individuals. For his part Hasan asserts: "I'm not going to get out on the sly because beyond a point you're not fighting for yourself. It becomes a cause so that such treatment cannot be meted out to a fellow-teacher again." Is the government committed to any such values as the professor?

The present militancy in the Valley cannot be explained unless we take into account the rising power of the Jamaat in Pakistan ever since its founder Maududi fled to that country and built up the organisation there to what it is today. The Jamaat in Pakistan is not only behind the Islamisation programme, but is also a powerful political force. It is responsible for much of the persecution of non-Muslims in Pakistan. It will be recalled that it fomented the anti-Ahmedia riots in 1953, in which many Ahmedias lost their lives. The military court, which tried Maulana Maududi, sentenced him to death, but President Ayub Khan refused to carry out the sentence. As a result of such anti-Ahmedia riots, Sir Zaffrullah Khan, an Ahmedia, handpicked by Jinnah to be Pakistan's first foreign minister, was hounded out of the establishment. As Professor Abdus Salam, an Ahmedia and the only Nobel Prize winner from Pakistan, was treated as a second-class citizen, he chose to live in London.

The persecution of the Ahmedias has continued. In 1984, a new provision in the Pakistan penal code was introduced to prohibit the use of Muslim terminology by Ahmedias. Such use was made an offence, punishable with a minimum of three years' imprisonment and a fine. In 1986, another provision was made in the criminal law making blasphemy against Prophet Mohammad punishable by death. In 1992, this punishment was made mandatory. In 1993, it was enlarged to cover the Prophet's family and companions. Ahmedia mosques cannot be called mosques in Pakistan and Ahmedias cannot enter Mecca for Haj.

Pakistan repeatedly refers to genocide against the Kashmiris and repression of minorities in India. In this regard Saeed Naqvi, a well-known Indian journalist, has written: "I hate to share contemporary jingoism, but the fact of the matter is that the atrocities committed by the Muslim Pakistan army on Muslims of what is now Bangladesh would compare more with Bosnia than what is happening in Kashmir now" (*The Pioneer*, 27 February 1994). Naqvi, however, does not have an answer to what will happen to Muslims in the rest of India if the Kashmiri Muslims vote for Pakistan in a plebiscite: "If Kashmir were placed in the balance of the Two-Nation Theory, by what logic are we going to incorporate India's 127 million Muslims in our agenda for the future? One shudders at the thought of what might happen."

It is high time that India realised that it should not be guided by politicians with regard to religion, nor by parties based on a communalised religious thrust, for they are likely to change their stances as and when exigencies demand. The worst example is our secular ideology as interpreted by politicians.

In his book *Bewildered India: Identity, Pluralism, Discord*, Professor Rasheeduddin Khan of the Jawaharlal Nehru University, New Delhi, holds that the trouble with the much publicised Vedantic ideal of equal respect to all faiths (*sarva dharma samabhava*) is that it has led to an attempt "at fusion of religious symbols, idioms, and social rituals, which has meant in effect reconciliation of multiple communalism, promotion of multiple obscurantism, universal superstition and mixing of all mythologies". In fact, the politicians, who are generally ignorant on most matters, had not only confused the people but also made the usual processes of adjustment – political and social – impossible. They are responsible for reducing every complex problem to simplistic terms and rituals: for example, with respect to the reading of scriptures from all religions at state functions as a symbol of the ethos of Indian unity and fraternity, Professor Khan says: "There can be no more spurious interpretation of secularism than this." He should have said this years ago. He further says that such an interpretation does not take into account the basic difference in approach of Hinduism and

Semitic religions. While the eclectic perception of Vedantic Hinduism is based on the essential unity of all religions, the dogma of Semitic religions like Islam and Christianity condemns eclecticism as heresy, he adds.

Professor Khan goes on to state that emphasising the ethical and humanistic dimensions of the Semitic heritage is to ignore the more appealing (to Muslims) dogmatic and ritualistic aspects. According to him "a more relevant strategy" is to "emphasise the civic-secular rational ideology of political culture and statecraft and leave the question of reconciliation of religions and belief patterns of voluntary social action and accommodation". But this is not a course favoured by politicians. Professor Khan takes to task majority communalism, but does not spare minority communalism either. He stresses that communalism of the minority manifests itself in "separatism, exclusivism, withdrawal and anarchism". Islamic fundamentalism is again threatening the life of Indian society. Once, it led to the partition of the country. If Muslim fundamentalism has not resorted to violence on a large scale, it is not for want of will. It is just this that it would be suicidal for the fundamentalists to challenge the Hindus at this stage. But in Kashmir the former are in a strong position. Hence their challenge.

But, how is it that the Muslims in the rest of India have not thought it necessary to condemn the outrages of the terrorists? It is their silence that encouraged the terrorists to threaten the Maulana with death. His is a lone voice, and it can be easily snuffed out, but if large numbers of Muslims had protested against the atrocities, it would have had a salutary effect on fundamentalists. It is this silence on issues of great importance to the state that has unnecessarily given rise to all sorts of apprehensions about the loyalty of Muslims.

The Muslim population may not be significant at present in terms of percentage (it is only 12 per cent, but in absolute terms they are about 120 million), but it is growing rapidly. It is already the second largest Muslim community in the world. But this is not what has been the cause of worry among the Hindus. They have a variety of concerns. For example, they ask, can a Muslim, holding a responsible position in society or government, be entrusted with the preservation of the Indian civilisation, which is largely Hindu? Again, will the Muslim use his numbers during elections for the general good of the country or to advance his community's narrow interests? The Muslims constitute the largest religious minority in many states of India – Assam (20 per cent), Bengal (20 per cent), Kerala (20 per cent), Bihar (12.9 per cent), Karnataka (9.9 per cent), Gujarat (8.9 per cent), Andhra Pradesh (8 per cent), Maharashtra (7.7 per cent), Rajasthan (6.9 per cent), Madhya Pradesh (4.3 per cent) and Orissa (1.2 per cent). They can use their numbers to make or break India.

It was in view of this growing clout of the Muslim community that a sense of extreme outrage was felt when V.P. Singh spoke of the need to combine the force of Muslims with that of the backward castes in order to capture power. As a man of very limited vision, he was not even aware of the dangers he was stirring up. Such a strategy would have produced a powerful backlash from the entire Establishment of India, not to speak of the growing middle classes. Only the Muslims and backward castes would have suffered from such a strategy.

India believes in accommodation and diversity, because it corresponds to its religious and world outlook. The Muslims should understand that the course of Indian civilisation – philosophical and social – has been set by Hindus through the millennia, and whether it be right or wrong, they are bound to follow its basic logic. Indian civilisation has been a quest for the ultimate truth. Unlike other religions, Hinduism does not claim that it has found the ultimate truth. The Hindu considers the quest itself as his way of life. Although there are other ways to salvation, the way of knowledge is significant for the Hindu. In short, for him, life is a process of discovery of the eternal. And each generation finds its bliss through its own effort. This is not the case with Semitic religions, which are religions based on books, in which it is claimed that God Himself revealed the wisdom. There is nothing beyond these books for man to seek. Thus, his life becomes a mere repetitive existence from generation to generation with no quest for the ultimate reality. These are religions with a finality. Remember, the Popes used to claim "infallibility" till recently. Such assertions are not only taboo in India but will be laughed at. For more than 3000 years, the Indian quest has continued, producing, in the process, a civilisation incomparable in depth and width. Apart from Hinduism, India has been the birth place of three other religions: Jainism, Buddhism and later Sikhism as also six distinct schools of philosophy. This quest was disrupted only with the Islamic conquest and the fundamentalist zeal of the conquerors. From the time of Ashoka, India's approach has been *sarva dharma samabhava* to different sects.

The Hindus would like to renew their quest again. They must, if they are true to their heritage. In this quest, Muslims cannot join; they would consider it blasphemous. Obviously, the ways of both religions are different and it is better to accept this reality. But that is no reason why we cannot live together. We must find a way to do so. After all, we must all live on this planet whether we are Hindus, Muslims, Christians or Buddhists. And ultimately all of us must work together to keep the world going.

It will be interesting here to recall what Nehru wrote on the parallel trends in Hindu and Muslim thinking on the subject: "Thus, it is interesting to note that the early waves of nationalism in India in the 19th century were religious and Hindu. The Muslims, naturally, could take no part in this Hindu nationalism. They kept apart. Having kept away from English education, the new ideas affected them less and there was far less intellectual ferment among them. Many decades after, they began to come out of their shell, and then, as with the Hindus, their nationalism began to look back to Islamic traditions and cultures and was fearful of losing these because of the Hindu majority" (*Glimpses of World History*, p. 437).

Nehru went on to say that Muslim nationalism had a strong appeal to the Muslim mind in India and a large number of Muslims took part in the struggle for freedom. "Yet," he contends, "Indian nationalism was dominated by Hindus and had a Hinduised look. So a conflict arose in the Muslim mind. Many accepted that nationalism, trying to influence it in the direction of their choice, many sympathised with it and yet remained aloof, uncertain, and yet many others began to drift in a separatist direction for which Iqbal's poetic and philosophical approach had prepared them" (*Discovery of India*, p. 304).

No doubt, Nehru is one of the very few thinkers of India who had given some thought to these matters. But even he was only vaguely aware of the depth and dimension of the subject.

That "separatist direction" led the Muslims to give credibility to the two-nation theory. According to Maulana Wahiduddin Khan, an eminent Muslim writer who has already been dubbed a renegade: "The two-nation theory should have disappeared after 1947, but, thanks to the superficial policy of certain ill-advised Muslim leaders, it continued to hold sway." Muslims should realise that as long as they embrace that theory, there will be problems.

Unfortunately, the question of nationalism is a pet subject of the Hindutva advocates. They say that a Muslim cannot be patriotic or nationalistic because he does not accept his country's heritage. This is, of course, partly true. But there is another issue which Indian scholars, more so Muslim scholars, should no more try to avoid. This is the strange religious practice among converts to Semitic religions of rejecting their own history. History is supposed to be the basis of nationalism. If a people reject their own history for the history of another people, then in what way can they be patriotic or nationalistic to the country where they live? We have avoided such a basic question. But this question calls for answers, not evasions.

The followers of Islam cannot make tall claims that Muslim rule in this country had been an unmixed blessing. Far from it. True, they contributed their art, literature and culture, and added to the overall richness of Indian society.

It was in India, in contact with Hindu civilisation, that Islam flowered. Says Dr. Akbar Ahmad, a Pakistani scholar, that he is proud of India's achievements and its tolerance which "provided space for Islam to flourish". He claims that the greatest contribution to Muslim thinking in this century has been made by South Asia. This would not have been possible, he asserts, "without the deepest synthesis with Hinduism".

Hindus, too, should show greater understanding. History has played foul with their destiny. But they cannot reverse anything now. If India was subjected to several invasions, this was because its rulers were weak and disunited. We must learn from past experience. A country with no deep historical sense could not have profited from its experience. We have a large Islamic and Christian legacy. We cannot disown it now. We must come to terms with it. Our minorities must also realise that after having denounced and rejected their ancestors (it is immaterial how they accepted the new faith, whether by force or choice) they have no natural claim to the patrimony. Minority fundamentalism is thus a continuing affront to the Indian heritage, to our pride in our civilisation. It is inimical to everything that India stands for.

11

Dangers of Plebiscite

The word "plebiscite" does not occur in Mountbatten's letter (27 October 1947) to Maharaja Hari Singh accepting his offer to accede to India. He only talks of the need to refer the question of accession to the people, when peace has been restored.

There is no provision for plebiscite either in the Indian Independence Act or in the Instrument of Accession. However, when Nehru made the announcement on accession, on 2 November 1947, he did commit the Government of India to a "referendum" under the supervision of an international agency. However, at the meeting between Mountbatten and Jinnah in early November, Mountbatten spoke of a "plebiscite" under UN auspices. Earlier, the idea was to hold elections under the Kashmir administration, a proposal approved by Nehru which was rejected by Pakistan. Later, there was a Pakistani proposal to hold elections under an "impartial" administration to be constituted under the governors-general of India and Pakistan. This proposal was rejected by Nehru. On his return to India, Mountbatten is reported to have persuaded Nehru to make an announcement on his acceptance of a plebiscite under UN auspices. Nehru made such an announcement on 11 November 1947.

If India refused to hold a plebiscite later, it was because Pakistan failed to withdraw its troops from the territory under its occupation. The UN Commission, in an *aide-mémoire* issued

147

on 14 January 1949, stated: "...in the event of Pakistan not accepting these proposals (plebiscite) or having accepted them not implementing parts 1 and 2 of the resolution of August 13, 1948 (i.e., withdrawal of its troops and tribesmen), India's acceptance of them should not be regarded in any way as binding..." (P.B. Gajendragadkar, *Kashmir: Retrospect and Prospect*, p.47). In other words, the question of plebiscite arises *only when Pakistan vacates the territory under its possession.* Instead of vacating the territory held by it, Pakistan has waged two wars with India to secure possession of Kashmir by force. Also, Pakistan has signed the Shimla Agreement (on 3 July 1972) under which it accepted that all issues between India and Pakistan, including Kashmir, would be settled peacefully and bilaterally, and recourse to any third party would be by mutual agreement. The Shimla Agreement supersedes all previous pronouncements on the Kashmir issue, and efforts by Pakistan now to take the Kashmir issue to the UN are in flagrant violation of this Agreement.

Plebiscite or referendum does not provide the only way to find out the views of a people. Regular elections in any democratic set-up serve this purpose. In the 1952 elections held in Jammu and Kashmir to form the Constituent Assembly, Sheikh Abdullah's party won all the seats. It was the most "popular" election that one can think of. His popularity was such that even in Jammu only two candidates were fielded to oppose his party.

In refusing to quit territory held by them, the Pakistani authorities seem to think: A bird in the hand is worth two in the bush. Legal experts have asserted that once the Indian Constitution was drawn up and it came into force, the Government of India could not have ceded any of its territory (this is what plebiscite amounted to – there was a chance in any case) to another party. This was an important factor. Then there was strong opposition to holding a plebiscite in view of Pakistan's military aggression on India.

Is India obliged to fulfil the UN resolution in these circumstances? Any obligation created under treaties or declarations are valid only under certain conditions. If the conditions change drastically, then the obligation ceases to be valid. Pakistan has waged war twice – in 1947 and 1965 – to seize Kashmir by force, causing immense loss of life and property to India, as also suffering to the people in J&K and elsewhere. After all this, India has no obligation to honour the resolution. In any case, Pakistan had rejected plebiscite and had accepted it only when faced with the prospect of a rout of its army in the areas held by it in 1947 and 1965. Then, again, how can Pakistan ask India to fulfil its part of the obligations under the UN resolution when the former was supposed to fulfil its obligation first? Any consideration of the UN process can be contemplated only when Pakistan withdraws its troops from the area now under its possession.

In this context, the former chief justice of India, P.B. Gajendragadkar, declares: "It seems to me completely fantastic for Pakistan to suggest that what it failed to achieve by force on two occasions, she should be allowed to attempt to secure by the holding of a plebiscite. The plea that a plebiscite should be held cannot, on elementary considerations of international propriety and decency, be permitted to be raised by Pakistan having regard to her conduct in 1947 and 1965. The act of aggression committed by Pakistan in 1965 makes any plea for holding a plebiscite by Pak wholly illegitimate and untenable" (*Kashmir: Retrospect and Prospect*, p. 118).

The Kashmiri Muslim is under no oppression. He has already exercised the right of self-determination when he elected the Constituent Assembly, which drew up the state Constitution. Since then the state has always had an elected government, except for brief periods. If elections were not fair, and if the leaders are venal, the remedies are also with the people. In any case, these phenomena are not peculiar to Kashmir. Elections in other parts of India are also sometimes rigged. As for venality, we have enough of such people in the country. It is for the electorate to set right their rulers, for there is no other force which can do this. As for autonomy, the state already enjoys a large measure of it.

But let the people in the Valley also take a look at what is happening in PoK. There they have no self-government after four decades; no democracy; no progress or development; and no say in planning their future. The fate of the Valley would have been worse if Pakistan had succeeded in grabbing it in 1947.

If the principle of self-determination is applied to any group but a nation, it can lead to anarchy in most of the countries. This principle cannot be applied to fragment a country or allow secession. In any case, such a process would close the windows of all societies to outside influences, for then no nation will permit foreigners to settle down among its people, allow conversion of its people to other religions or allow free flow of foreign ideas. India takes pride in the fact that it has a tolerant society and that it has a diversity of religions. If self-determination is to be allowed to people on some ground or the other, then India will cease to exist. Under no circumstances will it, therefore, permit such a development.

Mohammad Haroon Ahmed, a Pakistani writer, raises an interesting issue: "The Quaid-i-Azam had once said in Dhakka after the establishment of Pakistan: If we begin to think of ourselves as Bengalis, Punjabis, Sindhis, etc., then Pakistan is bound to disintegrate.' That is what we have witnessed from 1971. What is the guarantee that the Kashmiris will not meet the same fate as the Sindhis or Bengalis?" And he wants to know whether it would be right to put the future of Pakistan into jeopardy by fighting with India if the Kashmiris are really for independence (cited in *The Kashmir Question*, edited by A.G. Noorani, p. 65). A very sensible question. But he forgot to mention that it was Jinnah's strident tirades in terms of Hindus and Muslims which brought about the disintegration of India. The same sectarian spirit cost Pakistan one wing in 1971. What is left may also break up if Pakistan pursues "*Kashmirmania*".

Benazir Bhutto's call for "*aazadi*" (freedom) a few years back proved rather confusing, for she was, in fact, not in favour of Kashmir's independence. She wanted Kashmir to merge with Pakistan.

Similarly, the JKLF (Jammu and Kashmir Liberation Front) too had to give up its ambiguity. Its declaration of independence as its aim, while receiving support from Pakistan, did not appear to be logical. Once Benazir had made it clear that she was for the merger of Kashmir with Pakistan and not for Kashmir's independence, the JKLF had to clarify that "Pakistan is our friend, not our master". Even this position was not free from ambiguity. That is why Yasin Malik, president of the JKLF, had to make the goals of his organisation more specific. His emphasis is no more on "*aazadi*". He is in favour of a non-violent agitation and for a pluralistic society, secular in character, and for the return of the Pandits to Kashmir.

Ms. Bhutto is now definitely opposed to a plebiscite and is toying with the option of independence for J&K. Her calculations are realistic. She says that the Hindus there will naturally vote for India, while the Muslims will be divided into pro-independence and pro-Pakistan groups. There is one more element that she chooses to conceal: that there are sizeable numbers of Muslim refugees in various camps. That is why Benazir admitted in an interview to the *New York Times* (15 May 1994) that Pakistan could "lose" a plebiscite if the option of independence was open to the people. This apprehension also explains why she is strongly opposed to independence as an option today. She must now be convinced that the Valley people are against the Jamaat-e-Islami. This became evident during the funeral procession of Qazi Nissar, shot dead by the Hizb-ul-Mujahideen on 19 June 1994, when more than a lakh of people raised anti-Pakistan slogans.

But mischief continues to be afoot. Of late, a mission of the International Commission of Jurists, which visited the state, questioned the legality of accession. But others have questioned the Commission's interpretation. Professor Maurice Mendelson, for instance, an authority on international law, opines that Kashmir has no right for self-determination under international law. According to him, the 1952 election gave the most popular verdict on the issue of accession to India, when Sheikh Abdullah declared the accession as final. It was plebiscitary in that sense. His views were published in the Commission's report titled "Human Rights in Kashmir: Report of a Mission" (*The Times of India*, 25 May 1995). The Government of India has endorsed Professor Mendelson's opinion.

Professor Mendelson has totally disagreed with the ICJ mission's opinion that "the people of the State acquired the right to self-determination at the time of partition of India in 1947 and that the right still exists because it has neither been exercised nor abandoned". However, the mission was not in favour of plebiscite for the whole state.

Professor Mendelson has also questioned Mountbatten's right to concede "a reference to the people". "Once the accession was over, J&K became a part of the Indian Union," he emphasised. He added that Mountbatten was not legally empowered to impose conditions on accession. If at all anybody could do so, only the head of the state could. In any case, clarified the professor, what Lord Mountbatten said cannot have binding power: "... it could only be binding as a matter of internal law if the Governor-General was legally entitled to make such promises. I doubt if he was."

As for the 1947-48 UN resolutions, Professor Mendelson affirmed they have become redundant and obsolete, especially after the signing of the Shimla Agreement.

Professor Mendelson further felt that the ICJ mission had drawn "incorrect inferences" in that the Indian government made its acceptance of the accession in October 1947 conditional on "a reference to the people". In fact, India had rejected such claims. He recalled the fact (few experts have done so) that while ratifying, in 1979, the International Covenants on Civil and Political Rights and on Economic, Social and Cultural Rights, India made the following observation: "The Government of Republic of India declares that the words 'the right of self-determination' appearing in Article I apply only to people under foreign domination and that these words do not apply to sovereign independent states...."

12

Mosque-based Politics

D
r. Karan Singh, a former governor of J&K, has said that the Hazratbal incident (in October-November 1993 when the Indian army laid siege to the mosque after receiving reports that the locks of the safe containing the holy relic had been tampered with) was a "municipal issue" and that it was not for the army to intervene. One is inclined to agree with him. Yet, the incident snowballed into an international scandal due to our inept handling of the episode.

The Government of India is not responsible for the upkeep or security of temples, churches, mosques and gurdwaras. This is the job of the communities to which they belong. But if any of these holy places is threatened by communal violence, then the Central Government or state government has to step in. This was the case with the Babri Masjid in December 1992.

Neither the Centre nor the Kashmir administration is responsible for the maintenance or security of the Hazratbal mosque. If Muslim militants had turned this mosque into an armed camp, it was the job of the Muslim Auqaf Trust to throw them out. The Trust could have asked the police for help. The trustees must have been aware of the Central Government policy – that places of worship are not to be misused for political purposes. There were precedents in Punjab. Yet the Hazratbal authorities had permitted the terrorists to use the mosque for their activities, and the Kashmir administration looked the other way.

Our policy should be clear and unambiguous. It is not the duty of a secular state to storm a holy place to flush out militants if they hole themselves up inside it, nor should the law-enforcing authorities make a body-check of pilgrims as they enter a holy place. These functions are for the community authorities to perform. But once it becomes known that a religious place is being misused, people who go in or come out of it after worship should be subjected to a thorough search for arms and other clandestine materials. If militants take shelter inside a holy place, it is not for the state to decide whether or not the place has been desecrated; it is for the community to do so. Unfortunately, the Centre has no clear policy on any of these matters even after our bitter experiences in Punjab. Why can't the governor of Jammu and Kashmir ask the trustees of the Hazratbal mosque to furnish a monthly report that it is not being misused for political purposes and that no militants have taken shelter inside? These are routine administrative precautions, which any decent administration will enforce. But the governor has taken no such initiative to make the trustees responsible in the first instance; hence the burning incident at Chrar-e-Sharief in May 1995.

It is said that no Muslim would attack a mosque and that Chrar-e-Sharief could have been burnt down only by the Indian army. This is utter nonsense. Were there not fundamentalists who attacked the Grand Mosque in Saudi Arabia, the holiest place for Muslims? And, in Karachi, have not Shia and Sunni fundamentalists been attacking each other's mosques regularly? Yet, Abdul Ghani Lone, a Kashmiri leader, declared on Doordarshan that no Muslim could have torched the Chrar-e-Sharief mausoleum.

Coming back to what happened at Hazratbal, it is now clear that there was practically no coordination of approach among the various official authorities. The Centre, the Governor and his administration, as also the army, all acted on their own and at cross-purposes. That is why this episode becomes interesting, for it again demonstrates that the Central Government has not even laid down a proper drill to deal with an emergency, and allocate responsibility to each authority. This state of affairs explains the total ineptness in the handling of the episode. This is the situatiion in a state which has faced a series of crises from 1947 onwards.

It is widely believed that the siege of Hazratbal was undertaken on the basis of a report that two locks of the room which contains the holy relic were tampered with. There was no effort made to verify the report. It could have been a planted story. Governor Krishna Rao says there was no time to verify the truth. He could have, in that case, denied the report and ordered an examination of the locks. In any case, whose job is it to report such an event? And to whom should it be reported? Is there no drill or guideline for these matters? Did we learn nothing from the December 1963 incident?

Protection of the relic is the primary responsibility of the mosque trust. It was wrong for the security forces to lay siege. As for the militants, they had been using the mosque for a long time. When the government got the report, why did it panic?

Governor Rao says that he was forced to order the siege because loss of the relic could have created unprecedented violence as in 1963-64. If his administration was so concerned about the holy relic, why did it not post a regular police guard? In 1964, after the theft of the relic, the state administration allowed the Sheikh's followers to fully exploit the incident for political purposes. The authorities should have known then that the same method could be used by anyone else to create mischief. Yet the Kashmir administration failed to arm itself with a proper response to such challenges.

Having laid the siege, there was no effort on the part of the governor to allot specific tasks to the army and the civil administration. In any case, he was in conflict with the army. The idea of flushing out the militants holed up inside the shrine was given up. It was decided by the army to starve them into submission. But what was to be done with the pilgrims? Here was an excellent opportunity to use the pilgrims to break down the will of the militants, but the softies at the Centre and in the state administration decided on a different course. There were foodgrains inside the mosque. So the militants could have held out. But with the depletion of food and water, the pilgrims would have raised a howl against the militants. The militants would have been compelled to finally let them go. Instead, the Kashmir administration (more precisely Wajahat Habibullah, the divisional commissioner) ordered the supply of hot *biriyani* to the people inside the mosque. The army naturally asked: what then was the siege for? Neither Governor Rao nor his administration had an answer. Serving food defeated the army's objective. It was immaterial as to who ate the food. The army decided not to let the militants have a telephone facility. This was overruled by the Kashmir administration. As a result, the militants could remain in touch with ISI agents and foreign media. The army would have liked each militant to surrender with his respective weapons so that he could be identified and kept in a camp. Instead, it was decided to give safe passage to all, including the foreign mercenaries and let them leave their weapons in designated dumps.

Most of the negotiations were conducted by the administration, and the army had no hand in them. However, the army opposed the deal worked out by the administration which allowed the militants safe passage from inside the shrine. The army is reported to have objected to this deal as it would have appeared like a moral victory for the militants and their supporters in Pakistan and as a major setback to the Indian army. The deal was to hand over the shrine to the police in order to let them allow the militants to escape under the cover of darkness and transport them to special places from where they could flee.

The day after the siege began, General S.M. Zaki, adviser to the governor, claimed that a decision had been taken to cut off water and power. Later, it was reported that there was a well inside. But the point is: the employees of the concerned departments refused to carry out the decision and no action was taken against them. In fact, they refused to carry out any orders against the militants. So the army had to carry out the order. Yet when it was seen that the militants were collecting water from the Dal Lake, the water supply was promptly restored by the administration. Habibullah was responsible for all these soft approaches and he used to claim Governor Rao's authorisation. Even when the militants refused to accept food from the government, Habibullah did not give up the idea of feeding them.

Instead, he came up with the proposal that the supply of food should be entrusted to a private caterer.

One can only say here that even a permissive state like India should draw a line beyond which it should not allow its citizens to stray. Such a line has not been drawn by our rulers because they do not want themselves to be bound. Instead, they follow the policy of adhocism, judging issues as they come along, making arbitrary and contradictory decisions. "They are our boys," they say about the militants. This is the usual refrain of the politicians, especially the softies, with regard to rebels who have taken up arms against the rest of the population, against our state, for they do not want to be identified with any drastic decisions against the militants. These "boys" are, in reality, our enemies, for they intend to kill us indiscriminately in order to advance their own cause. In fact, they want to enjoy total power and edge out their opponents. They do not believe in the ballot, and in sharing power. In any case, India is not a tyranny. It has a buoyant democracy, and although it is by no means perfect, here we can change things through the power of the ballot. The process may take time, it may be frustrating, but things do change. As for other problems, the rebels should understand that India is a confederation of equal states and that the Centre has a responsibility to look after the uniform development of all states. If there have been failures in this aspect, it is because some states want to march ahead of others by exploiting Central resources or because those who are denied equality are not strong enough to protest. There is no way by which the Centre can bestow special advantages on a state. In any case, Punjab has the highest per capita income and the Kashmir Valley comes second.

Advocates of "our boys" should know that justice cannot be different for different people. How is it that a bank robber has to languish in prison for years, while a militant who robs dozens of banks goes scot-free? This is the easiest way to destroy the sense of justice and respect for law and encourage political revolt. This way we have already created a privileged community of criminals in a number of states, particularly in Punjab and

Kashmir. These people are not likely to give up the "privileges" they have enjoyed.

Thus, in the entire episode, the army personnel were made to look like fools, for while they wanted to pursue the general objective of bringing the militants under control, the governor and his administration wanted to give them a safe passage. Can there be worse contradictory policies? The militants must have understood from the whole episode that there is no unity of will among those who are entrusted with the task of containing militancy.

This is not to say that the army alone has a solution to the problem or that it is beyond blame. In fact, it has given cause for embarrassment to the Central Government whenever it over-reacted to provocations by the militants. This was the case at Bijbehara, where 37 persons died and over 70 were wounded in army firing (on 22 October 1993) in reply to serious provocation by the militants. Such incidents are bound to be blown out of proportion by human rights activists and Western press and media hostile to India. The army officers must know that years of their good work can be damaged by a moment of wrong reflexes.

13

Militants' Pressures on the Press

The Indian media has played a major role in promoting the wayward nature of Kashmiri politics. It chose to lionise local leaders and treated the Valley as something "special" from the very beginning. By overlooking the growth of corruption and want of principles in various state administrations of J&K, the media has tolerated violation of democracy. In short, the media has had a hand in creating areas of distortions which only helped the militants.

The press in Kashmir is not much different in its basic orientation from the one elsewhere in India. The proprietors are after higher circulation and profits. This explains why, in a small Valley, there are so many newspapers and magazines – 30 dailies and 100 weeklies – and why all are able to flourish.

The Kashmir press has, by and large, been terrorised by the militants. Only few papers ever dared (or dare) to criticise them.

Most foreign correspondents were the first to distort the truth of Kashmir events. But, then, they have always been hostile to India and pro-Pakistan. They have an axe to grind – the West had wanted Kashmir for its strategic importance. The foreign correspondents were naturally in the good books of fundamentalists and militants. At different times, the Government of India had to restrict their entry into the Valley. But they can always raise the bogy of press freedom and this would frighten New Delhi's image-builders.

As for the Indian national press, which carries greater responsibility, it was selectively interested in Jammu and Kashmir. In fact, journalists are not interested in most of the states. The usual refrain is: Why waste money on correspondents when there was nothing significant happening there? Most of them were, therefore, content to use agency stories. But agencies never sent their senior correspondents to Jammu and Kashmir. They were at best reporters, who could never understand the real story behind the official handouts. Today, no correspondent wants to take up a job in Srinagar and would prefer to operate from Jammu. As for the few newspapers which had posted their own men in the Valley, they soon discovered that they were surrounded by hostile forces. There was no way correspondents could gather and report the truth from the Valley. If they ever managed to get at the truth, they were soon warned off. They learnt by slow experience that it was wiser to mute one's voice and say the least. This explains why there are a thousand questions about the state of J&K for which there are no answers. Knock at the door of the ministry for information and the usual answer is: we do not know. Today, no Indian journalist can write against the militants and hope to stay alive in the Valley. The militants have put fear into their hearts by selective killing of Kashmiri journalists. No Indian correspondent or newspaper has, however, been honest enough to admit that the reports he (or she) or it writes or publishes are doctored. But there are some journalists who seek out the militants for "inside" stories so that they can sensationalise them to promote either their paper's circulation or their own career. Their mercenary approach has already done incalculable damage to the interest of the country. S. Sahay, a respected senior journalist, after a visit to the Valley on behalf of the Editors' Guild, wrote in *The Tribune* (20 February 1990): "As far as Indian journalists are concerned, some feel that one's nationalistic fervour should not colour one's professional outlook. Others (including this writer) feel that a journalist is a citizen too and he cannot act in a vacuum." No such thought restrains many journalists. One can understand why the human rights activists write on "state violence" in Kashmir. But how can any Indian correspondent talk of "state violence" when he knows that our army and paramilitary forces have a long tradition of civilised behaviour? If there had been exceptions here and there, they call for careful scrutiny. Surely, the Indian journalist or human rights worker is not trying to say that the militants are innocent victims of a terrorist government? The wonder is that the Indian armed forces, even under the greatest provocation, have not lost their cool. If militants have died, so have Indian paramilitary and army personnel. And their death is in no way less painful to their kith and kin. As for real "innocent" civilians, it is unfortunate that some are caught in the crossfire. But they are not always innocent, for, in many cases, they are active storm-troopers of the militants. Those who sympathise with terrorist causes should understand that the world has no sympathy for terrorists today. Theirs was a romantic movement of the last century, when rebels took to violence against landlords and capitalists. Today, even genuine revolutions will find no supporters, for no revolution has produced a just society. The cost has been vastly disproportionate. We have examples of the USSR and China, where almost 50 million people died for the "cause". This being so, the world cannot accept terrorism (i.e., plain murder of people) as a means to bring about favourable changes in society. The point is: you cannot hang a Hitler a million times, but only once, for his crimes. That terrorism has destroyed the freedom of the press in Kashmir has not worried these apologists of the militants.

It is part of the militants' strategy to trap the security forces in situations wherein the latter would react in a rather violent manner. Such a reaction would invariably lead to deaths of innocent people, especially of old people, women and children, in the crossfire. In turn, this would ensure the worst publicity for the security personnel. Sometimes, kidnappings of foreigners or other prominent persons are also resorted to, which generate adverse publicity.

That the aforementioned activities are in themselves grave human rights violations by the militants does not find much appreciation in the media. More than two lakh people have been turned into refugees in their own country (over a lakh of Pandits and Sikhs and nearly a lakh of Muslims). These are cases of extreme human tragedy. Apart from everything else, such persons have been economically ruined and will find it difficult to recover. The human rights activists and the national press mostly ignore all these factors and concentrate on a few instances of army "atrocities" on militants, more often provoked by the militants themselves.

Regarding human rights concerns of Western agencies such as Amnesty International and Asia Watch, Dr. Chrangoo, a spokesman of Panun Kashmir, says: "It baffles me why Amnesty or Asia Watch, who visited the Valley, could not pay even a single visit to the refugee camps" (of Pandits).

The state government itself has issued a handout on the human tragedy involving the Pandits, which reads as follows: "Never before in the history of the J&K such a vast exodus of any community (over two lakh Kashmiri Pandits, Sikhs and Muslims) was seen as in 1990-91. This was a great human tragedy." There were about one lakh Pandit families in Srinagar. Today, not even 10 per cent survive. They have lost almost everything.

B.G. Verghese, former editor of *The Hindustan Times* and *Indian Express,* and an independent journalist, visited the Valley with Vikram Rao, another senior journalist, on a fact-finding mission on behalf of the Press Council of India to investigate "army atrocities". In his report, Verghese asserted that many of the stories filed by correspondents were "distorted, fabricated and exaggerated". He made the following significant remark: "The two most serious allegations against the army, namely, the so-called Dudhi killings and the mass rape of women at Kunarn (Kupwara) are without foundation." Verghese's report came down heavily on those journalists and human rights activists as also on alleged victims and propagandists (Pyare Lal Kaul, *Crisis in Kashmir*).

Most of the human rights organisations of India have sent their representatives to the Valley to make on-the-spot studies. The Committee for Initiative on Kashmir (CIK) has, in the process, done more to misguide than guide the world on Kashmir. These human rights activists buy their stories from either the militants or journalists who work for these outfits.

On the rape of women by Indian armed forces in Kupwara district, which allegedly took place on 22-23 February 1992, Verghese wrote: "The Kunarn (Kupwara district) rape story, on examination, turned out to be a massive hoax orchestrated by militant groups and their sympathisers and mentors in Kashmir and abroad as part of a sustained and cleverly contrived strategy of psychological warfare.... The loose ends and contradictions in the story expose a tissue of lies by many persons and at many levels." The report further said that the "raped women were tutored to say so against their human dignity". This shows how bold the militant outfits can be, and how well they are served by disinformation agencies in the Valley. Obviously, the Pakistan intelligence has trained them well in how to conduct propaganda.

The Verghese Committee investigated four incidents: (1) killings of 73 militants at Dudhi while crossing the line of actual control on 5 May 1991; (2) mass rape at Kunarn on 22-23 February 1992, (3) army firing on 1 March 1990 at Zakoora; and (4) mass rape at Pazipora on 10 August 1990. The following points are noteworthy:

1. The 73 militants reported killed were crossing the line of actual control, and when challenged by the Indian soldiers they fired at them. The Pakistan army was providing them with covering fire for the crossing. The Indian army could not have arrested them as the human rights activists suggested.

2. On the mass rape at Kunarn, the report states: "Few incidents have aroused as much controversy, indignation and publicity, both within Kashmir and globally, as the alleged mass rape of women in a cordon-and-search operation...the account was raised ten days after the event as part of a motivated propaganda campaign by militants and their mentors to discredit the armed forces...." The Verghese Committee found out that Kashmiri women preferred to go to the military clinic in Kunarn rather than to the civil hospital even after the reports came out in the press. The Committee's visit to Kunarn and its meeting with the dramatis personae proved the falsehood of the video cassette

fabricated by militants. "The video recording was a carefully rehearsed piece of disinformation made and marketed to arouse anger and hatred against India among viewers unacquainted with the facts, to intensify alienation and win their sympathy", the Committee noted.

3. As regards the Zakoora firing, the report was that of the Committee for Initiative on Kashmir (CIK), which claimed that the army resorted to unprovoked firing. The army's case was that an army bus was carrying children back from school to their homes and that a crowd started stoning it. The army security personnel had to resort to firing to disperse the crowd. The CIK reported that there was no school on that day, as it was closed. On further enquiry, it was found that the school was functioning and that the children were indeed going back home in an army bus.

4. As for the Pazipora story, on 10 August 1990, an army patrol in Didikot village (Pazipora) was ambushed. In the ensuing battle, 25 persons were reported killed, eight to fifteen women raped and several houses burnt. The story was widely reported in India and abroad. *The Illustrated Weekly of India*, unfortunately, carried it under the heading "Protectors or Predators?"

The Verghese Committee could not visit the site, but interviewed several people connected with the incident, especially a former chief justice of the Jammu and Kashmir high court.

Incidentally, according to Verghese, the most "colourful" story was given by this high court judge. On this story the Verghese Committee reported: "The extravagance of the language used by the former Chief Justice and the firm conclusions he for one has arrived at without attempting to cross-check or assess the evidence or the probability is breathtaking". The Committee notes the judge visited the place only once on 15 August and that it was a fact that in an encounter some people died (the actual number is difficult to assess). All other stories are concoctions, the report concluded. *The Illustrated Weekly* should have been more careful.

Although the Verghese Committee has exposed the lies of the press and human rights activists, the latter have in no way ceased their ill-conceived activities. This approach shows that they are really not interested in the truth. Most human rights organisations have focussed attention on the wrongs done to the militants, ignoring what these hired assassins have done to keep the Valley in turmoil. The PUCL (People's Union for Civil Liberties) and the Committee for Initiative on Kashmir have not bothered to be impartial observers. They put the blame on the security forces for all the problems the citizens are facing. The CIK claimed that there is "ample evidence" to prove that killings, maimings, arrests, etc., are carried out as part of official policy. A four-member women's team visited the Valley and came to the amazing conclusion that most women have been raped by the security forces!

A four-member team of the Press Council of India, which visited the Valley recently, found the press and the electronic media under the constant threat of violence, arson and bomb attacks by the militants. The team, headed by *Tribune's* then editor, V.N. Narayanan, observed that the Kashmiris were overawed by fear and that life in the Valley was entirely under militant control. Only a few newspapers possess the courage to defy the militants. Interestingly, the newspapers which carry out militants' orders get more advertisement support from the government, while those who oppose them are deprived of support! The same pattern holds good with regard to house allotment. The team reported that some proprietors of offset presses (mostly owned by government officials and ruling party members) print anti-national material. It also found the role of some journalists, particularly those representing the foreign press, TV and radio, as also some correspondents of the Indian national press, dubious. It wanted closer scrutiny of their activities.

Amnesty International knows very well that it is Pakistan which is motivating, training, arming and financing the activities of the militants, yet not a word to condemn Pakistan is ever written. Such deliberate distortions are not expected from an impartial international body. In fact, Amnesty's approach violates the very spirit of the Declaration of Human Rights. By concentrating its attention on governments and not on terrorists, Amnesty is engaged in the "politics" of human rights. This fact comes out clearly from its stand; i.e., while taking the Government of India to task, it is silent on Pakistan.

There is no unanimity among the human rights organisations. For example, Asia Watch reported: "Kashmir militants do not deny that they receive support from Pakistan...sources have reported that the Pak army's field intelligence unit helped to organise the Jammu and Kashmir Liberation Front in the Indian-held Kashmir Valley as early as 1964. In 1988 Pakistan's Inter-Services Intelligence (ISI) Directorate had begun to establish training camps in Pak-occupied 'Azad Kashmir' manned by retired Pak army officers."

Asia Watch went on to say that militant organisations have issued death threats and have assassinated members of the minority Hindu community and those Muslims who have not supported their separatist cause (*The Hindustan Times*, 6 May 1991). These stories show how the reports appearing on Kashmir in the Indian or foreign press suffer from so many infirmities.

On the question of allowing representatives of Amnesty and Asia Watch for an on-the-spot investigation in the Valley, Dr. K.N. Pandita of the Friends of Kashmir organisation asks whether anyone in the Valley can speak the truth today? He believes that people are so scared that they dare not say a word against the militants.

It is not that all sane opinion has been snuffed out in the local press. *Al Safa*, an Urdu paper published from Srinagar, dared to criticise the wanton killings of innocent people by militants. It asserted that the excesses of militancy were tolerated because they were all part of the situation. It further pointed out: "In every society, there are bad and good people. But everybody does not have the capacity to decide what is right and what is wrong.... The very first defect of the militant movement (in Kashmir) has been that everybody arrogated unto himself the right to declare what is right and who is wrong and award punishment accordingly. Thus, an illiterate person, who does not have the vision of greatness, does not have the historical sense and is not aware of the basic message of religion, issues statements like a Mufti Azam or a judge. Thus, this position creates a notion in him that he is a Messiah or a Prophet of his times. Whatever he says is the truth, and whatever he does is the right thing. This illusion about one's own self will be highly dangerous for that society where such a person lives. More so when he has destructive material in his hands. In the Valley, there are more than 150 chiefs of units, district commanders, and section commanders belonging to different militant organisations wielding power and clout. They can do whatever they want. There are only a few amongst them who have the sense to observe bounds, (others) consider themselves authorities on religion, morality, politics.... Basically, the urgent need of the hour is to define the role of the gun and discuss the limits of its use" (Anil Maheshwari, *Crescent over Kashmir: Politics of Mullaism*).

The limits of the gun have been well examined by eighteenth, nineteenth and twentieth century political philosophers. Change and flux are present in every society, but change invariably harms or adversely affects some people. That is why they offer a great deal of resistance to change. But if change is resisted for too long, the price of change is bound to increase. People are likely to lose faith in peaceful processes. And sometimes they take to the gun. But if the gun is the only way to bring about changes no civilised society will be possible. We must build societies based on reason and peaceful ways. By taking to the gun, we are merely raising the price of change.

The point is: those who take to the gun because they do not believe in any argument must perish by it. We cannot argue with those who have made the gun argue for them. Society has the crucial task of telling them that they will not get any sympathy, and that they will be finally eliminated. It is in failing to explain the precise limits of the democratic process that we have allowed corruption and arbitrariness, violence and waywardness and, now the very challenge to civilised society, to threaten us. So, a messsage should go out to one and all that the gun is not a civilised way and that those who do not believe in the democratic process will get nothing by taking to the gun.

14

Shades of Geopolitics

Kashmir and the United Nations

When Jawaharlal Nehru referred the invasion of Kashmir by Pakistan to the UN in January 1948, little did he realise that that region was going to be sucked into the vortex of geopolitics. He perhaps believed that the matter was a simple one, and that the UN would give India a fair verdict. Instead, he found India in the dock. This reversal of roles was brought about by the USA and Britain. Nehru bemoaned: "Instead of discussing and deciding our reference in a straightforward manner, the nations of the world, sitting on the Security Council, got lost in power politics" (P.B. Gajendragadkar, *Kashmir: Retrospect and Prospect,* p. 76). This is what Gandhiji had feared and it came true.

Several historians and political analysts believe that this was yet another blunder committed by Nehru. More so because he was not unaware of the power politics within the UN. So, in the final analysis, he is to be held responsible for this act and its consequences.

The Government of India's case was no doubt a simple one. Its complaint, lodged on 1 January 1948, in the Security Council ran as follows: "The Government of Pakistan be asked to prevent tribals and Pak nationals from taking part in the fighting in the State of Jammu and Kashmir and to deny to the raiders access to and use of its territory in operations against Kashmir, military and other supplies, and all other kinds of aid that might try to prolong the fighting in Kashmir" (Gajendragadkar, *op. cit.*, p.63). Three persons – Gopalaswamy Ayyangar, a former prime minister of Kashmir, M.C. Setalvad, one of the ablest lawyers of India, and Sheikh Abdullah – constituted the Indian delegation to the UN. Pakistan denied the entire Indian charge, including the presence of Pak troops in Jammu and Kashmir.

Sir Zafrullah Khan, the foreign minister of Pakistan, presented his country's case. He called for ceasefire, withdrawal of all forces, rehabilitation of refugees who had left the state, setting up of a joint administration under the two governors-general and induction of either UN or Commonwealth forces into Kashmir.

Even at the initial stages it became evident that the USA and Britain had an axe to grind. So they deftly turned the case into an Indo-Pakistan territorial "dispute" even in the face of protests by the Soviet representative, Andrei Gromyko. Very soon, the emphasis shifted to plebiscite. The plea by the Indian side that the first task of the Security Council should be to expel the raiders was ignored.

The Security Council recommended the setting up of a three-member commission to investigate the case. On 29 January the Council chairman (a delegate of Belgium) introduced two resolutions. The first declared that the "fate of Kashmir should be decided by a plebiscite under international control" and the second called upon the commission to ensure the end of hostilities. At this stage, the US delegate, Warren Austin, declared that only when the tribesmen were "satisfied that there will be a fair plebiscite" would they agree to withdraw. As if he had a brief for them! In other words, he was in favour of a neutral administration under UN or Anglo-American auspices. In reply, Ayyangar contended that the issue before the Council was not the future of Kashmir, and that neither the Council nor Pakistan had any jurisdiction over the form of government to be set up in Kashmir. In frustration, India decided to recall its delegation from the UN, but this move was opposed by the Anglo-Americans, who called upon the Council to go ahead with its plans. Only the firm opposition of the USSR put a stop to this mischief.

The UN Commission arrived in Karachi on 7 July 1948, when Zafrullah revealed for the first time that Pakistan had three of its army brigades stationed in Jammu and Kashmir. This revelation threw new light on the entire matter. Zafrullah offered some lame excuses for the military presence. But what surprised one was the fact that the commission did not take any action on the basis of this new fact nor did it report the matter to Nehru when its members met him. But they could no more ignore the issue of ceasefire.

As the war continued, the commission drew up ceasefire and truce agreements (on 13 August 1948) in three parts. Part I called for immediate ceasefire (both sides not to raise troop strength). Part II outlined the truce agreement, and Part III suggested steps towards a plebiscite. While Part II (a) called for the withdrawal of Pak troops from Kashmir, II (b) called on Pakistan to secure the withdrawal of the tribesmen. Only after Pakistan had carried out these stipulations was the plebiscite question to be taken up. In the event, Pakistan put up so many amendments that it was tantamount to a rejection of the ceasefire proposal.

Meanwhile, India pushed ahead with its own plan to clear out the raiders. In the process, it gained more territory. Pakistan, therefore, realised that its aggression was proving futile. It, therefore, proposed a ceasefire, but suggested certain new steps with regard to plebiscite. It wanted a UN plebiscite administrator; perhaps this idea was instigated by the USA. But India insisted that, before plebiscite, there should be ceasefire and withdrawal of Pakistani troops and tribals and the disarming of "Azad Kashmir" forces. The plebiscite administrator was to be appointed by the J&K administration although chosen by the UN Security Council.

On 1 January 1949, the truce came into effect. Nehru was at Allahabad then, where, he declared: "We stopped a victorious army. We could have settled conclusions. In obedience to the Charter we restrained the action of our military forces. Instead of obtaining what we could have obtained by the use of force, we continued to negotiate" (*The Hindustan Times*, 2 January 1949). This was yet another of Nehru's blunders. India could have at least reclaimed the northern areas. The UN secretary general appointed a "UN military observer group" consisting of 50 persons, 24 of whom were Americans.

In February 1949, the Czech representative in the UN Commission exposed its bias. To make matters worse for the Commission, Pakistan began to violate the truce agreement. It augmented its military strength and refused to withdraw its troops or tribes. Instead of preparing to vacate the area held by it, Pakistan consolidated its position and created a new "Azad Kashmir" force of 32 battalions. It, however, offered to withdraw its troops, but insisted on parity with India. India disagreed with these new demands.

The UN Commission did not expect Pakistan to consolidate its position. In its interim report, it admitted failure in anticipating this development: "It is reasonable to suppose that if the Commission had been able to foresee that the ceasefire period would be prolonged and that Pakistan would use that period to consolidate its position in the 'Azad [Kashmir'] territory, the Commission would have dealt with this question in Part II of the resolution of August 13" (Pyare Lal Kaul, *Crisis in Kashmir*).

In the meantime, the USA was making a study of the strategic value of the Valley and the northern areas. It drew up plans for setting up army bases and airfields. The Anglo-American members of the Commission were keen to place the "Azad Kashmir" territory, including Gilgit, the area contiguous to the USSR, under combined Pak and Anglo-American control.

The Commission next turned its attention to the appointment of a plebiscite administrator, one of its strategies to gain control of Kashmir despite the fact that Pakistan had not carried out its part of the Commission's resolution. On 22 March 1949, UN Secretary General Trygve Lie appointed Admiral Chester Nimitz, the former chief of US Naval Operations, as plebiscite administrator. He was given wide powers. But India refused to accept him.

On 15 April 1949, the UN Commission presented modified truce proposals, this time more favourable to Pakistan. In the meantime, the US held out food aid to India (then reeling under a famine) as a bribe to accept the truce proposals. On its part, the Commission threatened that this was the "final" proposal and failure to accept it would compel it to refer the whole matter back to the Security Council.

At this stage, Nehru was not willing to make any more concessions. So he insisted on the disbandment of "*aazad*" forces and on the entry of Indian troops into the northern areas. As Pakistan was not agreeable to any of these conditions, the Commission's proposals were dropped.

The Commission now turned to new tactics, i.e., arbitration. This ruse helped bring Nimitz in through the back door by making him an arbitrator. President Harry Truman approved the move and the British PM, Clement Attlee, sent a personal message to the prime ministers of India and Pakistan recommending the arbitration move. Pakistan promptly accepted the new approach in which both parties were put on an equal footing. But India found the proposal highly arbitrary. The area of arbitration and the methods were left to Nimitz. So, on 8 September 1949 India rejected the arbitration proposal, foiling the US-UK plans to foist Nimitz on Kashmir.

Consequently, the Commission could make no further progress. Hence, the two mediators, Sir Owen Dixon and Dr. Frank Graham, returned to Geneva and reported failure. But in its final recommendation, the Commission suggested a single mediator. Considering the failure of the Anglo-Americans to get their way, the US and the UK media put forward proposals for the partition of the state. While the UK press was for partition and for plebiscite in the Valley, the US press called for the total withdrawal of India and Pakistan from Kashmir. This move was perhaps to prepare the ground for the independence of Kashmir.

The proposals of the two mediators are of some interest. Dixon recommended the withdrawal of Pakistan and the demobilisation of "Azad Kashmir" forces as a prelude to the withdrawal of Indian forces. Dixon recognised the accession of the Maharaja as a legal act and Pakistan's entry into the state as a violation of international law. According to Dixon, plebiscite should have taken place only in areas where voting was uncertain. Such an area was the Valley. The Dixon plan did not find favour with either India or Pakistan.

The US involvement in the Korean war (1952) turned international attention away from developments in Kashmir. However, during the Commonwealth Conference, an effort was made to find a compromise by placing Kashmir under Commonwealth forces before the plebiscite. While Pakistan accepted such a compromise, India did not, because it was not prepared to accept foreign troops in Kashmir.

Meanwhile, events were not marking time in Kashmir. The National Conference decided, on 27 October 1950, to convene a constituent assembly with a view to framing a constitution for Jammu and Kashmir and to hold elections in this regard. At this decision, there was consternation in Pakistan, which called for an emergency meeting of the Security Council. This call was promptly supported by the Anglo-Americans because India had, in the meantime, declared its neutrality with regard to the Korean war. As was expected, the resolution passed by the Security Council was loaded against India. This resolution called for a UN force to hold the fort and also for early steps to conduct the plebiscite. India was painted in the worst colours. Nehru called such denigration as a "challenge to India's self-respect".

On 30 April 1951, Dr. Graham was again appointed as the UN mediator. He came with a large entourage of assistants. He worked between 20 June 1951 and 27 March 1953, but was not able to make any headway. In the meantime, relations between India and Pakistan steadily worsened as Pakistan sought entry into Western military alliances. Nehru warned Pakistan that if it moved into Kashmir, a full-scale war between the two nations could erupt. Dr. Graham also failed to induct Nimitz into Kashmir. However, he was able to reinforce the UN observer team.

On 17 January 1952, at the UN, Jacob Malik of the USSR accused Britain and America of imperialist motives. He opposed the induction of foreign troops into Kashmir. This effectively halted the Graham initiatives. In April 1952, Dr. Graham reported failure. But the UN Security Council had no plan to close the issue, and asked Dr. Graham to continue his mission. But Dr. Graham's main effort was directed to bring in Nimitz, although Pakistan's failure to carry out its part of the UN resolutions continued to block success. (This question remains valid even today.) Finally, Dr. Graham wanted to rope in Nimitz as his adviser, but India opposed this move.

The Anglo-American attempt to seize Kashmir was thus foiled, for from 1952 onwards the USSR used its veto power to block all Western proposals on Kashmir. However, the Anglo-Americans did not give up their plan. They merely changed their tactics. This time they tried to win over Sheikh Abdullah by tempting him with the offer of assistance for an independent Kashmir.

The Sheikh in Search of a Sheikhdom

The framing of J&K's Constitution brought to light the innate differences in the approach of various political personalities of Kashmir. From the very outset, the Sheikh was for internal autonomy. But others were not so sure, for all other states which signed the instrument of accession (for defence, foreign relations, and communications) had gone back on their demand for internal autonomy so that they could gain the advantages of formal merger. Abdullah, however, decided to retain internal autonomy (conferred on J&K under Article 370 of the Indian Constitution). But he was not content with the measure of autonomy he was enjoying.

Of course, there was growing opposition to the Sheikh at various levels. His land reform measure was a failure, for, once the landholders knew the ceiling on the land they could own, they distributed the surplus land among their kith and kin. Thus, there was not much land left for distribution to landless people. Again, the endemic famines afflicting the state, especially at a time when India itself was facing a serious food scarcity, made the task of feeding the Kashmiri people difficult. Crops failed in 1949-50 and 1950-51 in the state. Although the Centre met a large part of the demand for foodgrains, they were diverted into the blackmarket by unscrupulous officials of the Food Control Department. Although the peasantry was in a tight situation, the administration continued to procure foodgrains from them at a nominal price. This brought the National Conference and the state food minister Mirza Afzal Beg into a head-on clash. As for cooperative stores, which handled food distribution, they were riddled with corruption.

It was in this kind of atmosphere that the Sheikh and Beg began to berate India for their own failures. They told the Kashmiris that accession was a mistake and that Kashmir must secure its independence. They also shared such thoughts with Western correspondents. On 5 July 1953, Robert Trumbull in a despatch from New Delhi told *The New York Times* readers: "Sheikh Abdullah is said to lean towards independent status as this would solve many of his problems, both political and financial, and thereby strengthen his personal support which now appears to be falling off."

The agitations in Jammu that followed the death of Dr. S.P. Mookerjee, president of the Jana Sangh, in June 1953, while in detention, made the Sheikh furious. He took the view then that since Jammu was "a hotbed of communalism", it could not remain in association with Kashmir. This view revealed new trends in his thinking.

In the meantime, the Sheikh entertained the idea that Kashmir could have the status of Switzerland and that Kashmir's neutrality could be guaranteed as in the case of Switzerland. On 19 December 1952, the *Christian Science Monitor* came out with a story by its correspondent in Delhi, Gordon Graham: "With Soviet Russia and Communist China towering to the north, Sheikh Abdullah sees Kashmir's future as a matter of alignment rather than accession, and of [the] largest measure of independence compatible with safety. His dream, perhaps, is that one day Kashmir may be the 'Switzerland of the East' not only in the physical resemblance which is already so strong, but also in the neutrality guaranteed by all the nations surrounding it."

The story of the Sheikh is that of a patriot who, through vaulting ambition, turned an opportunist. Early in May 1953, the US Senator Adlai Stevenson met the Sheikh in Srinagar several times. Even Beg was not present at these meetings. There was only one subject for such a lengthy discussion and that was the independence of Kashmir and how it could be sustained.

In his Id-ul-Fitr broadcast on 14 June 1953, the Sheikh spoke to the people of the three alternatives before them: accession to India, accession to Pakistan and independence and friendship with both India and Pakistan.

In 1953, John Foster Dulles, the US secretary of state, visited both India and Pakistan, and is reported to have discussed with both countries the future of Kashmir, including independence. Robert Trumbull of *The New York Times* reported on 5 July 1953 that, according to Dulles, "a solution of the Kashmir dispute envisages a special status for the Kashmir Valley, possibly independence guaranteed by both countries, and partition of the rest of the State along lines now occupied by the opposing armies under a ceasefire agreement".

The Working Committee of the National Conference, which was headed by Bakshi Ghulam Mohammad, opposed the new ideas of the Sheikh. In May 1953, the Working Committee discussed these ideas for three weeks, but the Sheikh failed to convince its members. The committee passed a resolution supporting the Delhi Agreement, which secured 15 votes against four. This came to be reflected in the cabinet, in which three out of five came out openly against the Sheikh. They declared: "You have tended to act in a manner that has generated uncertainty, suspense and doubt in the minds of the people of the State in general, and of those in Jammu and Ladakh in particular.... Under these circumstances, what seems inevitable is that interested foreign powers may well take advantage of and exploit the situation for their own selfish purpose" (Gajendragadkar, *op. cit.*, p.101). Bakshi claimed that the Sheikh had lost the confidence of his cabinet. A copy of this letter was sent to the Sadr-i-Riyasat (Karan Singh) who dissolved the council of ministers, dismissed the Sheikh and invited Bakshi to form a new government. The Sheikh and some of his close friends were arrested at Gulmarg.

For a Place in the Cockpit

Kashmir, where three empires (British, Chinese and Tsarist) used to meet, can be considered to be "the cockpit of the world". In the post-colonial era, Kashmir's importance has not lessened; it has, in fact, increased.

The United States, the only surviving superpower today, has a special interest in this region. And for the same reason that once inspired the British. Apart from strategic considerations, the US has economic interests in Asia, especially in the oil-rich regions of the Middle East and the Gulf. The US depends on outside sources for 10-15 per cent of its oil consumption. But more important to the US is the fact that American companies handle a large part of the production and distribution of oil and oil products in the world. As supplies dwindle, the US interest in preserving its turf is on the increase. That is why Pakistan is gaining in importance in the eyes of Washington. Apart from being a leading Muslim state, it is the only Muslim country which possesses nuclear weapons.

"Nuclear weapons have now become a key to Pakistan's assertive strategy in Kashmir", according to a US Republican Party report (*The Times of India*, 27 February 1995). The report further states that Benazir Bhutto believes that Pakistan's growing nuclear capabilities will shield USA's assertive policies.

The strategists in Washington are alarmed over the growth of Islamic fundamentalism, especially in the Gulf region, and must be working out plans on how to come to terms with the 1000 million Muslims of the world, for unlike the Indians, the Muslims are spread virtually all over the world. They can cause greater harm to US interests than India. These factors are at present more significant for Washington.

As for the EEC (European Economic Community) and Japan, both of which too are dependent on the Middle East and the Gulf for oil, their dependence is going to decrease as Russian economic recovery and oil production gain momentum. Thus, these two major global actors – the EEC and Japan – have no significant interest in Pakistan. It is more likely that both the EEC (particularly Germany and Britain) and Japan will move closer to India in the coming years. Apart from economic attractions, they see India as a stable factor in a turbulent world.

On the international scene, we are already seeing that Japan is moving out of the shadow of the USA; that Germany is planning a new strategy; that China, while still cultivating its connection with the USA, is opposed to the growth of American influence in the northern territories of Kashmir; and that Britain is no more ready to ditto everything the Americans are doing. As for Russia, although internally weak, it cannot permit the growing influence of America in Central Asia.

Thus, although there are major changes taking place in the world, the geopolitical interests of major actors in the region have hardly changed.

Foreign policy objectives of the great powers continue unchanged. Way back in 1947, when Britain took the decision to hand over power and quit India, both London and Washington exchanged notes on their residual interests in the region. They discovered a common strategic interest in Kashmir and in the subcontinent's manpower. But while Britain wanted to keep India as a closed preserve for British trade and industry in the name of Commonwealth preferences, Washington wanted Britain to scrap the Commonwealth preferences and throw open the closed markets of the colonies. Here, their interests clashed. But this was not the case when it came to safeguarding Western dominance over the world, or the dominance of the capitalist system over the global economy. Here, they all stood together. And, when it came to containing and rolling back communism, the USA and the UK had two common objectives: to pass their financial burden on to the newly free nations and, at the same time, to keep them within the Western fold. Thus, Washington spent little during the final débâcle of communism, while it gained much in the process. But this is a strategy the US has worked to perfection.

The recent US attitude towards India seems to indicate that "there is a vacuum in President Bill Clinton's foreign policy". We would be naïve to fall for this stand. This is the usual plea of apologists.

Apologists dismiss the Clinton letters to the sympathisers of the militant cause as "proforma in nature". These letters are no more proforma in nature than the statements of State Department officials casting doubts on the legal validity of Kashmir's accession to India. Way back in 1948, the legal adviser to the UN Commission for India and Pakistan (UNCIP) affirmed that the accession was legal. It was on this basis that Pakistan was asked to withdraw its armed forces from the state. Nevertheless, his letter to Ghulam Nabi Fai, a Kashmiri separatist, Clinton gave an assurance "to work with you and others to bring peace to Kashmir". To the Democratic representative, Gary Condit, Clinton said that he shared the latter's desire "for a peaceful solution, that protects Sikh rights". Maybe these are routine replies. But what about the US decision to waive the Pressler Amendment? And what about the US stand on the Indo-Russian cryogenic deal? Did these factors also come out of the "vacuum" in understanding? One cannot ignore the convergence of other significant happenings – the European Conference in Brussels on Kashmir and the seminar held in Washington.

US "think-tanks" claim that their country's interest in the region is not "marginal", that the US had taken roots in the region during the long years of the Afghan war, that the US should not leave the region, and that it can still influence Central Asian and South Asian developments.

Professor Stephen Philip Cohen, an authority on South Asia, holds (quoted by I.K. Gujral, India's former foreign minister, in *The Hindustan Times*, 13 February 1994) that even if the US has "no vital interests in South Asia — something worth going to war over — it must sustain its presence and advance a new South Asian Regional Initiative (SARI), and for this it must keep pressing India regarding Kashmir". So, Kashmir is central to US policy today. It is true that American foreign policy does not always look rational or even intelligent. But whatever the confusions at the individual level, there is a certain direction and consistency that can be missed only by the blind. And even deliberate confusions can sometimes be engineered to explain away the apparent anomalies. Gujral also observed: "Our policy makers would be well advised not to believe that the 1953 strategic doctrines of the USA regarding this region have died with the end of the Cold War" (*The Hindustan Times*, 13 February 1994). There are many in India ready to forget the US role.

The US has offered its mediation in Kashmir unasked, and we have rightly rejected it, for having gone in for a bilateral settlement, we could not have killed the very spirit of the Shimla Agreement. In any case, wherever the USA has intervened, it has left that country in shambles. Let us consider the latest example: Afghanistan. That country is in ruins and is not likely to recover for decades. The USA went there to liberate it from Soviet occupation. But the world knows today that Afghanistan had peace and prosperity only when it had a regime supported by Moscow.

In his address to the UN in 1995, President Clinton declared: "Let me start by being clear about where the United States stands. The United States occupies a unique position in world affairs today.... The US intends to remain engaged and to lead." But the leadership has brought neither glory to the United States nor peace to embattled states. That is why a man like George Kenan, the father of post-War US foreign policy, warned the United States leaders in his book *Around the Cragges Hill*: "I should make it clear that I am wholly and emphatically rejecting any and all messianic concepts of American role in the world, rejecting the image of ourselves as teachers and redeemers to the rest of humanity, rejecting this illusion of unique and superior virtue on our part...." Obviously, Clinton seems to be blissfully unaware of what his mentors in America have said.

Kenan was perhaps forced to make such an observation because, behind the veneer of messianic intentions, America relentlessly pursued its national goals. Let us take one instance: the case of terrorism. America was perhaps the first country to turn against terrorism. But, when terrorism was directed against the United States or its friends, Washington was ready to bomb both Libya and Iran in the name of anti-terrorism because both these countries were openly hostile to US interests. However, Washington turned a blind eye to the terrorism sponsored by Israel. Similarly, it refused to declare Pakistan a terrorist state (it did so in the case of Sudan) although there was enough evidence, because Pakistan was a long-time ally and Washington still needed that alliance. The point is: Washington was ready to bomb Libya; but would it stand aside if India were to bomb the training sites of the Pakistan-sponsored terrorists? That is why I feel that India's undue concern to be prim and proper in its foreign policy behaviour is a misplaced commitment. It is certainly not in the interest of the country.

Unfortunately, many of our policy makers and political commentators thought that with the end of the Cold War, America would be opening up a new chapter in its foreign policy and providing a more constructive leadership. In fact, this was the hope of the entire world. America did nothing to cast doubts on this hope, for it was busy, in the meantime, using the favourable opportunity to promote its new policy of globalisation of economic development – a major strategy to infiltrate the world economy. Washington even proposed to supply defence equipment and sensitive technologies to India, and carried out some joint naval exercises. All these ploys gave the impression that Washington had given up Pakistan as a strategic ally, especially in view of the fact that the Soviets had withdrawn their troops from Afghanistan. Our foreign policy experts and our captains of industry were thrilled by the prospects of globalisation, but they gave no thought to the real objectives of the "new world order" Washington wanted to promote. Globalisation was expected to boost the American economic presence throughout the world and, simultaneously, its political power would have grown.

Samuel P. Huntingdon in his book, *The Clash of Civilisations*, writes: "Decisions made at the UN Security Council or in the IMF that reflect the interests of the West are presented to the world as reflecting the desires of the world community.... Through the IMF and other international economic institutions, the West promotes its economic interests and imposes on other nations the economic policies it thinks appropriate...the West, in effect, is using international institutions, military power and economic resources to run the world in ways that will maintain Western predominance, protect Western interests and promote Western political and economic values" (p. 132).

Our own advocates of globalisation hardly thought that, in such a short time, America would utilise other elements of its game plan to block nuclear and missile development programmes and deny advanced technology to India. The USA has already made a great success of the globalisation plan as far as India is concerned. As the Indian PM Narasimha Rao has reiterated time and again: there will be no going back on globalisation. This is music to Washington's ears. But more is needed: India's signature on the nuclear NPT (non-proliferation treaty). It was with this objective that Washington decided to resurrect the Kashmir question – a vulnerable issue for India. Of course, there can be two objectives to a single policy. In the case of Kashmir, Washington had earlier wanted to use this state as a watch-tower to observe and influence developments in the USSR, China, South Asia and the Gulf. Those objectives are still there – more so, now that the USSR has broken up. The break-up of Central Asia remains an unfinished business. Today, the US wants to prevent the Central Asian states from going back to Russia to form an alliance – either military or economic. It also wants to prevent India from emerging as a new Asian power to upset the balance of forces in the region. Washington is reconciled to China becoming a nuclear power, but a nuclear India? No. The US believes that a nuclear China can checkmate both Russia and Japan.

In all these cases, Pakistan can play a useful role as far as US interests are concerned. Pakistan itself cannot aspire to be a major power for lack of resources, but it certainly wants to be the leader of the Islamic world. Although this goal is not easy to attain, the very fact that Pakistan aspires to such leadership has certain implications for the rest of the world. Speaking at the World Affairs Council in Los Angeles in May 1995, Benazir Bhutto maintained that Pakistan was a frontline state in the effort to shape and define the Islamic world. Yes, as one of the states to initiate Islamisation, introducing barbarous practices of an ancient past, Pakistan is certainly trying to redefine the Islamic state. Islam's leadership has fallen on the shoulders of the fundamentalists, not on that of the reformers. And Pakistan is the vanguard of the fundamentalists. Washington may agree to pay this price, although in doing so, it is running some grave risks. The point is: India is not likely to play second fiddle to any power. It aspires to be an independent actor on the global stage. This aspiration does not suit Washington. So, to gain its own objectives it must reduce India's influence in the region and thus frustrate its aspirations. That is why Washington began to arm Pakistan way back in 1953 and has continued to do so. It is the same calculations which have come into play now in clandestinely helping Pakistan's nuclear ambition and in stirring up the Kashmir issue again.

Asia is emerging as a powerful economic rival to Europe. In terms of resources, Asia is better endowed. Japan and China have already established themselves as powerful nations. And there are the Asian tigers, whose combined strength is not to be scoffed at. That is why Washington cannot countenance with equanimity the rise of another major power – India. Perhaps India cannot be stopped; but its growth can be halted for a long time. That is the objective behind the present US efforts. As before, Pakistan serves as a useful instrument for the achievement of this objective. But times have changed for everyone. Britain stood by helplessly when India burnt in 1947. Worse can happen if we allow Kashmir to go to Pakistan.

With this background in mind, let us return to the Kashmir imbroglio. As we have seen elsewhere, America encouraged Sheikh Abdullah's ambition to have an independent Kashmir. In fact, Loy Henderson, the US ambassador, spoke to him several times. Henderson also spoke to Nehru. In a telegram to the US State Department, Henderson asserts that "so far as Kashmir was concerned, he (Nehru) would not give an inch" (quoted in Dennis Kux, *Estranged Democracies*. Kux was a former State Department official). Nehru had become adamant on Kashmir once he saw through US intentions.

As for arms supplies to Pakistan, Prime Minister Liaquat Ali Khan of Pakistan had approached Secretary of State George Marshall for military aid as early as 1948 "to bolster Pakistan and the Muslim states against the communists". But Marshall did not respond. However, John Foster Dulles did. Although, at first President Dwight Eisenhower went along with Dulles on the issue of arms aid to Pakistan, he regretted it later. According to Dennis Kux, Eisenhower called for an end to the policy of Dulles, and told the National Security Council that non-alignment was not against US interests and that the tendency to seek out new allies was "not very sensible". More specifically, he said that the pact with Pakistan was "perhaps the worst kind of pact we could have made. It was a terrible error, but now we seem hopelessly involved in it". This involvement decreased during the regimes of John F. Kennedy and Lyndon Johnson, but increased significantly during the tenure of Richard Nixon. Later, although President Ronald Reagan was not opposed to India, he decided to involve Pakistan in a big way in the proxy war against the USSR in Afghanistan.

With Bill Clinton in the White House, Pakistan is back as a favourite, because his administration has decided to resurrect the imperialist interests of America. No one can convince India that human rights have become such a hot issue to Washington overnight, when millions are dying in Africa due to starvation and civil war, malnutrition and diseases. But the rich nations have washed their hands off these concerns by reducing/eliminating official development aid (ODA), which drew protests from the Pope.

After a decade of silence, Washington has again brought up the subject of Kashmir. In his address to the UN on 27 September 1993, President Clinton clearly linked Kashmir with the NPT. Clinton's main theme was how the world should adjust itself to the post-Cold War situation. He remarked: "Thus, we marvel at these bloody ethnic, religious and civil wars [that] rage from Angola to the Caucasus to Kashmir." Then he went on to point out how destructive weapons in the hands of a country like Iraq could be. He said that ways had to be found to control these weapons and "reduce the number of states that possess them". Obviously, this was an oblique reference to the need to force India give up its nuclear and missile development programme.

Dinesh Singh, foreign minister of India, told the Asia Society in New York the same day: "India has certain basic security concerns, as we are situated next to China and Pakistan. These have to be addressed. Our indigenous technology in this context cannot be given up unless others do the same and our security is assured. The same also applies to our missile technology."

Although India has expressed its stand on these matters *ad nauseum*, Washington has not tried to appreciate India's point of view. Instead, it has seized every opportunity to twist India's arm. Linkage of the NPT with Kashmir is the latest exercise.

In order to impress the world about the dangers posed by India's nuclear programme (no word from him on Pakistan's bomb in the basement), Clinton has cautioned one and all against a nuclear exchange between India and Pakistan.

Bill Clinton has claimed that he "shares human rights concerns with Pakistan". And Secretary of State Warren Christopher, for his part, has stated that he has no evidence of Pak support to terrorism. These are deliberate statements – no "vacuum" in understanding here – meant to confuse the world, if not to convert it to "Americanism".

But the world refuses to be converted to the American way of thinking. Memories are still fresh with regard to US Cold War precepts and practices. While America was the champion of democracy as a precept, in practice, it was instrumental in creating the worst forms of tyranny and the maximum number of despotic states. They still fester here and there.

During his press conference at the UN Correspondents' Club in New York on 9 April 1990, Amanullah Khan, head of the JKLF, revealed his involvement in murder and mayhem. In response to this revelation, the US State Department spokesperson, Margaret Tutwiler, said on 12 April: "We are deeply disturbed by the statements attributed to Amanullah Khan during his press conference in New York. If accurate, we believe that the statements promote terrorism...we consistently and unequivocally condemn terrorist acts by any organisation, including the JKLF." Now, the Clinton administration seems to say that it will be ready to work with Amanullah Khan for the protection of human rights in the Valley! However, in 1990 the State Department had ordered the cancellation of Khan's visa, upon which the Pakistan embassy announced full diplomatic protection to the rebel. Pakistan also threatened that if the visa were cancelled "there will be a very, very strong reaction in Pakistan and elsewhere" (*Frontier Post*, 27 April 1990). What a reversal of policy!

Pakistan's own "track record" is not very encouraging. Ever since its inception, it has more often than not been under military dictatorships. There has been little freedom of the press till recently. And Pakistan has proclaimed to the world that it is a theocratic state. The members of the Hindu minority have steadily left their homes and those of the minority sects of Islam, such as Ahmedias were, and are, being persecuted. The Pak Supreme Court had prohibited the Ahmedias from using Islamic symbols. But worse was to come: the loss of East Pakistan in December 1971, because the ruling clique of Pakistan (mostly Punjabis) did not know how to deal with the subnationalism of Bengali Muslims. Pakistan perpetrated the most horrendous genocide, which is why the Bengali Muslims, not normally aggressive, took to violence to gain their liberation. The drama, now being re-enacted in Karachi, with the Mohajirs (Muslims from India who opted for Pakistan after partition) being branded as "not of Pakistani blood". Pakistan thus has no ground to accuse India of failures on the issue of human rights. And Washington should be aware of these realities.

When Ms. Bhutto was fulminating against India on its human rights record, the human rights activists of Pakistan were castigating Pak authorities on its own record. Till now, Pakistan has not passed the basic legislation to safeguard the human rights of minorities, women and children. Amnesty International has charged that 85 per cent of the women in police custody have been raped or otherwise abused. The death sentence or extreme penalties for blasphemy are resorted to.

Pakistan was born in an atmosphere of hatred and violence, and it cannot redeem itself from this curse. It is a country ruled by mullahs and calls itself an Islamic state, where only a Muslim can become the president or prime minister. There was fierce opposition from mullahs to Benazir Bhutto, a woman, becoming the prime minister.

We do not expect Washington to follow a truthful policy. The US chose to state that Pakistan had no nuclear weapon programme for several years, when it needed Pakistan as an ally in its proxy war in Afghanistan. Pakistan, indeed, has the bomb. But instead of putting pressure on Pakistan to give up its nuclear programme, Washington has chosen to put pressure on India to sign the NPT. In a similar way, Washington is ready to ignore the role of Pakistan as a terrorist state because it needs that country for the pursuit of its Central Asian and South Asian policies.

As for drug trafficking, Pakistan, according to Bill Clinton, is a "victim" of the drug trade, not its promoter! The fact is: Pakistan is one of the major merchants of the drug trade today and accounts for a fifth of all the heroin consumed in the USA according to the *The Washington Post* (29 April 1994). And the CIA has the necessary evidence to prove that the top brass of Pakistan's armed forces and its top bureaucracy and political leadership are involved in this trade. A study commissioned by the CIA concluded that the heroin trade has penetrated "the highest policy circles" of Pakistan and "is becoming the life blood" of the economy and government in the strategically located South Asian country. It further comments that the Pak military intelligence agency has used heroin profits to fund separatist movements in India. But more on this topic in Chapter 15.

The recent visit of a mission of the International Commission of Jurists (ICJ) to the state of Jammu and Kashmir, perhaps inspired by Washington, was an important event, for its report has created considerable controversies. This report has called for expert legal opinion, and India sought one from Professor Maurice Mendelson, QC, and a well-known expert on international law. I propose to give a brief review of Professor Mendelson's report on "Human Rights in Kashmir: Report of a Mission". But before doing so, it would be relevant to recapitulate the circumstances of the case.

Have the people of J & K a right to self-determination? Under the Indian Independence Act, 1947, the choice of accession lay with the rulers of princely states. So, once the ruler acceded to India, J & K became a part of India. To open the subject of self-determination at this stage is tantamount to secessionism.

The ICJ mission's recommendation that a plebiscite be held in Muslim majority areas is, first of all, a religious approach. The mission showed no concern for the minorities living in Muslim-majority areas. In fact, the ethnic cleasing resorted to by the fundamentalists finds favour with the ICJ mission, for, on this issue, the mission is silent. In fact, by reviving the two-nation theory, the mission has created a dangerous situation. If states are to be broken up on the basis of ethnicity or religion, there will be no peace anywhere. The mission ignored the fact that India has more Muslims than Pakistan. India cannot but take into account the 1947 communal holocaust and how a new partition can bring about a "repeat performance". The secretary general of the UN was definitely opposed to the introduction of such concepts. This was further affirmed by the World Conference on Human Rights (1993) which laid down that the right to self-determination "shall not be construed as authorising or encouraging any action which would impair, totally or in part, the territorial integrity or political unity of sovereign and independent states conducting themselves in compliance with the principle of equal rights and the self-determination of peoples and thus possessed of a government representing the whole people belonging to the territory without distinction of any kind".

The mission's report itself admits: "It is doubtful whether a right of secession exists at all and it is clearly not at the present time a generally accepted principle of international law."

It is also interesting to cite here the opinion of Asborn Eide, an expert member of the UN Subcommission on Prevention of Discrimination and Protection of Minorities, presented to the forty-sixth session of the subcommission in August 1994: "The purpose of Minority Protection is not, and should never be, to create privileges or to endanger the enjoyment of human rights, on an equal level, by members of the majority." As for self-determination, Eide says that it does not imply "achieving statehood nor can it challenge the territorial integrity of the state, but it expresses the right of the whole people to continue to govern itself through a representative government freely elected through participation by members of all groups in society".

The mission report is full of contradictions and is a blatant attempt to reactivate the involvement of Security Council in the Kashmir issue, although the UN resolutions are already obsolete.

In any case, the report admits that the matter is bilateral. "The Shimla agreement is clearly binding on Pakistan and deprives the Pak Government of locus standi to intervene in J & K", says the report. If so, how can you reactivate the UN involvement?

Professor Mendelson says that there was only one member in the ICJ mission who was familiar with international law. On the claim that the right to self-determination includes the right to secede from India and become independent or apparently even to join Pakistan, Professor Mendelson affirms: "In my view, this is wrong in law."

Self-determination in the sense of seeking freedom from foreign rule is now a legal right. But on other issues, there is no clarity. In any case, if religious and ethnic self-determination is accepted, the entire international system would collapse.

Professor Mendelson wonders whether Mountbatten had the legal powers to impose any condition on accession (condition of plebiscite). He believes the people had no right to self-determination during the rule of the Maharaja. Yet the mission report makes much about Mountbatten's promise. "Even if he (Mountbatten) did and had (this legal right), (a) this would not bind India under international law and (b) the invasion he referred to has still not been terminated", adds Mendelson. "In short, under international law, as it stood at the time, the accession was valid; and the inhabitants of J & K had no right to be consulted. Accordingly, for them to have such a right now, as the report claims, they would have had to have acquired it subsequently. I have shown that subsequent developments in international law did not confer right of secession on a non-colonial people such as the inhabitants of the Indian state of J & K", asserts the report. As for oppression, the report states that this activity has not reached such a stage that one could ask for secession. So the only grounds for a claim to self-determination are the Security Council resolutions. "However, these resolutions were passed under Chapter VI, not VII of the Charter and were, therefore, not binding on the parties"., clarifies Professor Mendelson. Both India and Pakistan rejected Resolution 47 (1948) and India rejected Resolution 51 (1951). Admittedly, they both accepted certain resolutions of the

UN Commission for India and Pakistan, which envisaged a plebiscite. However, the plebiscite was expressly conditioned on other stiputations being met, including the withdrawal of Pakistan troops and irregular forces. These stipulations were never met. In any case, even acceptance of a plebiscite does not mean that the people have a right to plebiscite. In the event, the Security Council and the UN Commission for India and Pakistan reached an impasse.

Under the Shimla Agreement, India and Pakistan have taken the Kashmir issue out of the hands of the UN. The ICJ mission report notes that the Shimla Agreement could not have deprived the people of J & K of any rights of self-determination to which they were entitled at the time of the agreement. But "since for the reasons given they did not have any such right at that time, the argument is of no avail".

It is contended that the 1977 elections held in J & K were rigged and did not reflect popular will. However, the report of the mission says that the 1977 election was fair. In this election Sheikh Abdullah won a thumping majority. The same Abdullah had entered into an agreement (the Indira-Sheikh Accord), two years before, in which he reaffirmed J & K's accession to India.

Now, again, if the people of J & K are seeking the right to self-determination, the process should encompass the entire population including the people of PoK. But the report hardly mentions PoK except to say that it supports Kashmiri militancy. In fact, the report concentrates on the Indian part of Kashmir. This is a queer way of looking at the problem.

Professor Mendelson, in his concluding remark, says that he is surprised that a body of jurists could ever produce such a report!

15

Narco-Terrorism: Its Ramifications

Today, trade in narcotics has come to play a major role in Pakistan's proxy war against India. In this war, the Afghan mujahideen leaders occupy an important position. In a similar way, the Kashmiri Mafia of Lahore has also made its presence felt in a big way by fostering and sustaining militancy among the Kashmiris in the Valley. India had been unaware of these linkages till recently. But the conspicuous presence of Afghan mujahideen in the Valley revealed the hand of Afghan leaders, such as Gulbuddin Hikmatyar, in the Kashmir insurgency. Similarly, India was unaware of the role played by the Kashmiri community of Lahore till the publication of a CIA report on "Heroin and Pakistan" in 1994.

Heroin is becoming the lifeblood of Pakistan's economy and political system. Those who control the production and international transportation of heroin are using their resources to purchase protection, to gain access to the highest political circles in the country and to acquire a substantial share in the banks and industries being sold to private investors. Apart from the military, no major national institution or law enforcement agency has remained free from significant penetration by the narcotics network. Some Pakistanis believe that only the military now has the capacity to control and finally defeat this network.

However, according to a CIA report: "Some Pakistani experts hold a different view. They believe the military is significantly involved in narcotics. They point to numerous reports that military intelligence (the Inter-Service Intelligence Directorate ISID) used heroin profits to help finance the war in Afghanistan and has developed similar funding arrangements with Sikh militants and the insurgents in Kashmir. They also believe that as Prime Minister Nawaz Sharief used drug money to buy off top army generals and keep himself in power" [reproduced from *The Friday Times* (no date) of Pakistan].

Pakistan is a major producer of opium as also Afghanistan. The tribal heroin cartels of Pakistan control the cultivation and marketing of opium in Afghanistan. After the end of the Afghan war, and as a result of the protection opium cultivation has received from the Afghan mujahideen leaders, Afghanistan has emerged as the world's largest opium-producing country (about 2000-3000 tons per annum). The Pakistani cartels carry out the refining of opium, mainly in mobile laboratories in the Pakhtun tribal areas. Thus, at present, the "Golden Crescent" has become a dangerous region, which can not only promote Islamic fundamentalism but can also set off "bush fires" in many parts of the arc stretching from East Africa to the Philippines. Mafias in Pakistan control the overland movement of drugs into international channels through India, Iran, Dubai and, by sea, to Amsterdam and Hawaii. Ever since the end of the Afghan war, conduits have been opened through Central Asia to Turkey and onwards to Europe and America.

Pakistan gains an enormous amount from this narcotic trade. According to one estimate, this figure could be 120 billion dollars. In 1992, the National Development Finance Corporation of Pakistan estimated that opium trade was contributing about 32.5 billion dollars yearly to black money in Pakistan. So, we can well imagine the quantum of this illicit money available to the narcotic Mafia and its patrons in the Pakistani Government. Before Washington began to pump money into Afghanistan, Pakistan military authorities were freely using these drug funds for their proxy war against the Soviets. Now these funds are available for other uses.

There are different opinions with regard to the narcotic trade in the Golden Crescent. Some claim that President Reagan and the CIA director actively encouraged narcotic trade in Afghanistan hoping to dope the Soviet soldiers. This did not happen. Instead, the drugs went to Europe and 'he USA through other channels. Washington remained indifferent to this trade till the drugs hit the shores of America. Whatever the truth, narcotics brought fabulous wealth to a lot of important people – smugglers, producers, and politicians. And this huge amount of money was laundered by the Bank of Credit and Commerce International (BCCI), which is now under liquidation. (Perhaps it was created for this purpose alone.) All these facts have been revealed in a recently published book, *The Outlaw Bank,* by two correspondents of *Time* magazine, Jonathan Beatty and S.C. Gwynne.

If skirmishes in Afghanistan continue unabated even today, they are not the result of differences over Islamic issues (these are forgotten), but over who should retain the benefits of the narcotic trade, which is now flowing through Afghanistan, Central Asia, the Balkans and beyond. When Soviet soldiers were in Afghanistan, the trade partly flowed through India which had blocked most of it. Hikmatyar, the Pakhtun leader, who has been the principal beneficiary of the narcotic trade, wants to control this trade, but both Burhanuddin Rabbani and Ahmed Shah (both Tadjiks) are opposed to him and they can effectively block this trade through Central Asia. So can General Raschid Dostum – an Uzbek. So the war of attrition continues. In the meantime, Hikmatyar, the fundamentalist, has turned his attention to Kashmir (by the way, does poppy grow well in Kashmir?).

The warlords of Afghanistan and their Pak friends have enjoyed the benefits of billions of dollars of drug money for a decade or more. They are in no mood to give up these benefits and allow Afghanistan to settle down in peace. In the meantime, they will disguise their nefarious objectives with calls for Islamic jehad.

Pakistani experts believe that drug money is financing the political system of their country, supporting party organs and election campaigns. Known drug lords sit in the National

Assembly and in the Provincial Assemblies of the North-West Frontier Province, Punjab and Baluchistan. In Sindh, the Assembly is full of *patharidars*, who protect the drug traffickers. Some narcotic traffickers of Punjab are related to Nawaz Sharief by marriage and participate in the inner councils of the Sharief family. The law enforcement agencies are full of officers who cooperate with the drug Mafias.

Three decisive events shifted the drug trade to Pakistan. The first was the Iranian Revolution of 1979, which led to the banning of all narcotic production and use of drugs in that country. A few drug lords were hanged by the new regime under Ayatollah Khomeini. Many other Iranian drug lords moved into Afghanistan or Pakistan along with their followers and their trade. They also financed opium cultivation in the Helmand Valley of Pakistan. The second event was the ban imposed by Zia-ul-Haq on the production of opium and its distribution. This ban pushed the narcotic business underground, and into the hands of the Pakhtuns and Punjabis. Opium came to be cultivated in the vast semi-autonomous tribal regions of the North-West Frontier Province. Export of heroin brought huge amounts of money to the smuggling gangs, which, in turn, flooded the markets of the subcontinent with consumer goods such as electronic gadgets and garments. The third event was the Soviet invasion of Afghanistan which disrupted the old smuggling routes between Afghanistan and Europe. Consequently, the trade began to be routed through other regions such as Baluchistan and India.

The North-West Frontier Province remains the cradle of the heroin trade. Largely populated by the Pakhtun tribes, these areas were known for a flourishing smuggling trade even before narcotics came on the scene. There are four major smugglers' bazaars operating in the Khyber Agency, where heroin is freely available among other smuggled goods. These are Landi Kotal, Jamrud, Bara Bazaar and Dara Adam Khel. Dara is also known for its cottage industry in manufacture of guns. Most of the drug lords in these places are Pakhtuns. Among them mention may be made of the Yusufzai and Khattak tribes of the lowlands. Both these tribes are firmly placed in the elite political, military and industrial circles of Pakistan. The leading families intermarry and spread their sons across all the key private and public institutions – the military, civil service, police, banking, industry, MNCs, etc. Blood and kinship command the strongest loyalties in Pakistani society and nowhere more so than in the Frontier.

The smugglers and narcotic traffickers seek safety through marriage, gifts, business deals or by providing services to these clans. Such was the case of a number of people around Zia-ul-Haq. Two of his pilots used the presidential aircraft to smuggle heroin to America. And Zia's banker and chief financial adviser, Hamid Hasnain was arrested in Norway for his heroin-smuggling activities in Europe.

According to the CIA, no group is more important to the future of narcotics trafficking in and through Pakistan than the Afridi Mafia. They hold the Khyber Pass. The Zakha Khel (clan) is the largest, and it heads the Afridis. The "wildest and most lawless" of the clans, this clan also occupies a strategic region. The Adam Khel clan members are experts in weaponry and the Afghan war helped them master the technology of many weapons. They are the main suppliers of weapons in South Asia and Sri Lanka.

Air Marshal Asghar Khan is an Afridi. The Afridis control a good part of the transport from the NWFP to Karachi. This helps them in their drug trafficking. The Afridis took to heroin business from the very inception. As a result they are leading in the heroin business today, controlling about 60 laboratories in the Khyber Agency. One of the colourful characters of the heroin trade of this Agency was Malik Wali Khan Kuki Khel, who was also a member of Pakistan's National Assembly. The Government of Pakistan had to use a whole brigade to bulldoze his factories. After Soviet withdrawal from Afghanistan, the Afridi tribes have extended the poppy cultivation to Afghanistan. According to Pak experts, five or six Afridi Maliks are running major heroin operations out of the Khyber Agency. They maintain good relations with the Afghan mujahideen and with the Government of Pakistan. Three of them – Malik Waris Khan Afridi, Malik Momin Khan Afridi and Malik Rehman Shah Afridi (owner of the *Frontier Post*) – and Malik Mohammed Ayub Khan Afridi, also known as Haji Ayub Zakha Khel, allegedly the biggest drug baron in Pakistan, play a decisive role in the drug trade. Haji Ayub supported General Zia, and cooperated with the ISI in its large-scale efforts to arm and assist the Afghan mujahideen.

In brief, we can conclude that, after the Afghan war, the mujahideen have not yet been disbanded. They are still in the employ of the various warlords who, in turn, are beholden to the drug lords. And they are all flush with funds. That is why the Afghans have a prominent presence in the Kashmir Valley. These mujahideen mercenaries are mostly beholden to Hikmatyar who is close to a number of drug lords of the tribal belt.

Punjab and Kashmir and the Heroin Mafia

According to a CIA report (1994): "Punjab province is where the focus of military and political power resides in Pakistan and it is here that heroin edges closest to the seat of power in the country." The Pak army is 72 per cent Punjabi and 26 per cent Pakhtun and stands behind the conservative political coalition of old landed families and tribal chiefs, the industrialists, the military, and moderately reformist orthodox clerics.

Because heroin is easily available in the tribal belt, enterprising young Punjabis have taken to freelancing in heroin trade and heroin gangs operate in every city and town of Punjab. Political groups use heroin to fund themselves and also to buy arms.

The heroin trade came to Lahore in 1980, and the key figure was Haji Iqbal Beg, an accomplished smuggler, who had established his routes in India. Belonging to the Mughal *biraderi*, a small group, he sought alliance with the Kakkazais, a bigger group, to secure his interests and to play the two big groups of Lahore – the Arains and Kashmiris – one against the other. Beg not only used many small tribes in his heroin operations but also the Arains and Kashmiris. Two of his protégés – Sohail Zia Butt, a Kashmiri, and Chaudhry Shaukat Bhatt – have taken over from Beg and have emerged as the new drug lords.

Beg was known as the "king of the Indian route" because of his control over the Indian traffic across the border. This made him a player in the murky world of intelligence, insurgency and arms smuggling. He assisted the ISI in organising support for the Sikh insurgents and carried heroin across the border to India in return for weapons and money. Beg's contacts in Delhi and Bombay moved the heroin further into the international market. Beg and many others went into the real estate business in Lahore, Rawalpindi and Islamabad. Beg was particularly interested in the new cooperative banking societies of Lahore. Such societies made large loans to the Sharief family, which have now taken on the dimensions of a scandal. Millions of small investors were ruined when these societies collapsed because their funds had been manipulated by Beg and others to advance their own interests. Beg is now in jail in Karachi.

Lahore politics has veered around the two dominant communities – the Arains and Kashmiris. Arains are agricultural people living in the city periphery, while the Kashmiris are the city people, mostly engaged in trade. Both of them are equally powerful, having connections in all key power centres. Zia-ul-Haq was an Arain, although he hailed from Jalandhar. The original home of the Lahori Kashmiris is Srinagar, but most of them have been living in Lahore for a century or more, pushed out of Srinagar by famines and Dogra tyranny. Nawaz Sharief is a Kashmiri. His father came to Pakistan via Amritsar during partition.

With their links in the old city, several Kashmiris have strong roots in the underworld, which provide the muscle power for street politics. In fact, many Kashmiri politicians in the Punjab Assembly and National Assembly have risen from these city crime syndicates. The arrival of heroin has not made any change in the patron-client relationship except that now the scale of operation and money involved are stupendous.

The underworld of Lahore is run by six gangs, all of which are answerable in some way to the city crime boss Sohail Zia Butt, an extremely well-connected Kashmiri who is called "king of Hira Mandi". The police, too, is deeply involved in the heroin racket, sometimes arbitrating between the gangs and allocating territories.

The old city gangs form the base of the "Kashmiri Heroin Syndicate". Sohail Zia Butt is a key figure. He was a close lieutenant of Haji Beg and is related to Nawaz Sharief. His career prospered along with that of Sharief. In 1990, he stood for election to the Punjab Assembly on the IJI (Islami Jamhoori Ittehad) ticket. In 1991, when Beg was sent to prison, Sohail took control of a large slice of the Beg empire.

The Kashmiri Mafia is keenly interested in the fortunes of its compatriots in the Valley. It will be recalled that Mohammad Maqbool Butt spent considerable time among the Lahori Kashmiris before he launched the JKLF with the money offered by the Kashmiri Mafia. Indian intelligence has not given any serious thought to this connection, which is unfortunate. When Nawaz Sharief was the prime minister, the future of Kashmir had assumed great importance to Pakistan. It was largely because of him that the insurgency got a boost and ISI involvement was stepped up.

The Kashmir insurgency, like the Punjab insurgency, is a proxy war under the direction of the ISI, but financed largely by the money provided by the drug lords of Pakistan. That is why one has to take this war seriously, for there can be no end to it as long as the narcotic trade flourishes. Now, there is also an endless stream of foreign money pouring into the Valley from various Islamic fundamentalist sources. All these factors make the task of India much more difficult.

16

Conclusions

Sir John Macdonald, a British administrator, wrote in 1825: "I am decidedly of the opinion that the tranquillity, not to say security, of our vast oriental possessions is involved in the preservation of native principalities (Princely States) which are dependent on us for protection. These are also so obviously at our mercy, so entirely within our grasp, that besides other and great benefits we derive from their alliance, their co-existence with our rule is of itself a source of political strength, the value of which will never be known till it is lost" (Sisir Gupta, *Kashmir: A Study in India-Pakistan Relations*, p. 13).

This observation explains why the British administration in India gave a free hand to the princes and why the states remained so backward. In his *Autobiography*, Jawaharlal Nehru wrote: "The Indian states represent today probably the extremist type of autocracy existing in the world." He was naturally appalled by the misery of the people. Only a few of the 500-odd princes showed any awareness of their responsibility to their people. Others were playboys, voluptuaries and tyrants. They were not even conscious of the cynical contempt in which the British held them. No wonder, the ruler of Jammu and Kashmir lived like a lotus eater.

Mishandling Partition

The partition of India was mishandled by both British and Indian leaders. They could have avoided the holocaust and the Kashmir

199

problem. What would happen to the minorities in the two dominions should have been their first concern. But it was not. Constitutional experts, both British and Indian, did not have a clear idea of what partition and independence meant in the Indian context. The British did not conceive of an independent India as the natural legatee of the British Government. That is why it proposed that, on the expiry of British paramountcy, the 500-odd princely states would revert to their independence. A more absurd proposition could not be imagined. It was only a strong protest from the All India Congress Committee that saved the situation. Or, was it a conspiracy on the part of the British to balkanise India? The Kashmir problem is a reflection of these anomalies and confusions.

Secret British Plans

Britain wanted to detach Kashmir and the northern territories of the state of Jammu and Kashmir from India. Lord Louis Mountbatten wanted the Andaman and Nicobar islands to go to Pakistan as a link between the two wings of Pakistan. The significance of these islands became evident during the 1971 Indo-Pak war, when the two wings were literally cut off from each other. On the other hand, Pakistan's possession of the Andamans would have been a serious threat to India. But as a naval man, Mountbatten was keen to retain British dominance in the region and this was possible only if the Andamans went to Pakistan.

Hari Singh, the Hero

In J & K was a ruler who did not understand the importance of his state. Although Hari Singh favoured independence (a vaulting ambition), there is no evidence to show that he was preparing his state for it, for his regime collapsed in the face of a few thousand raiders from Pakistan. He had made no provision to defend it. Hari Singh neither was aware of the significance Britain attached to his state in its geopolitical calculations nor did he know that the British were instigating the Muslims of his state against the Hindus. In fact, he handed over the administration of the state to a wily Briton. But, then, there is no point in singling him out for condemnation. None, except a few of the princes of India, had established a better record than Hari Singh.

Sheikh Abdullah: The Man and the Legend

Sheikh Abdullah could be viewed as a leader of the people of the Kashmir Valley. He had little interest in Jammu or Ladakh. For that matter, he was even afraid of a challenge to his leadership from the Muslims of the Punjabi-speaking areas of the state. That is probably why he advised Nehru to halt the march of the Indian army into these areas. What he probably wanted was to convert the Valley into a small hereditary sheikhdom. Nehru was once a close friend of the Sheikh. But it is doubtful whether they were sincere to each other after 1953.

The Sheikh was in favour of India because he had burnt his boats with Mohammad Ali Jinnah and Liaquat Ali Khan. He would have joined Pakistan if he could have obtained better terms.

Autonomy Demand: Veiled Separatism

It was a grave mistake on the part of the Government of India to grant "special" autonomy to the Valley in view of Muslim separatism and its inevitable consequence in the form of partition of the country. It appears the Indians learned nothing from the partition. While Jammu and Ladakh wanted full integration, only the Valley wanted autonomy. But having granted the autonomy, it would be unwise to now withdraw it in haste. Article 370 was not a permanent arrangement. But, in the name of autonomy, the separatist politicians want to make this Article permanent. That is why further extension of autonomy is not desirable, though certain adjustments can be worked out. The new offer of "anything short of *aazadi* (freeedom)" by the Indian Government is an open invitation to disaster.

Dr. Farooq Abdullah continues to talk of Kashmir's autonomy. In a recent interview, he said: "We want autonomy in Kashmir and we want to know from the Government of India the quantum of autonomy they are prepared to give us. They also must open their doors to other organisations, be it the Hurriyat or the JKLF. So, we want a clear-cut policy in relation to all matters – development projects, Ladakh, Jammu, everything". It is clear from this statement that Farooq has not changed much. He should know that experiments in autonomy during the past three decades have failed. It appears that the demand for greater autonomy is nothing but a demand for a free hand for the Valley politicians to do what they want.

US Stand against India

There is no doubt that it is the strategic significance of Jammu and Kashmir that has attracted the attention of American strategists. The state can be an excellent watch-tower for the vast area stretching from Central Asia to the Pacific. But this is not the only reason why America chose to befriend Pakistan and not India. At the turn of this century, America itself was on the road to becoming an imperialist power, and it was Nehru who remarked way back in 1927 that American imperialism would be a greater menace to the world than the British one. This proved true. Independent India naturally turned against American imperialism and became a formidable opponent of Washington. One need not go into the long history of Indian opposition to American foreign policy and how the entire struggle of the Non-Aligned Movement against US imperialism was spearheaded by India. Even today any opposition to American excesses in the world will have to come from India. Washington knows this. Overriding all these forms of conflicts is the competition at the economic and social level. No American entrepreneur can dismiss the Jews, Japanese, Germans or the Indians, for these people have the capacity to overtake America even in the most complex technologies or production processes. All these factors constitute a perennial challenge to the West in general and to America in particular.

America looks upon China in the same way, but with less trepidation. All these conflicts and competitions may appear very common and harmless to most naïve people. For example, competition for satellite transmission may appear as economic competition for advertisement revenue. Yet, ultimately, it is part of the competition for the minds of men – it is part of the civilisational conflict.

The sudden spurt in Washington's interest in Pakistan has something to do with the future of Central Asia. Central to the present US policy is the plan to prevent the spread of Iranian influence in Central Asia. In other words, this is a long-term policy and Washington hopes to maintian a vigil all along the arc from East Africa to the Philippines (1) to safeguard its oil lifeline, (2) to prevent Islamic fundamentalism from affecting its interests adversely and (3) to carefully monitor Iranian moves in Central Asia.

So, America seems to have a long-term interest in keeping India under check and prevent the country from becoming a major power. Under no circumstances can America be expected to promote the economic and military might of India.

It may appear that I am exaggerating the dangers. I am not. For us, our civilisational values are important. So is our way of life. These values have given us a great heritage and hidden reserves of strength. There is no means of knowing that the way chosen by the West is the best. Under these circumstances, we must follow our own way.

The Valley's Power Monopoly

Experience shows that the power of the Valley over the state of Jammu and Kashmir (a result of the dominance of Sheikh Abdullah) must be reduced. The National Conference, a party restricted mainly to the Valley people, does not want to share power with other parties. It had serious conflicts with both the Congress and the Janata Party. In fact, the Valley politicians are after monopoly of power so that they can have a free hand. But the National Conference has no influence over either Jammu or Ladakh. However, it wants to rule over these two regions too by being the dominant party in the Valley. This anti-democratic tendency must be curbed. There is a need for the presence of all parties in the Valley so that the people can make a choice among several programmes.

It is also necessary to examine in what way the dominance of the Kashmiris in the administration can be counterbalanced. This dominance has not benefited the state. Both Sheikh Abdullah and his son, Farooq, were against officers of the Central cadres being posted in Srinagar and favoured local recruitment. This is understandable. However, if Jammu and Kashmir is to remain a part of India, then, in the name of autonomy, it would not be proper to allow local cadres, under the patronage of local politicians, to dominate the administration.

We had hoped that with progress and industrial development, religion would be marginalised – a Marxist fallacy. The fact is that with improvement of living standards and levels of education, the people have become conscious of their identity and aware of their history. Interestingly, in certain cases this awareness has led to the growth of communal factors. Nehru did not pay much attention to minority communalism – for example, the much advocated belief that Muslim and Sikh religion and politics could not be separated. Nehru also believed that majority communalism was dangerous, without stressing simultaneously that minority communalism could be equally dangerous.

In the fairly permissive society of India, orthodox Islam was bound to come into conflict with the Indian spirit of enquiry and tolerance of diversity. And it did, except for a brief period under Emperor Akbar. The Sufis tried to find a common identity for Hindus and Muslims. But they obviously failed. Thus, while Christianity got Indianised to some extent, there is an apparent resistance to any such move in the world of Islam, thanks to the influence of the fundamentalist mullahs.

The Congress Party, which bore the brunt of the Muslim League's communal politics, was out to woo the Muslims right from the first general election held in 1952. In the process, it dealt a death blow to some of the features of secularism and prevented self-introspection among the majority of Muslims. Subsequently, most political parties have resorted to communal politics. It is not secularism if you appeal for the votes of religious minorities. That is communalism. It is not secularism if you appeal for votes on the basis of caste. That is casteism. It is not secularism to finance denominational schools or Haj pilgrimages. This is appeasement. This is how a section of Hindus looks at the issues of secularism and communalism.

The Representation of the People's Act, 1951, states that the application for registration as a political party to the Election Commission should be accompanied by a specific declaration of commitment to secularism. Still, many political parties which came up on communal lines were able to get themselves registered. This is how the spirit of the Constitution has been trampled upon.

In spite of all this, India has managed to remain a tolerant and non-communal society. Father Peter Hans Kolvenbach, superior general of the Society of Jesus (Jesuits), during his recent visit to India, emphasised that India's example of tolerance was vital for the world: "How in India people with many languages, religions and cultures live together is a lesson to learn! India has an important role to play in shaping the destiny of mankind." Kolvenbach condemned the growing cult of fundamentalism.

Speaking of the fear of "Hinduisation" among minorities, Kolvenbach clarified: "It is Indian culture we are adopting, not Hindu culture. We are following the same practice in many other countries. In Africa we are adopting the African culture." But what is Indian culture? No one knows, and it will never be defined.

Never before, as Nani Palkhivala, the well-known public figure and jurist, pointed out, were prejudices more widely mistaken for truth, passion for reason, fundamentalism for religion and myth for history as in modern India.

The Alienation Factor

It is glibly stated that the people of the Valley are alienated. But how many? No one knows. And from whom or from what are they alienated? If anything, their alienation is self-inflicted. India has done nothing to deserve their hatred.

Ved Marwah, adviser to Governor Jagmohan and former director general of Delhi Police, has written: "It is a matter of great concern that a national problem of such dimensions is used, at times, to settle personal scores" (*Indian Express*, 16 September 1993). According to him, it is political and administrative mismanagement which is responsible for the alienation of the people of the Valley. Legitimate grievances, he says, have been left unattended for far too long by successive governments. Others have also confirmed this view. Who is responsible for this state of affairs? Only the leaders of the Kashmiri people; not the Government of India. In the final analysis, what made the difference was the fact that while people can change their corrupt governments in the rest of India, the people of J&K could not. They have been forced to live with the same politicians and their corruption. The Kashmiri leaders attribute all the state's problems to the machinations of New Delhi. To some extent, they are correct, but not because of machinations but because of the Centre's incompetence. What is more, New Delhi cannot denounce these Kashmiri politicians as it has to depend on them for its political·games in the Valley.

Separatism: Meeting It Head On

We do not want to reply to violence with violence. But do we know how to answer it with words? We do not. We could effectively counter neither the Muslim League's espousal of the two-nation theory nor its demand for Pakistan. In fact, the demand could have been silenced by effective arguments and subtle threats. The same situation is developing at present in Kashmir. We are reluctant to wield the gun against the militants, which is understandable. But why are we silent against the propaganda of the militants? It is not enough to brand them as bad or that they are anti-national. This is the novice's way of tackling the arguments of the militants. The point is: the politician prefers to be mute, for he does not want to lose votes. That is why this job of articulating our views on communalism and separatism cannot be left to political parties and politicians. The people must take over this task.

In Kashmir, a few thousand people hired by a foreign intelligence agency have taken up arms against the state and the Central authority. They do not believe in sitting across the table, because the issue at hand does not pertain to their bread and butter. The issue is religion: whether the Valley should be part of India or of Pakistan. That is why the militants do not want to enter into a discussion. Already two wars have been fought over the issue with enormous losses of men and material. Will India give in to a few paid militants when it has not yielded to Pakistan's armed might? The militants must develop a sense of realism. Obviously, they do not appear to be a realistic people. In these circumstances, we must isolate them by accelerating the political and economic processes. It is because nothing worthwhile is happening in the Valley that the people remain preoccupied with the propaganda of the militants.

Self-Determination: Dangerous Implications

If the principle of self-determination is applied to any entity except a nation, it can lead to anarchy in most of the countries, for there are very few homogeneous societies in the world. On the basis of this principle, ethnic groups can fragment countries. And one should not be oblivious of the larger implications of self-determination, of which most people are blissfully ignorant. What will happen to small ethnic groups when such a principle is universally accepted? The majorities, in that case, will drive out the minorities. America, the melting pot of all races and creeds, will drive out, first of all, the Asian immigrants. So will the Gulf states. And no conversion will ever be permitted, not to speak of giving asylum to foreigners. Human society will go into retrogression. One should remember that the New World accepted the "refuse" of the Old World in the name of humanism. But in a world of self-determination, there will be no scope for humanism. India has, however, no intention to close either its windows to foreign ideas or its doors to people who want to take shelter here, after keeping them open for thousands of years. Even now thousands of people from Pakistan and Bangladesh pour into India every year. We have been an open society all these centuries and that is how we wish to remain. This is the unique element of our civilisation. That is why we will not entertain further division of our country. Nor can we allow our goodwill to be paid back by perfidy.

The Muslim Factor

Why should the three million Muslims of the Valley join the 100 million Muslims of Pakistan and not the 120 million Muslims of India? The Kashmiri Muslims cannot claim that they are closer to Pakistani Muslims. What is more, they stand to gain nothing, for they enjoy a far higher standard of living compared to the Muslims of Pakistan and India. As for self-determination, they have had control over their destiny since 1947. They could have shaped their fortune as they wanted to. If they failed in this task, it is not the fault of New Delhi. They must blame their own leaders. They must now set their house in order.

The Benefits of Integration

All the states in the Indian Union interact with each other and with the Centre for their own good; more so, states such as Goa and the "seven sisters" of the north-east. Jammu and Kashmir is in no way unique. It must be integrated with India. But the integration of India will not stop at that. There is a far more challenging task before it: the integration of half the Hindu population (the backwards, scheduled castes, tribals) with the mainstream of Hindu society. The integration of this half will take a long time and will depend on how quickly the other half of Hindu society can adjust itself to the new realities. Such integration will call for drastic changes in our "vote bank" politics, which was designed to perpetuate the divisions within our society. Only through full integration can a state secure the full benefits of integration.

The Innate Conflict

Pakistan calls Kashmir the "unfinished business" of partition. But is it? Will such "business" end with a solution to the Kashmir problem? Certainly not, for Pakistan will, in that case, invent a new problem. Without a permanent animus towards India, Pakistan cannot justify the two-nation theory. In fact, as long as there are Muslims in India (and there will always be) Pakistan will contend that the business of partition must continue, as if it is the godfather to Indian Muslims. It is for the Muslims in India to repudiate such claims. Some people had thought that with the break-up of Pakistan in 1971, the two-nation theory would be buried. But that did not happen. What is more, the Muslims of India have not yet firmly rejected the two-nation theory. They must do so now in no uncertain terms.

The Shimla Agreement

There is only one solution to the Kashmir imbroglio and that is to accept the partition of Kashmir and the line of control as a de jure boundary. This was the intention of the 1972 Shimla Agreement between India and Pakistan. All other solutions are fraught with grave dangers.

T.N. Kaul, a former foreign secretary and a participant at the Shimla talks, related in a recent newspaper article how Zulfiqar Ali Bhutto promised at Shimla to settle the Kashmir issue "in two weeks". Bhutto apparently told Mrs. Gandhi: "If I accept any settlement of Kashmir here (Shimla), I shall be accused by my people of having given in to pressure. But I assure you, madam, within two weeks of my return to Pakistan, I shall prepare the ground for such a settlement." (This settlement was the acceptance of the ceasefire line as a permanent border.) However, Bhutto also did not want to return empty handed. So, he persuaded India to commit itself to release the 90,000 Pak prisoners of war as also hand over the 5000 sq. km of territory it had seized from Pakistan.

Once India made the commitment known, Bhutto felt free to resume his attack on India, and he made no effort to carry out his part of the agreement. But the understanding was there. Why not accept the line of control as the permanent border? The alternative is war, which neither country wants.

Many historians have acknowledged that the ceasefire line of 1949 follows a broad cultural-ethnic divide. It gave greater importance to Kashmiri identity, while the Punjabi-speaking areas ("Azad Kashmir") and northern areas fell on the other side of the line. This reduced the dominance of Jammu and gave Kashmiris the feeling of importance.

Lessons from Punjab

Punjab has some lessons for Kashmir. So long as the politicians were allowed to meddle in Punjab, militancy grew. But once the army was brought in and the Punjab police was given a free hand, militancy began to decline. The same process must apply to the Valley.

No Future without a Past

The Jamaat-e-Islami, which is behind the militancy in the Valley, must know when to put a stop to the process of Islamisation, for if it thinks that it can create a pure Muslim society in the Valley, it is mistaken. The Pandits – all of them – will have to go back to Kashmir, or, if necessary, to a "homeland" of their own in the Valley. And their presence in the Valley will be a constant reminder of the Valley's multireligious past. So, let not the Jamaat think that it can wipe out the memory of Kashmir's past, even if that memory makes it feel uncomfortable.

Adopting Ashoka's Ideal

The concept of equal respect for all religions, which we constantly advocate, can be traced back to the policy propounded by Emperor Ashoka, who, although a missionary dedicated to spreading Buddhism, exhorted his followers to respect all sects. It is interesting to note that this exhortation has been repeated in so many edicts all over the country that it became a central feature of Indian life. Such exhortations cannot be found in Semitic religions. That is why the great historian Arnold Toynbee called Ashoka the greatest of all emperors.

Such respect for all religions explains how, for centuries, Hindus, Buddhists and Jains co-existed and flourished in this country despite the fact that they had fierce disputes among themselves. This phenomenon also explains the long tradition of tolerance among Indian kings. Nowhere did Ashoka claim pre-eminence for Buddhism, nor did he ever resort to violence to spread his faith. This spirit of India's quest for truth can be traced to the Vedas, too. A Vedic hymn runs as follows:

Ah, what are words, and what are mortal thoughts!
Who is there truly knows, and who can say,
Whence this unfathomed world, and from what cause?

The Vedas thus express a profound doubt. No certainty here
like in Semitic religions. Yet, the Vedic seers visualised a supreme
power. They called it THAT. "That" became the source of
Sankara's monotheism.

But Ashoka did not want the votes of the Hindus. Today, it
is the craze for power which has destroyed every ideal.

The Myth of Neglect

Many political commentators and historians as well as sociologists
have time and again asserted that the state of Jammu & Kashmir
has been neglected. This is yet another myth created by those
opposed to India.

Like any other state in India, J&K also launched the process
of development with the First Five Year Plan. As a consequence
of state intervention, the economy did undergo a structural
transformation. The net state domestic product (NSDP)
registered a compound growth rate of 5.9 per cent, on the basis
of current prices, from 1960-61 to 1990-81. The figures of
growth of per capita income worked out to be 1.2 per cent.
The pace of development of the state is evident from the fact
that the share of the primary sector in SDP decreased from 67.3
per cent in 1960-61 to 51.95 per cent in 1985-86 with a
corresponding increase in the secondary and tertiary sectors from
8.82 per cent to 22.63 per cent and 19.37 per cent to 28.68
per cent, respectively.

There have been substantial changes in land relations.
Jammu and Kashmir has undertaken thorough implementation
of land reforms. All agricultural development indicators, such as
the use of fertiliser and high-yielding variety of seeds, cropping
intensity, and irrigation intensity and frequency, registered a
significant increase during successive Five Year Plans. And, as
a result, the foodgrain production increased from 0.33 million
tonnes in 1951-52 to 1.4 million tonnes in 1985-86. The

cropping pattern also experienced a shift which is more pronounced in the Valley. For instance, there has been growth of orchards, increase in saffron and hops cultivation, and a shift to commercial crops, which include vegetables and sugarcane, and fodder in the Jammu region.

The process of industrialisation picked up during the 1970s and the 1980s. The industrial sector recorded a manifold increase both in the number of units and the rate of employment. For instance, registered factories and their employment potential recorded a 15-fold and five-fold increase, respectively, between 1952 and 1985. Although most of the factories were located around Jammu and Srinagar cities, dispersal of the factory sector was quite visible in the recent past. The most spectacular aspect of growth was of registered small-scale industrial (SSI) units: their number increased from 2203 in 1973-74 to 26,322 by March 1989 and employment grew from 17,000 in 1978 to 1.15 lakh in 1989. The number of registered SSI units recorded an 11-fold increase with a seven-fold increase in employment in less than two decades.

There has been an equally remarkable growth in handicrafts, handloom and village and *khadi* industries. The value of goods produced by such industries increased from Rs.3.21 crore in 1978 to Rs. 20.63 crore in 1986. They registered a nearly six-fold and three-fold increase in production and employment, respectively, in about two decades (Y.P. Chathley, Kashmir Crisis: Economic and Political Dimensions, *The Tribune*, 22 June 1994).

The dominance of the Valley over the state's administration has not helped the people of Jammu and Ladakh, who feel neglected. Their representation in the Assembly also has been distorted. As things stand, power will always remain with the Valley.

There is, therefore, an urgent need to set up independent development councils for all the three constituent units -- Jammu, Kashmir and Ladakh. A way must be found to distribute equitably the revenue of the state among the three units. As for Central assistance, this must be allocated directly to the three development councils. These three councils may have an apex council to coordinate their activities.

For a long time, the Kashmiri politicians have been able to divert the attention of the people from the basic issues to subjects such as autonomy. There is thus need to shift the focus to development. The Centre has promised a package of assistance, but only when militancy comes to an end. In the meantime, New Delhi has made a major commitment to improve the communication and transport systems in the state and its links with the rest of India. The railway line from Udhampur to Srinagar is an investment for the future. It is necessary to take up similar projects which will have not only an economic but also a psychological impact on the region.

Plebiscite Prospects

There is the lurking fear that if a plebiscite is held in the Valley, the verdict of the people might go against India. There may be some element of truth in this. But, in reality, very few Muslims would vote for Pakistan.

There is a variety of sociocultural and linguistic groups within the Valley, but hardly any serious attempt has been made to understand their diversities. A majority of the people living in the Gurez Valley (located along the north of the international border in *tehsil* Bandipore of Baramula district in the Kashmir division), for example, happen to be Muslims of the Kashmir region but they speak a different language (Sheena) and blame the Kashmiris of Bandipore for their misfortune. Similarly, a substantial number of persons living along the line of actual control speak Punjabi and do not share the perception of a section of Kashmiris regarding state autonomy. The people living across the line of control in PoK and just inside it not only speak a common language but also possess a similar culture. The inhabitants of the two border districts of Baramula and Kupwara in the Valley are Pahari-speaking Rajputs, Mughals, Afghans and Gujjars who constitute a kind of buffer between the Kashmiri-speaking Muslims and the Punjabi-speaking inhabitants of PoK. Only a very small area of Kupwara and Handwara *tehsils* consists of Kashmiri-speaking people. They are particularly very small in number in Uri *tehsil* which is mainly inhabited by Pahari- and Gojari-speaking people (Y.P. Chathley, Kashmir: Conflicting Layers of Perception, *The Tribune*, 22 May 1994).

In the Valley, a variety of calculations will come into play. The more prosperous people there would opt for India because they visualise greater opportunities. The Sunni population, which is the dominant group, is divided between "*aazadi*" and being "pro-Pakistan". What proportion of this group will vote for Pakistan is not clear, but its choice cannot be taken for granted. As for the Shias in the Valley, they will definitely not vote for Pakistan. And there may be differences between the perceptions of the converts and the outsiders who came from Afghanistan, Iran and Central Asia. The converts are more likely to vote for independence, whereas the outsiders who are under Jamaat influence are likely to favour Pakistan. Our political commentators generally miss all these nuances of the situation.

As for the Pandits (about a lakh of them have fled the Valley), their votes must be taken into account wherever they live. They are for India and are now in favour of creating a homeland of their own.

The local and regional specificities of social structures along with diverse perceptions of different ethnic groups about their current situation need to be understood and nurtured to strengthen the political process in Kashmir.

In this context, Y.P. Chathley (1995) elaborates that "apart from the division between Sunni and Shia sects among the Kashmiri Muslims, there are also caste-like divisions, though less rigid than among Hindus. For instance, a majority of the Sayeeds possess land. They have lately started entering services, trade, etc., resulting in shifting of their activities to urban centres. They have been quite active in the politics of the state. The *Kamgars* too enjoy relatively high social and educational status. A majority of them have marginal and small landholdings. They have also been entering services, transport and trade and a section among them have already achieved affluence. They are the original Kashmiris. Most of the political activists, such as *Lone, Bhat, Wani, Malik*, etc., come from among the Kamgars. A section

CONCLUSIONS || *215*

of the *Pathans*, who too are relatively better placed in the social ladder, possess marginal landholdings and have also started entering services."

Chathley goes on to add: "The *Gujjars* and *Bakarwals* [or *Barkerwals*] are quite low in the social and educational hierarchy. The major concentration of the Gujjars is in the Kandi area of Kashmir Valley. Though they have started developing some land connections, they are essentially cattle rearers. They speak Gojari. A section amongst the Gujjars go to the Jammu areas and/or outside the state for labour, such as, wood-cutting, working on dams, canal construction work, etc. Most of the Gujjars and Bakarwals do not side with the main political and other issues of the Kashmiris and they constitute, by and large, the support base of the Congress. The other Zat/Karams among the Muslims in the Valley are the *Watul* and the *Musali* who are very low on social hierarchy and are mostly illiterate. They are involved in menial work. The *Nangars* in the Valley are in the medium category at social scale. Before land reforms, they had been landless tenants. Land reforms of 1952 gave the majority of them land. Most of the Nangars possess small landholdings. They are the original Kashmiris. Presently, most of them are involved in the work of functionaries."

A plebiscite will also give rise to other questions: for example, what is to be done with the 5000 sq. km of territory given to China by Pakistan? What is to be done with the northern areas which have been incorporated within the federal structure of Pakistan? And what will happen to the PoK area?

The point is: plebiscite may not give a clear verdict, but it can stir up a number of conflicts and controversies. In any case, we have rejected plebiscite as a solution in view of the altered circumstances.

Mosque-based Politics

When it comes to the Valley, a double standard prevails with respect to New Delhi's policy. How else is one to explain the difference in the approach of the Centre to the mosque-based politics of the Valley? There exists a law in India prohibiting the use of religious places for political purposes. Although this law is strictly enforced in the rest of India, in the Valley the opposite is true. Nothing has been done to put a stop to this topsy-turvy practice. The events at the Hazratbal mosque and later at Chrar-e-Sharief have not stirred the Central authorities to evolve a suitable policy with regard to the mosque-based politics of the Valley Muslims.

Weakness Does Not Pay

Bhutto and his ilk failed to honour the Shimla Agreement. Today, his successors even repudiate it. Instead of accepting the line of actual control as a permanent border, Pakistan continues its efforts to grab the whole state. As T.N. Kaul observes: "We could and should have resisted these attempts of Pakistan rulers, but did little. The result was that Pakistan is fighting a cheap proxy war against us in Kashmir and we are paying heavily for it" (Shimla and After, *The Times of India*, 17 October 1993).

Similarly, we did not respond adequately to Zia-ul-Haq's "Operation Topac" (1983). We should have made it clear then itself that we would bomb the training camps and should have done so. Pakistan would not have dared to declare a proxy war against India then.

The proxy war has gone on for over a decade, aided and abetted by Pakistan. The time has now come for taking risks. We must be ready to punish Pakistan, short of war, or bring about radical changes in the state of Jammu and Kashmir to stop the insurgency.

Ethnic Differentiations

Kashmir Valley, with a predominantly Muslim population (95 per cent), both rural and urban, has just 4 per cent Hindu and 1 per cent Sikh population. The top and junior administrative positions had once been occupied mostly by Dogra and Kashmiri Pandits under the former Dogra rulers. The Kashmiri Pandits had a preference for education and government jobs. Most of them also possessed landed estates and *jagirs*. Kashmiri Muslims, on the other hand, were mostly cultivators and tenants, and a small section among them was involved in domestic industries such as weaving and shawl making.

Jammu division had also been a Muslim majority region prior to accession and the Pakistani invasion in 1947, after which, the religious composition changed in favour of non-Muslims. A substantial number of Hindu and Sikh traders from Mirpur, Kotli, Sardoli, Muzaffarabad and other "Pakistan-occupied areas" replaced the Muslims in the urban areas of the Jammu region. Presently, Muslims constitute a majority in the districts of Poonch, Rajouri and Doda in spite of their being in a minority in the Jammu region as a whole.

There is a variety of ethnic groups in the Valley. A thorough understanding of the ethnic differentiation is very important to work out any possible solutions to the Kashmir crisis. Apart from the division between Sunni and Shia sects among the Kashmiri Muslims, there are also caste-like divisions, though less rigid than among Hindus.

Chathley (1995) observes that "the new social groups emerging as a result of economic and political changes have continued to dominate the political scene of the state. A section among them who stick to National Conference have been returning to power in almost every election, even if it be by electoral rigging or manipulations, or unopposed, particularly up to 1970. This process has distorted democratic practice in the state. This has accentuated the process of alienation among Muslim masses, who had been promised a functional democracy by their leaders at the time of the accession of the State to India. Understanding the Kashmiri Muslims as a homogeneous group may not help since social groupings have been more on ethnic lines than on religious ones. Even the newly developed colonies in Jammu city show ethnic concentrations. Ethnic differentiations are also reflective [sic] in the broad ideology, rank and profile, identification of issues and programmes of action of the dominant militant groups".

The Role of Elections

No normal election has been held in Jammu and Kashmir ever since its accession to India. Elections have been systematically rigged either by the National Conference or the Congress, the only two parties which mattered in the state. But a few seats more to either of the parties through rigging might not have mattered much. Ultimately, there was hardly any difference between these Tweedledums and Tweedledees. They were both corrupt and venal. Both of them made a mockery of elections, which is one reason for the rise of militancy in the Valley.

The forthcoming election may be boycotted by the militants. But they have never counted for much at the hustings. Even the Jamaat had failed to get more than five seats in the Assembly. If the militants can gain more seats today, it can be only because of the gun, and not because of their mass appeal. In these circumstances, one has to evolve a practical approach to the proposed election. In Jammu and Ladakh, the militants cannot prevent the holding of the election. There are 11 reserved constituencies. And the militants cannot exercise their sway in all districts of the Valley. Moreover, no one is going to look askance at the result of this effort at restoring democracy.

Many of the problems of Jammu and Kashmir arose for want of a democratic tradition in the state. There was a shift from the feudal rule of the Maharaja to the personal rule of Sheikh Abdullah. Unfortunately, the National Conference did not even approve of the existence of the Congress in the state. All these practices must go: lock, stock and barrel. The state must have a powerful, independent media and a pluralistic approach in every field. And its economy must be freed from the clutches of politicians. What is more, the accounts of the state must be audited by Central authorities. There can be no exception on this count. All these aspects cannot be left to either the state administration or local politicians. These must be supported by the national media and the mainstream political parties.

The Need for a Political Dialogue

Of course, the starting of the political process is a complex and complicated exercise in today's terrorism-infested atmosphere. The fear of the gun, which is too overpowering, has virtually silenced the saner elements among the Kashmiris. They do not open their mouth and are afraid of coming out openly for the restoration of political normalcy in the state. Nevertheless, this vicious trap has to be broken.

The prevailing political vacuum only gives a free hand to the gun-toting militants and the mercenaries. The real challenge today is how to overcome the fear of the gun and involve the people in the installation of a popular government. A number of approaches can be evolved and pursued simultaneously. We all know that there are various prominent leaders belonging to different communities such as Kashmiris, Gujjars, Bakerwals, Gojris and Sheena, which are spread all over the state. A process of discussion can begin with them. In fact, the nominees of the various groups representing varied social and economic interests such as students, apple growers, the tourism lobby and the handicrafts association can provide a nucleus to build a new democratic infrastructure. This will be a somewhat unorthodox approach in the absence of structured democratic institutions and the lack of normalcy in the state. But it will be worth trying.

It is through a series of dialogues with these community interest groups that a broad-based superstructure can be created. Such an approach is feasible only if the Centre evolves a clear-cut policy on the parameters of the dialogues and inducts the right types of people to undertake this painstaking job. There can be no shortcuts to the democratic process in the Valley. If peaceful answers have to be evolved to silence the guns of the militants and the mercenaries, then there has to be a precise and determined approach to men, matters and issues.

Power to the People

To set the democratic process in motion, one initial step could be giving power to the people at the grassroots level. With the 73rd and 74th amendments (relating to Panchayati Raj) to the Constitution of India having been implemented, it should be made mandatory to conduct elections to local bodies in Jammu and Kashmir. But what do we hope to achieve through elections in J&K has not been explained properly so far. To merely reiterate that elections should be held so that self-rule can be restored to the people is to be naïve. It is not as simple as that.

After fighting an insurgency backed by foreign powers and obscurantist forces for more than five years, our objective cannot be to hand over the governance of the state on a platter to these very forces. We may get caught a trap if we hold Assembly elections without preparing the ground. If the insurgents and their proxies decide to stand for the elections and get elected, they may spell further trouble. At best, we can try to ensure that they do not secure a majority in the Assembly. This may not be easy in view of the prevailing fear of the gun.

We keep on reiterating that the state is an integral part of India and that we would not tolerate any further division of the country. And, yet, the prime minister has told the people that he is ready to give anything but *aazadi to* J&K. If this is so, we should be ready to follow the logic of these two stands. We must give operational freedom to the people at three levels: at the panchayat level, at the autonomous council level and at the Assembly level. Nothing can be more demonstrative of our intension to give them self-rule at the grassroots.

But first things first. By holding panchayat elections first, we can test the real wishes of the people, of which we know almost nothing as far as the Valley is concerned. This way we can also test the strength of the insurgents in the countryside. The panchayat election has one advantage: neither the people nor the militants would like to expose themselves as secessionists. So, the people are more likely to vote for moderate candidates. And once these moderate candidates establish themselves (they should, if the new panchayat powers are given to them, as also control over finances), they would prefer to send moderate candidates to the Assembly too when elections are held. In other words, the policy should be to bring to the forefront the moderate elements backed by the people. This is where the mainstream parties can play an effective role. But for this first step, it is necessary to break the backbone of militancy. Unless the fear of the gun is removed, we will never know the true choice of the people.

This exercise is necessary in Kashmir because we are in the dark about the real desires of the people, unlike in Punjab where we were sure that the people were opposed to terrorists. Once it is known that the majority of panchayats are opposed to insurgency, the latter is likely to collapse. In any case, we can easily isolate the militants.

We must also make political power less attractive to the rebels by decentralising power among the three divisions – Kashmir, Jammu and Ladakh. It is absolutely necessary that the proposed autonomous councils have complete power over factors such as economic development, finance and employment. Once the militants see that their nostrums are being effectively bypassed by these councils, their enthusiasm to stick their neck out for merger of the state with Pakistan will diminish.

The success of our policy will depend on the manner in which we explain to the people how we propose to strengthen their autonomy and how we propose to give them more powers in the fields of politics and economics. The attractiveness of this package, against the offer of merger with Pakistan that the militants are offering the people, should be obvious to anyone in the light of the deadly ethnic strife in Pakistan and the demand for an independent Mohajir state.

J & K state has 6477 villages with 1469 panchayats. This means that if elections to the panchayats are held then about 1500 *panches* and *sarpanches*, in addition to about 500 other elected members to the municipalities, corporations, etc., would directly participate in the developmental process of the state. This phenomenon would have a three-pronged effect. First, about 2000 families, from which one representative each gets elected, are closely related to 10 other families, which means about 20,000 families. In other words, about one lakh persons would directly contribute to the development of the state and it would be in their interest to ensure law and order and resolve other related problems in the area. Second, when money comes straight to the panchayats and other elected bodies at the grassroots, a new and healthy competition will start which will automatically help checkmate the subversive tendencies. Third, individuals representing different religious, caste and ethnic groups and speaking different languages will be elected who, in turn, can voice their demands to counter the dominant superficial demands for an "independent" or "pro-Pakistan" Kashmir.

There is thus an opportunity for India to involve the people in the democratic process, especially now that there are clear signs of fatigue in a sizeable section of the militants and the growing disenchantment among ordinary Kashmiris at the way in which the foreign-inspired mercenaries are posing a threat to the basic ethos of their life and culture, which they greatly cherish.

What we have to do is to adopt both direct and indirect methods to involve different segments of the people first in a constructive dialogue and, then, in creating conditions for holding elections at the earliest possible time. Mere shadow-boxing cannot take us very far. Equally crucial is the adoption of a tough posture towards the cult of the gun so that the people feel reassured that a shift away from the protective militant umbrella would not mean the absence of a parallel state security umbrella, which a government anywhere in the world is expected to provide to its citizens. A genuine people's democracy is the only answer to Kashmir's complex problems. It fits very well into the rest of India's political milieu.

Select Bibliography

Abdullah, Farooq, *My Dismissal*, Delhi: Vikas, 1985.

Abdullah, Sheikh Mohammad, *Aatish-i-Chinar*, Srinagar: Ali Mohammad and Sons.

Abdullah, Sheikh Mohammad, *Flames of the Chinar* (English translation of *Aatish-i-Chinar*), Viking, New Delhi, 1993.

Agarwal, H.O., *Kashmir Problem: Its Legal Aspects*: Allahabad: Kitab Mahal, 1979.

Ahmad, Mirza Mahmud, *Duties of Inhabitants of Kashmir*, Quadian, 1931.

Akbar, M.J., *India: The Siege Within*, London: Penguin, 1985.

Akbar, M.J., *Kashmir: Behind the Vale*, New Delhi: Viking, 1991.

Anand, A.S., *Development of the Constitution of Jammu & Kashmir*: Delhi: Light & Life Publishers, 1980.

Argyris, C., *Organisation and Innovation*, Illinois: The Dorsey Press, 1965.

Bamzai, P.N.K., *Socio-economic History of Kashmir (1846-1925)*, New Delhi: Metropolitan, 1987.

Bamzai, P.N.K., *History of Kashmir*, New Delhi; Metropolitan, 1973.

Bannerjee, Sir Albion, *Kashmir: Retrospect and Prospect* (other details not available).

Baru, Raina, *Field Study Note in Jammu & Kashmir,* Delhi: National Atlas Organisation, 1968.

Bazaz, Prem Nath, *History of Struggle for Freedom in Kashmir*, New Delhi: Pamposh Publications, 1954.

Bhatt, Ram Krishan Kaul, *Political and Constitutional Development of Jammu & Kashmir State*, Delhi: Seema Publications, 1984.

Bhushan, Vidya, *State Politics and Government, Jammu & Kashmir*, Jammu Tawi: Jay Kay Book House, 1985.

Bhutto, Zulfiqar Ali, *The Myth of Independence*, Karachi: Oxford University Press, 1967.

Birdwood, Lord Christopher, *Two Nations and Kashmir*, London: Robert Hale, 1956.

Biscoe, Tyndale, C.E., *Kashmir in Sunlight and Shade*, 2nd edn., London: Seeley Service and Co., 1925.

Breacher, Michael, *The Struggle for Kashmir*, New York; Oxford University Press, 1953.

Brunton, Paul, *Search in Secret India*, Delhi: B.I. Publications, 1970.

Campbell-Johnson, Alan, *Mission with Mountbatten*, London: Robert Hale, 1951.

Chagla, M.C., *Kashmir: 1947-65*, Delhi: Publications Division, Ministry of Information and Broadcasting, Government of India, 1965.

Chandra, Bipan, *Communalism in Modern India*, Delhi: Vikas, 1984.

Chathley, Y.P., Kashmir: Conflicting Layers of Perception, *The Tribune*, Chandigarh, 22 May 1994.

Chathley, Y.P., Kashmir Crisis: Economic and Political Dimensions, *The Tribune,* Chandigarh, 22 June 1994.

Chathley, Y.P., *Education, Population and Development: A Regional Perspective of Northwest India*, Centre for Research in Rural and Industrial Development (CRRID), Chandigarh, May 1995.

Chathley, Y.P., J&K: Panchayat Poll to Peace, *The Tribune*, Chandigarh, 20 August 1995.

Dhar, Somnath, *Jammu & Kashmir*, New Delhi: National Book Trust of India, 1976.

Dhar, S.N., *Kashmir – Eden of the East*, Allahabad: Kitab Mahal, 1945.

Dogra, Ramesh C., *Jammu & Kashmir* (a selected and annotated bibliography of manuscripts, books and articles together with a survey of its history, language and literature from *Rajatarangini* to modern times), Delhi: Ajanta Publications, 1986.

Doughty, Marion, *Afoot Through the Kashmir Valley*, Delhi: Sagar Publications, 1971.

Durand, Colonel Alergnn, *The Making of a Frontier*, London (other details not available).

Engineer, Asghar Ali, *Secular Crown on Fire: The Kashmir Problem*, Delhi: Ajanta Publications, 1991.

Faroquee, M., *Pakistan Policies that Led to Breakup*, New Delhi, 1973.

Fazili, M. Hassan, *Kashmir Historiographer*, Srinagar: Gulshan Publishers, 1983.

Fischer, Louis, *The Life of Mahatma Gandhi*, New York: Harper & Row, 1983.

Gajendragadkar, P.B., *Kashmir: Retrospect and Prospect*, University of Bombay, Bombay, 1967.

Gauhar, G.N., *Sheikh Nuruddin Wali,* Delhi: Sahitya Akademi, 1988.

Giasuddin, Peer, *Understanding Kashmir Insurgency*, Delhi: Light & Life Publishers, 1992.

Governor: Sage or Saboteur? Delhi: Roli Books, 1985.

Gupta, N.S., *Socio-economic Development of Jammu & Kashmir*, New Delhi: Jay Kay Book House, 1988.

Gupta, Sisir, *Kashmir: A Study in India-Pakistan Relations*, New Delhi: Asia Publishing House, 1966.

Hari Om, *Special Status in Indian Federalism*, New Delhi: Seema Publications.

Hassan, K.Sarwar (ed.), *Documents on the Foreign Policy of Pakistan: The Kashmir Question*, Karachi: 1966.

Hassan, Mahibul, *Kashmir under the Sultans*, Calcutta: Iran Society, 1969.

Hassnain, F.M., *Heritage of Kashmir*, Srinagar: Gulshan Publishers, 1980.

Hodson, H.V., *The Great Divide, Britain, India, Pakistan*, London: Hutchinson, 1969.

Hugel, B.C., *Kashmir and the Punjab: A Particular Account of the Government and Character of the Sikhs:* Delhi: Light & Life Publishers, 1972.

Hussain, Majid, *Geography of Jammu & Kashmir State*, New Delhi: Rajesh Publications, 1987.

Hussain, Syed T., *Reflection on Kashmir's Politics*, Delhi: Rima Publishing House, 1987.

Iqbal, S.M., *The Culture of Kashmir*, New Delhi: Marwah Publications, 1978.

Jagmohan, *My Frozen Turbulence in Kashmir*, New Delhi: Allied Publishers, 1991.

Kak, B.L., *Changing Shadows in Ladakh*, New Delhi: 1978.

Kapur, M.L., *History of Jammu & Kashmir State: The Making of the State*, Vol. 2, Jammu: Jammu & Kashmir History Publications, 1980.

Kapur, M.L., *Kingdom of Kashmir*, Jammu: Jammu & Kashmir History Publications, 1983.

Kaul, P.N. and Dhar, K.L., *Kashmir Speaks*, London: Lazac & Co., 1950.

Kaul, Pyare Lal. *Crisis in Kashmir*, Srinagar: Suman Publishers, 1991.

Khan, Ghulam Hassan, *Freedom Movement in Kashmir (1931-40)*, Delhi: Light & Life Publishers, 1980.

Koal, P.A., *Geography of Jammu & Kashmir*, Delhi: Light & Life Publishers, 1925.

Lamb, Alastair, *Kashmir: A Disputed Legacy, 1846-1990*, Hertfordshire: Roxford Books, 1991.

Lapierre, Dominique and Collins, Larry, *Mountbatten and Independent India*, New Delhi: Vikas.

Lawrence, W.R., *The Valley of Kashmir*, Srinagar: Kesar Publishers, 1967.

Lidhoo, M.L., *Kashmir Tribals: Child Rearing and Psycho-Social Development*, Srinagar: Minakshi Publishers, 1987.

Madhok, Balraj, *Jammu & Kashmir and Ladakh: Problem and Solution*, New Delhi: Reliance Publishing House, 1987.

Madhok, Balraj, *Kashmir: Centre of New Alignments*, Delhi: Deepak Prakashan, 1987.

Mahajan, Mehr Chand, *Looking Back: An Autobiography*, New Delhi: Asia Publishing House, 1963.

Maheshwari, Anil, *Crescent over Kashmir: The Politics of Mullaism*, New Delhi: Rupa, 1993.

Menon, V.P., *The Transfer of Power in India*, Bombay: Orient Longman, 1957.

Menon, V.P., *The Story of the Integration of the Indian States*, New Delhi: Orient Longman, 1985 edn.

Mohammad, Yasin (ed.), *History of the Freedom Struggle in Jammu & Kashmir*, Delhi: Light & Life Publishers, 1980.

Mountbatten, Louis, *Time Only to Look Forward: Speeches of Rear Admiral the Earl Mountbatten of Burma*, London, 1949-50.

Mullik, B.N., *My Years with Nehru: Kashmir*, New Delhi: Allied Publishers, 1971.

Neve, Arthur, *The Picturesque Kashmir*, Sand, London, 1900.

Neve, Ernest F., *A Crusader in Kashmir,* London: Seeley Service & Co., 1928.

Neve, Ernest F., *Beyond the Pir Panjals: Life among the Mountains and Valleys of Kashmir,* London: T. Fisher Unwin, 1912.

Noorani, A.G. (ed.), *The Kashmir Question,* Bombay: Mankatalas, 1964.

Panikar, K.M., *A Study of Kashmir and Jammu,* London: Oxford University Press, 1948.

Panikar, K.M., *Gulab Singh: The Founder of the Kashmir State,* London: Allen & Unwin, 1953.

Peissel, Michael, *Zanskar: The Hidden Kingdom,* London: Collins and Harvill Press, 1979.

Phadnis, Urmila, *Towards Integration of Indian States,* Bombay: Asia Publishing House, 1968.

Puri, Balraj, *Abdullah Era,* Srinagar: University of Kashmir, 1982.

Puri, Balraj, *Communalism in Kashmir,* Calcutta: Institute of Political and Social Studies, 1962.

Puri, Balraj, *Jammu & Kashmir: Triumph and Tragedy of Indian Federalisation,* New Delhi: Sterling, 1981.

Puri, Balraj, *Jammu – A Clue to Kashmir Tangle,* New Delhi: Photo Flash Press, 1966.

Puri, Balraj, *Kashmir: Towards Insurgency,* New Delhi: Orient Longman, 1993.

Puri, Balraj, *Simmering Volcano: Jammu's Relations with Kashmir,* New Delhi, Sterling, 1983.

Raina, A.N., *Geography of Jammu & Kashmir,* New Delhi: National Book Trust of India, 1977.

Raina, Dina Nath, *Unhappy Kashmir: The Hidden Story,* New Delhi: Reliance Publishing House, 1990.

Raina, N.N., *Kashmir Politics and Imperialist Manoeuvres 1848-1980,* New Delhi: Patriot Publishers, 1988.

Rajan, M.S., *India in World Affairs,* Bombay: Asia Publishing House, 1964.

Sanyal, S., *The Boats and Boatmen of Kashmir,* New Delhi: Sagar Publications, 1979.

Saraf, M.Y., *Kashmir Fights for Freedom,* 2 vols., Lahore: 1978-79.

Saxena, K.S., *Political History of Kashmir (300 B.C. to A.D. 1200)*, Lucknow: The Upper India Publishing House, 1977.

Sharma, B.L., *The Kashmir Story, 1959-61*: Bombay: Asia Publishing House, 1967.

Sharma, D.C., *Kashmir: Agriculture and Land Revenue System under the Sikh Rule (A.D. 1819-46)*, New Delhi: Rima Publishing House, 1986.

Singh, Karan, *Autobiography (1931-67)*, New Delhi: Oxford University Press, 1981.

Singh, Karan, *Sadar-e-Riyasat*, New Delhi : Oxford University Press, 1985.

Singh, Tavleen, *Kashmir: A Tragedy of Errors*: New Delhi: Viking, 1995.

Sufi, G.M.O., *Kashir*, Vol. I, Delhi: Light & Life Publishers, 1974; *Kashir*, Vol. II, *Islamic Culture in Kashmir*, 1977.

Taseer, A.R., *Tehreek Hurriyat Kashmir, 1931-39,* Srinagar: Mahafiz, 1968.

Teng, Mohan Krishan *et al.*, *Kashmir: Constitutional History and Documents*, Delhi: Light & Life Publishers, 1977.

Thorpe, Robert, *Cashmeer Misgovernment*, London: Longman Green & Company, 1870.

Verma, P.S., *Jammu & Kashmir at the Political Crossroads*, New Delhi: Vikas, 1994.

Wakhlu, Khem Lata and Wakhlu, O.N., *Kashmir: Behind the White Curtain*, Delhi: Konark, 1993.

Wani, G.M., *Kashmir Politics: Problems and Prospects*, New Delhi: Ashish Publishing House, 1993.

Weiner, M.(ed.), *State Politics in India,* New Jersey: Princeton University Press, 1968.

Zutshi, U.K., *Political Awakening in Kashmir*, New Delhi: Manohar, 1986.

Index